Praise for *To Drink from the*

A compelling chronicle of th[illegible] a deeply religious young woman finds herself condemned and rejected by the only faith community she has ever known. Anna Redsand provides a prophetic witness against the grievous damage that exclusionary religious teaching inflicts on LGBT believers . . . . A rich source of inspiration for spiritual pilgrims of all stripes. Highly recommended.
—Reverend Mark Achtemeier, author, *The Bible's Yes to Same-Sex Marriage*

So much of what shapes us has more to do with the agenda of religion and society than it does with who we are at the core of our being. Few of us can hear the sensuous whisper of the voice of God competing above the tumultuousness of everyone else's definitions of how we are to live our very individual lives, a voice which only asks: "Where *are* you?" Anna Redsand managed to discern God's voice and dared to explore this, the very first question Creator asked First Human. In so doing, she found herself exiled from the embrace of a spiritual communion that had enwombed her and nurtured her from childhood on. Anna's journey is skillfully and entertainingly chronicled in this delightful and inspiring read.
—Rabbi Gershon Winkler, PhD, author, *Magic of the Ordinary: Recovering the Shamanic in Judaism,* and co-author, *The Invitation: Living a Meaningful Death*

From Navajo dwellings in New Mexico to Scandinavia to the evangelical Midwest, Anna Redsand's beautiful, heroic story is for anyone who has ever felt outcast from a community they love and tossed into the desert of doubt and despair. Here you will find spiritual hope embodied, and the promise that, no matter where we are lost, it is possible to find our way home to new communities of faith, compassion, healing, and belonging.
—John T. Price, author, *Daddy Long Legs: The Natural Education of a Father*

To Drink from the Silver Cup breaks new ground by situating the reader in a spiritual and physical landscape that is familiar to anyone longing to break free from imposed belief; yet its roadmap is beautifully fresh with each turn of the page. I could not put the book down as I let Redsand's honesty and kindness raise my awareness of what is most sacred about the human experience—authenticity.

—Paul Renigar, Assistant Professor of Language and Technology, University of Alabama; gender, language, and identity researcher

In *To Drink from the Silver Cup*, Anna Redsand has written a brave, graceful, and intelligent account of her struggle to rediscover her lost faith and find acceptance of her sexuality. She depicts a journey filled with doubt, pain, joy, and ultimate affirmation.

—Arnold Johnston, playwright, poet, fiction writer, translator, author, *The Witching Voice: A Novel from the Life of Robert Burns*

By sharing her unique and deeply personal faith journey, Anna Redsand illustrates universal truths about the human person: that every person is sacred, that it is in our human nature to seek to know God however we might define that Presence, and that we all long for peace within ourselves and within community. In lyric prose, she tells her story with elegance and grace. She is a writer and person to be admired.

—Ann Przyzycki, Editor, *Isthmus*

The central character of this beautiful, seeking memoir is a woman who is unwilling to be kept outside the gates of the church because of the way God made her. Maybe someday, we will stop treating church and faith like a closed club. Until that time, Anna's book reminds us that He calls all of us to the table to drink from the cup.

—Molly Jo Rose, columnist, "In and Of the World," *U.S. Catholic*

In *To Drink from the Silver Cup,* Anna Redsand graciously invites us into the captivating story of her own spiritual journey, from her early years in fundamentalist Christianity through the pain of exile because of her sexual orientation to her cautious and glad return to a faith community. In the process, she opens our hearts and minds to examine spiritual challenges with which many struggle, whether LGBTQ or straight. Her writing will make you laugh, cry, rejoice, question, hope, and perhaps see the grace of God anew.
—Reverend Catherine Robinson, minister, Presbyterian Church (USA)

If you have any interest whatsoever in religion, spirituality, sexuality, personal growth, family relationships, community, the search for meaning, the Navajo Nation, or finely crafted creative nonfiction memoir, you need to read *To Drink from the Silver Cup.*
—Monica Friedman, author, *Rosalind Franklin's Beautiful Twist*

Anna Redsand is a masterful storyteller. This intensely personal narrative of her spiritual journey struck a particular chord with me, an ordained minister who is also gay. However, it will resonate with anyone who has lost the faith of their youth but is seeking to reconnect with it in a deeper, more spiritually authentic way.
—Reverend Dwain Lee, gay minister, Presbyterian Church (USA)

Anna Redsand knows the language of the Bible the way you know the language of your mother tongue. She also knows that she won't be spiritually satisfied with any religion that views itself as the "only way." Before it can excommunicate her. Anna leaves her childhood church and sets out on a quest to find a new spiritual home. In the process, she opens herself —and her readers—to Native American spirituality, Buddhism, Protestantism, Calvinism, Judaism, Unitarianism, Christianity, and more. Read *To Drink from the Silver Cup* and think, learn, heal, grow—and *believe.*
—Jody Keisner, essayist and Assistant Professor of Creative Writing, University of Nebraska-Omaha

To Drink from the Silver Cup is the best kind of quest: brave, unexpected, and full of discovery. Redsand's voice is lyrical and honest. Her story will speak to anyone on a journey of the most difficult kind: growing up as the "wrong" sort of person in an unforgiving world. Her loving optimism in spite of it all is inspirational.
—Linden McNeilly, author, *Map Art Lab* and *War Torn*

As a gay man who came from the same denomination as Redsand, I eagerly gulped each chapter of *To Drink from the Silver Cup*. Many LGBT+ people are alienated from their childhood faith communities and long for that place of belonging. Too many give up. Redsand's story is a powerful journey of faith, alienation, and reconciliation that speaks of hope, inclusion, and belonging.
—Douglas Houck, former board member of Exodus International

Anna Redsand's memoir, *To Drink from the Silver Cup*, captures the complex journey of being true to herself and her family in a life-giving way while trying to reconcile and find a community of faith that saw her as beloved. Anna claims all her identities and complex relationships in the most gracious way. It is a powerful story.
—Annanda Barclay, M. Div., Co-Moderator of the National Board of More Light Presbyterians

To Drink from the Silver Cup shares the author's journey through the heartbreaking loss of family and church because of her need to live an authentic life. I recommend this book to anyone looking for ways to more deeply understand tender experiences often lost in theological discussion.
—Cara Oosterhouse, Board Co-President, All One Body

I am so blessed by Anna Redsand's writing. Great work, great experiences, and such a depth of spirituality as I've hardly ever known in anyone.
—Reverend Alyzsa Van Til, Unity minister

To Drink from the Silver Cup

Also by Anna Redsand

Viktor Frankl: A Life Worth Living

To Drink from the Silver Cup

From Faith Through Exile and Beyond

Anna Redsand

Santa Fe, New Mexico

Portions of *To Drink from the Silver Cup* have appeared in slightly different form as "A Good Stranger" in *Isthmus,* "Naturalization" in *Clockhouse Review,* and "Screened Kiss" in *Fireweed.*

Library of Congress Control Number 2016944138

Distributed by SCB Distributors, (800) 729-6423

Published 2016
Printed in the United States of America

Published by Terra Nova Books, Santa Fe, New Mexico.
www.TerraNovaBooks.com

ISBN 978-1-938288-72-2

For Susan

because you walked with me for such a long way

You cannot disown what is yours. Flung out, there is always the return, the reckoning . . . perhaps the reconciliation.

There is always the return. And the wound will take you there. It is a blood-trail.

—Jeanette Winterson,
Why Be Happy When You Could Be Normal?

Contents

Acknowledgments

I am grateful to Mae Kruis and the late Richard Kruis, my mother and father, who taught me that there is a life of the spirit and instilled in me a love for the words of spirit.

Thank you to all who read early versions of *To Drink from the Silver Cup* and gave your invaluable feedback and encouragement: the late Jo Doran, Monica Friedman, Kate Harrington, Fonda Kirchmeyer, Corliss Kruis Mock, Joshua Kruis, Pat Kruis Tellinghusen, Robert Kruis, Ryan Kruis, Eleanor Milroy, Paolo Renigar, and Sarah Rodlund.

Thank you also to Lydia Fasthorse for graciously checking some of my Diné language spelling. Any remaining errors are mine.

I owe the most profound gratitude to my early editor, Linden McNeilly, for being unstintingly demanding that *To Drink from the Silver Cup* be all that it could be; for our years of friendship; and for her and her husband Tom's generous hospitality in their Corralitos home as we discussed changes that needed to be made. What could have been a painful process became deeply meaningful, pleasurable days spent in communion with another writer.

Thank you also to the friends, acquaintances, and people previously unknown—too many to name—who read *To Drink from the Silver Cup* as a serialized blog on my website. I am especially grateful to those who took the time to comment and to engage with me in discussions about the book's stories and ideas. Their enthusiasm gave me the courage to continue seeking publication.

Thank you to my wonderful team at Terra Nova Books, first of all for believing passionately that *To Drink from the Silver Cup* is a story the world needs. My editor, Marty Gerber, devoted himself to a close read of the manuscript, making this a better, clearer book. My publisher and book designer, Scott Gerber, made it a beautiful book. Both of them have taught me so much about collaboration, which does not come easily to me. And they have become trusted friends.

I would be remiss if I did not acknowledge the foundational contribution that Tristine Rainer's book, *Your Life as Story,* made to my understanding of story structure.

As always, I am grateful to my daughter, Cheyenne Jansdatter, for being true to who she is and for always supporting and loving me as a writer. I count it such a privilege to be her mother. Thank you to Irene Dauphinee for always believing in me.

Preface

THIS IS THE STORY OF A JOURNEY AWAY FROM THE EVANGELICAL faith that was the core of my existence as a child, adolescent, and young adult. It is about the emptying out of faith, about longing for what was lost. It is about seeking a way to return when I no longer believed the things that my community had instilled in me as fundamental to the faith. It is a story for anyone who has left a faith community for any reason: disbelief, rigid morality, the choice of an unacceptable partner, finding science incompatible with religious teachings, sexual orientation, to name a few. It is for anyone who is questioning whether their faith still works for them. It is for people who have separated from their family of origin because of differing ideals or cultural pressures. It is for people who still live in their place of origin while caring about those who have left.

Leaving church and home also meant leaving a Dutch American missionary community situated in the Navajo Nation. *To Drink from the Silver Cup* centers on my spiritual journey while offering a taste of what it was like for a white girl to grow up in that place in the 1950s and '60s. I present only a flavor here because, in the end, it was necessary to move with the journey. I have completed the manuscript of a second memoir, which tells more about that life between two worlds.

One aspect of *To Drink from the Silver Cup*'s setting bears mentioning because is nearly unintelligible to many people today. My departure from my world began in a watershed moment when I started to realize that there would be no place for me, an innocent young lesbian, in my church community. It was 1964, and I had never heard *dyke, faggot,* or *queer* spoken. In 1953, a new meaning for the word *gay* entered the dictionary, but to me, at sixteen, it still meant *light-hearted.* When I read "The Lovesong of J. Alfred Prufrock" in 1964, my English teacher told me, "Most prostitutes are lesbians."

"What's a lesbian?" I asked.

Rigid sexual repression meant no one (except that teacher) mentioned homosexuality, not even to say it was wrong. I didn't know it existed. As my sexuality began to find expression, I moved into a vacuum where, as far as I knew, I had never seen another person we would now call gay or lesbian, bisexual or transgender. Paradoxically, this also meant that I was free to explore my sexuality in the beginning without realizing that anyone else would see it as wrong.

Moreover, *The Feminine Mystique,* although it had just been published, had not made it to the mission school I attended on the edge of the Navajo Nation. I only started to become aware of the unequal treatment of women through that same misinformed teacher, although only in the context of the mission.

I have written this story thematically rather than chronologically, so time is somewhat fluid. There will be occasions when readers want more detail about something that is mentioned only in passing. This is because I have tried not to be diverted from my main story. I hope that will not be dissatisfying in the long run.

Some readers of the manuscript have wanted to know more about how I decided to have a child, and how my daughter, Cheyenne, came into my life. That is certainly not a side trip for me, and although telling about it might satisfy some curiosity, it is not germane to my story's theme. Also, there are aspects of that choice that belong just to her.

Most people in this story have been given pseudonyms for reasons of confidentiality. I have altered some minor facts to protect the identity of the girl I call Grace, who was my first love. She followed a path different from mine, entering a heterosexual marriage. I can only guess that what was an important confirmation of my identity was an innocent exploration for her.

To Drink from the Silver Cup

Prologue

Leaving (1964)

. . . a stone, a leaf, a door. . . O lost, and by the wind grieved . . .

—Thomas Wolfe, *Look Homeward, Angel*

I LEFT BEFORE THE CHURCH COULD EXCOMMUNICATE ME. IT wasn't because I wanted to leave. I went quietly out the back door. I wanted almost more than anything to stay there in the security of all that I knew, there in the place where I'd belonged ever since before I could remember.

On a Sunday afternoon in early autumn, when I was sixteen years old—that was when I started to sense that I would have to leave. My mother, father, and I were rolling back into Gallup in the mission station wagon. My brothers had all stayed home that afternoon. As we rounded the corner onto Second Street, I saw the railroad arms descending. Red lights flashed, and bells clanged, and I brought the car to a stop.

My mother started talking about two women who worked at Rehoboth, the hub of our mission in the Navajo Nation. Jennie was a blonde, blue-eyed nurse. Alice was a stocky, slightly older Navajo woman who ran the laundry. "We're worried about Jennie," my mother said, "because she's been staying with Alice at night."

"What's wrong with that?" I asked, but already I was afraid.

My mother raised her voice and pushed her words out on heavy air. "They're living in sin. They should see a doctor."

I might have laughed at that odd juxtaposition, except that her two sentences gripped my belly in a pair of cold claws. My mother was a large woman, always worrying about her weight. At that moment, she became vast, filling the car and the space around it. My father seemed to have gone somewhere else, and I shrank to nothing but my knuckles on the steering wheel.

I fastened my eyes on the freight cars that rumbled by. Baltimore and Ohio. Orange. Brown water marks. Atchison, Topeka & Santa Fe. Rust-red. Grimy white words. My mind grasped at inconsequential facts: "No train ever stopped in Santa Fe." "The Santa Fe stop is in one-horse Lamy."

My mother might have gone on talking or not. I heard nothing but the bells going off inside my head.

At last I pulled into our gravel driveway. All I could think of was getting to my bedroom and destroying the piece of me that lay in a flat, powder blue cardboard box. Those twelve letters from Grace Vander Laan. Grace had discovered onionskin paper and cartridge fountain pens that summer. When I opened the box, I held the sheets of sheer, crinkly paper in my shaking hands. For one last time, I read her stories about being a mission volunteer in Los Angeles. "I'm nut-brown," she wrote, "from passing out gospel tracts in the poorest neighborhoods and lying out on the beach in between."

Then came what I needed to destroy: "Remember being on the bus on the way back from Toadlena? Holding hands, my head on your shoulder? Do you think Charlie is right, that you're my male substitute? I don't think so. I just love you for who you are, and I will always." My body summoned other moments of my junior year—holding hands with her in Reformed Doctrine class, pressing tight and close to each other during chapel, deciding whether to kiss on the mouth—a first kiss—during a pause while we practiced for our brass ensemble.

Grace and I never really talked about *us*. We just did stuff. But when we were on a school field trip, we shared a room with two other girls. Grace and I shared a bed. My legs and arms entwined with hers, I tried to breathe quietly, but my body wanted to pant and moan. Then Grace whispered, warm and moist in my ear, "This is wrong." I felt as if she'd blown ice water into my stomach.

I whispered back, "No, it's not. We're just friends who love each other a lot." But I was afraid. Was it because I might be sinning, or was I afraid of losing Grace, afraid she would want to stop because she thought it was wrong? We held onto each other tightly after that, waiting for sleep and whatever else might come.

While I reread Grace's letters, my insides trembled. I remembered us finally pressing each other's lips through the dusty window screen of my dorm room. We hadn't kissed in that pause during ensemble practice, but Grace wouldn't leave it unfinished. I was almost asleep that night when she scratched at the window. I was afraid Mr. Haverdink, the houseparent, would come by any minute and shine his flashlight under the door and up the walls. If he suspected that anything other than sleep was happening, he would barge in. Still, we had our first lip-to-lip kiss.

All the time I reread Grace's letters, I was nervous. At any moment, my mother might thrust open the bedroom door and tell me to set the table. If she did, I knew her telescopic eyes would read everything on those fragile pages. Before she could, I stuffed the letters back into the box and went into the kitchen to get matches.

"I want you to set the table," she said.

"I need to take some trash down. Can I do that first?"

"Okay, but hurry up. Mr. Vander Laan is coming for supper. He'll want to practice with you before we eat."

I'd forgotten that Grace's father would be playing the piano for hymn singing at the Twin Lakes Chapter House. He would also accompany me on my trombone solo. I took the letters and rushed down the steps to the rusty backyard burn barrel.

I lifted the lid off the blue box and carefully laid the onionskin envelopes on the bed of cold ashes. I lit a match and watched Grace's words of lasting love and banal mission activities turn into thin black flakes.

★ ★ ★

Roly-poly, jolly Mr. Vander Laan arrived, and my mother shooed my brothers outside so we wouldn't be disturbed. Grace's dad sat at the piano. He asked what I was going to play.

" 'The Holy City,' " I said. I didn't know how I was going to get my body to stop shaking so I could blow air into the horn and move the slide. At the same time, I sensed that this horrible quivering vibrated only inside me, that no one could see it. All my thoughts went into each movement I had to make: "Unpack the trombone." "Mr. Vander Laan is playing those ripples." "Attach the slide to the bell." "Mom hates flashy, ripply playing." "Warm up the mouthpiece."

Everything happened in slow motion, but at last, my horn was put together and I lifted it to my lips. At the second verse, Mr. Vander Laan said, "Let's draw out these phrases. Never play two verses exactly the same way. Otherwise, why play more than one?" He grinned up at me and winked. I nodded and mechanically did what he said.

When we were done, I put the trombone back in its case and left my father and Mr. Vander Laan talking in the living room. I could hear them from a few feet away where I brushed my hair with my bedroom door open. Dad went on and on about expanding his mission beyond the little gray stucco chapel at Tohlakai.

I'd only been half listening until Grace's dad said to mine, "Say, did you hear about those two teachers at the Christian school in Denver?"

"No, I don't think so. What?"

"They were roommates. Then at the end of the school year, one of them came to the minister—Huizenga I think it is—and told him that she felt she was a man in a woman's body."

"What?" my dad said. "What?" and for the second time that day, my stomach whirled. I held my hairbrush in midair.

"*Ja.* It happens, you know. I guess. They have surgery for it. Huizenga helped her. Him. I don't know what to say. Him, I guess. Huizenga loaned him men's clothes, and he had the surgery. So he came to school the next year a man. They say the kids didn't have any trouble with it. Probably more the adults."

"That can't be . . . ."

"Wait. There's more. He. She. He was in love with the woman teacher who was her, his roommate."

"That's not right. The Bible . . . Romans 1 says, 'God gave them up unto vile affections: for even their women burned in their lust one toward another.' Verse 26. It's not right. Plain as day."

I held my breath and hoped my mother wouldn't call me back to the kitchen. I needed to hear this. I didn't want to hear it.

"But that's just it. It wasn't two women anymore. I think it took a lot of guts for Huizenga to help him. Them. But you know what it made me think of? Those girls' parents. How did they react? How would you and I feel if that happened with one of our kids?"

Everything had gone still around me, like I was enclosed in a soundproof bubble so I couldn't hear my dad's response. Stillness around me, but my mind churning out one thought after another. "Does Grace's dad know something about us? Why else would he ask about those girls' parents? Is that what I am? A man in a woman's body?" I looked down at my well-developed breasts, my slim waist and flat belly, curving hips. "I don't think so. But I loved Grace. Grace is gone to college now. And I loved to touch and kiss her. Who am I?"

My mother called the boys in to wash up. I could barely choke down half a baloney sandwich and some lime Jell-O with pears. I tried to swallow my rising fear with the sandwich. Potato chips were a rare treat, but I didn't want any. No one noticed—one of the good things about sitting at the table with seven younger brothers and company besides.

* * *

At Twin Lakes, I played for the singing and then performed "The Holy City" the way Mr. Vander Laan wanted me to. The song is a joyful paean of children and angels singing loud and sweet hosannas—for the most part. The second verse, the flash-back or forward, depending on how you hear it, takes you to the dark hour of the crucifixion. That's the one Grace's dad wanted me to play like a quiet dirge. I was always good at imagining that horrible, gracious hour when Jesus hung on the cross to save me from my sins. I could take the idea and let it fill my chest with gratitude and sorrow. There and then, I let it fill my horn.

My dad started up a black and white movie about the life of the Apostle Paul. With my part in the service over, thoughts came rushing back. "Alice and Jennie are living in sin." "Was what Grace and I did together a sin?" "She said it was wrong." "But I loved her."

In the movie, I heard a man who sounded like he was in an echo chamber. He cried, "Come over into Macedonia and help us." It was Paul's call to his next mission.

That was one of my father's favorite verses, the call to preach the gospel. Any words about God's call could set him on fire. My father loved being a missionary. I loved those words too. I had been sure that one day, I would hear God call me to serve. That evening, my hope for a call was gone. I got up, glad that I didn't have to cross the light of the projector. Anyone who noticed me leave would think I was on my way to the outhouse.

A corral stood close to the chapter house, and I walked around it, listening to the tinkling of sheep bells, smelling the pungent manure soaked in goat and sheep urine. I held onto myself with both arms as I walked, head down. It was chilly after the sun went down. I held on for warmth, but also to keep from losing the only life I knew.

Part I
Communion

. . . when he reached the small villages, the little portable altar was set up in the school house or a private dwelling, a hymn or two sung with someone playing the accordion, or the banjo. It was always the same. It was not fine sermons they sought now in the long cruel winter. It was communion.

—Margaret Craven, *I Heard the Owl Call My Name*

~ 1 ~

Family Circle

I THINK OF TEEC NOS POS—T'IIS NAZBAS IN THE LANGUAGE OF the *Diné* (the Navajos' name for themselves)—as lying at the heart of the Navajo Nation, the land called *Dinétah.* In reality, Teec Nos Pos is near the northeastern corner of the Navajo Nation, close to where New Mexico, Arizona, Colorado, and Utah meet. During our family's first year on the reservation, we lived in the small town of Shiprock. Less than a year later, when I was nearly five, we moved to the mission in the small valley that was Teec Nos Pos. This was where I first felt rooted, and that is probably why I mentally mis-locate it in the center of the reservation. In some sense, I feel deeply that if there is place on Earth where I belong, it is there; at the same time, I am acutely aware now that I do not belong.

When we first moved to Teec Nos Pos, there were four of us kids: Dickie, Trudy, baby Danny, and me, the oldest. Later, Bobby, Eddie, and Ronnie would be added, and much later, the ones we always called The Little Boys, even when they were teenagers: Phil and Brian.

There were for us five concentric circles of belonging. The innermost was the family circle. We were most closely knit with one another while we lived in the embrace of the valley of Teec Nos Pos. When I turned nine, we would move to the small town of Gallup because my father was reassigned to the mission at Tohlakai, fifteen miles north of town. In Teec Nos Pos, we relied mostly on one another for our social needs; in Gallup, we had neighbors and acquaintances all around. Also, as we grew older, it was natural for us to move outward from the family.

In the sprawling adobe missionary's house at Teec Nos Pos, there was a corner room we called the *playroom*. It was the center of our home, and just about everything but play took place there. The only reason I can think of for the room's name is the large battered cardboard box that stood in one corner, filled with toys that seldom got used: a Buzzy Bee pull toy; wooden blocks; random pieces of a Lincoln Log set; ditto Tinker Toys; a small rubber doll named Patsy, so old the inner aspects of her elbows had become holes; little metal cars losing their paint; and at the bottom, marbles and wooden beads.

We ate every meal together in the playroom, except that Dad was often gone at lunchtime, out visiting Navajo hogans. We sat around the table, which was our family altar in the golden knotty pine room. Mom or Dad prayed, and then we kids chanted in unison: "We thank thee, dear Lord, for this good food and drink and home and parents and thy Word. For Jesus's sake, Amen."

Food came around—mutton chops from sheep my dad bought at someone's corral, boiled potatoes and brown gravy, steamed yellow crookneck squash, and thick acid red tomato slices from Dad's garden. We talked over and through each other, more than one conversation going at a time until someone said something that grabbed everyone's attention.

"We found a new dirt slide today," Dickie announced, mouth full of potatoes.

"Don't talk with your mouth full," Dad said.

"What do you mean, dirt slide?" Mom asked.

"It's this kind of like a tunnel that starts at the top of the arroyo and goes all the way to the bottom."

"What? Do you mean you get into the tunnel and slide down?" Mom asked.

Oblivious, we all said, *"Ja."*

"Don't you ever do that again. It might collapse and suffocate you." We looked at each other joylessly. "Do you hear me?" We nodded.

Dad changed the subject: "Say, do you see that goldfinch in the tree?" Banks of windows ran the length of the playroom's two outside walls, and, forgetting the forbidden slide, we watched the bright little bird hop from branch to branch. Another with much less yellow, more brown, joined it. "That's the female," Dad told us. "I bet their babies are grown by now. Time for them to fly south soon."

Then with a grin, he started to tell a story on himself. "Geronimo and I went to the Yazzies' hogan today. Their son was sick last time we were there. So I asked the mother how he was doing now. Everyone in the hogan started laughing. I couldn't figure out why."

He paused.

"Well, why?" Mom asked.

I said *niyaa'* instead of *niye'."* He started chuckling and then laughing hard. We all looked at him.

When he stopped laughing he said, *"Niye'* means *your son. Niyaa'* means *your lice.* So I asked her how her lice were."

We laughed.

At the end of the meal, Mom went to the kitchen to make chocolate pudding from scratch. Dad's eyes sparkled, and he said, "I'm thinking of someone."

We knew it would be a character from the Bible, and we took turns asking questions with yes or no answers. Everyone who could talk got a turn.

"Is it a man?" A safe start from me because I knew, even though I'd read *Ten Famous Women from the Bible* several times, that there are lots more male characters than female.

"Yes."

Dickie came next. "Was he in the Old Testament?"

"Yes."

Trudy's turn. "Was he one of the disciples?"

Dickie and I pounced in unison: "The disciples weren't in the Old Testament."

She looked crestfallen, and Dad said, "That's all right. She's learning."

Danny asked, "Was he a prophet?"

"No."

My turn. "Did God come to him in the burning bush?"

"Yes."

Our rule said that if you asked the defining question, you could guess the name, and then it would be your turn to think of someone. "Moses," I fairly shouted.

Dad grinned. "Yes."

We knew Moses, the lawgiver and man of the burning bush, Ruth, the foreigner, Peter, the brash and faithless, and Priscilla, the tent-maker, as well as we knew the kids we played with.

When we'd eaten our pudding, Dad got out the fat *Children's Story Bible Book.* He held the book open to show us the colored picture—Rhoda, the servant girl, her face filled with surprise to see Peter, released from jail by an angel and standing at the gate.

"Rhoda shouldn't have been surprised," Dad said. "Because the early Christians in that house had just been praying for God to save Peter. We should never be surprised when God answers our prayers. Rhoda was showing lack of faith."

In the mornings, it was Dad who made breakfast—never the same thing two days in a row—pancakes, creamed hamburger on toast, fried eggs and bacon pieces, french toast, cream of wheat, cornbread soaked in warm sweet milk, cornflakes. Mom poured juice and milk and made coffee, all the time reminding us to dress and wash up.

At the end of the meal, Dad opened *The Family Altar.* "Today's reading is from Matthew 25, the parable of the talents." In an aside to Mom, he said, "This month, the readings are by Reverend Broenige."

"Oh *ja.* Isn't he in Pella now?"

Dad flipped to the front. "Orange City, it says here."

My mind fluttered off to *The Secret Garden. The Family Altar* was for grown-ups. But when he was done reading, Dad brought the point home to us. "If we don't use the talents

God has given us for his glory, there will be consequences—weeping and gnashing of teeth." He looked around the table at each of us to make sure we'd heard. I squirmed, feeling guilty for wandering among the roses with Mary, Dickon, and Colin instead of thinking about how God wanted me to use the gifts he'd given me. While I was thinking about that, Dad was on to the next thing—finding out from the back of the booklet which missionary, someone working elsewhere in the world, we would pray for that morning.

At noon, if Dad was home, he read to us from one of the P's—Psalms, Proverbs, or one of the prophets. When he was out visiting homes, Mom had us memorize entire Psalms, which we chanted together, a verse at a time from the King James Bible. We learned Psalm 1 first. It was all about contrasting the wicked with the righteous, the believer with the unbeliever, a theme that ran like a thick thread through our lives: "Blessed is the man that walketh not in the counsel of the ungodly, nor standeth in the way of sinners." Psalm 23, the one read at even the most secular of funerals, is a song of eternal comfort: "The Lord is my shepherd; I shall not want. . . . Surely goodness and mercy shall follow me all the days of my life . . . ."

Psalms 19 and 91 were two of my favorites—Psalm 19 because it spoke of the glories of nature and its ability to touch the spirit: "The heavens declare the glory of God; and the firmament sheweth his handywork. Day unto day uttereth speech, and night unto night sheweth knowledge. There is no speech nor language, where their voice is not heard."

In Psalm 91, there was unfailing comfort: "He that dwelleth in the secret place of the most High shall abide under the shadow of the Almighty. I will say of the Lord, He is my refuge and my fortress: my God; in him will I trust. Surely he shall deliver thee from the snare of the fowler, and from the noisome pestilence. He shall cover thee with his feathers, and under his wings shalt thou trust. . . ."

Once in a while in the spring and summer, Mom made what we called "pickups" for lunch. She cut raw vegetables and cubes of longhorn cheddar and laid them out on a huge platter. We stood around the kitchen counter for prayer, but after that, we were free to grab slices of bell pepper, carrot, and celery sticks, and run around outside, coming back in for more.

Our little donkey, Bahe, might be lying on his side in the sun, and we could cuddle up to him while we ate. We'd race halfway up the hill to fly out on the board swing suspended from the gnarled oak towering over us. We loped across the road and climbed the pink-tinged, gray branches of the apple tree. Each branch had a name, and each of us possessed the one we sat on. Big and Little Buttermilk, Big and Little Texas, Montana, Wonderland.

"I'll trade you Big Buttermilk for Little Texas," Dickie said to Trudy.

"No, Little Texas is my favorite."

"How about you, then?" he asked me. "Big Buttermilk for Wonderland."

"Okay," I said and we jostled awkwardly so we wouldn't drop to the ground where there could be floods or hot molten lava. Settled, we plucked the tart little apples, slightly chalky for lack of water, and ate them for dessert.

No closing prayer or Bible reading on pickup days.

⋆ ⋆ ⋆

For third grade and until I went to the mission boarding school halfway through fourth grade, the playroom became my schoolroom and my mother my teacher. The Bureau of Indian Affairs (BIA) school in Teec Nos Pos, run by the Department of the Interior, ended after second grade. My school in the playroom was based on the Calvert Correspondence Course used by missionaries the world over.

I read *Robinson Crusoe* a chapter a day and hated having to wait for the next installment. I learned about Hera sleuthing after that good-for-nothing Zeus and about Jason and the Argonauts pursuing the golden fleece. Early U.S. history came to me through *Smiling Hill Farm,* a novel about a family that traveled from Virginia to Ohio in a covered wagon. Together my mother and I created a miniature farm of oatmeal, cracker, and saltboxes.

At a small wood-and-wrought iron desk, built at the beginning of the century, I sweated over arithmetic papers, grimy from erasures. Just before Christmas, Dad and Trudy and the boys rolled out yellow cookie dough on the table. They shook out sparkling red and green sprinkles and silver B-B candies and laughed and chatted.

"I want to make cookies too." I was close to tears.

"Quit your *brommen,"* Dad threw in the Dutch word. "You had all morning to do that multiplication. And what did you do instead?"

I bent over the hated work and swallowed hard.

Mom came in from the kitchen. "You can make cookies when you're done with that arithmetic. Not before."

I set my jaw and stopped working all together. I would show them. The cookies went into the oven and came out to cool. More trays went in, and I looked out the windows toward the chapel and watched snowflakes begin to fall out of the heavy sky.

* * *

By the time I was reading about Pegasus and Bellerophon, Diana and the wood nymphs, Dickie had started kindergarten at the BIA school. My first crush was on his teacher, Miss Holbrook, whose skin was a rich caramel color. She wore nubbly knit wool dresses, gold jewelry, scarlet lipstick, and heady perfume, and spoke with an accent from the Deep South. She let me come up the hill to her classroom after the students had left and chatter my heart out with her. When she finished marking papers, I sometimes went to her little green trailer with its blond wood paneling. While she fried up pork chops and made a salad, I nattered away. I walked around the trailer, marveling at all the little cupboards, her knickknacks, the salt and peppershakers that looked like tiny chefs.

One afternoon, when I got back just in time to set the supper table, it occurred to my mother that coming home late was becoming a habit. "Where were you?" she asked.

"I was at Miss Holbrook's."

"What?"

Her tone should have warned me, but I went on. "I help her after school. I clean the blackboards. Sometimes she lets me grade papers."

"All this time, you've been in her classroom?"

I hesitated, hearing it now. "Well. No."

"What then?"

"Sometimes I go to her trailer. With her."

"What do you do there?"

For a few seconds, I was confused. Then, "Nothing. I mean. She makes supper. I talk to her. I set the table for her." Grasping at a straw then, "I'm helping her."

"Well, she doesn't want you there. You need to stop bothering her."

Miss Holbrook had never made me feel like I was bothering her. But my mother must be right. After that, Miss Holbrook was relegated to my fantasy of hugging her, pressing my face into those nubbly dresses and smelling her perfume, to remembering the little things we talked about while she made supper.

* * *

The playroom carries my only memory of being held on my mother's lap. It happened on a winter evening when I was eight, just weeks away from my first stint at the mission boarding school. It was the first year I got to stay up a half hour later than the other kids. The room was dark when I walked in, and my mother was talking on the phone in a low voice. Something in her tone and her words about a baby made me ask after she hung up, "Who was that?"

"Esther Roanhorse," she said. Mrs. Roanhorse was the wife of the missionary at Redrock.

"Who had a baby?"

"Esther's sister Agnes."

I was confused. Agnes wasn't married, and I knew you had to be married to have babies. "How?"

My mother must have heard something more than confusion in the question because that's when she took me onto her lap. "Don't be afraid," she said. "Agnes loves her baby. What she did was wrong, but she'll go in front of the church and confess her sin, and the baby will be baptized. Esther and John will help her raise the baby. It will be all right."

I don't know what I understood of what my mother told me, but she was right about what I'd felt. Fear. I nestled into the luxury of being held and looked out at the night sky. If I was very still, my bedtime might be forgotten for a while.

~2~

A Circle of Trees

WHILE THE TABLE WAS OUR FAMILY ALTAR AND OUR tightest circle of belonging, the valley that embraced us formed the second of our five circles. In my heart, we belonged first to the long ridge of golden sandstone, topped by the three great rock guardians of the valley and situated immediately across from the mission. Everyone called the formation the Three Monkeys. Three Monkeys was there for climbing. Most often, we headed up without any plan. Other times, Mom helped us pack lunches of peanut butter and jelly sandwiches, carrot sticks, and apples. We filled ketchup bottles with water and were gone for hours. Sometimes we went up with Dad and his .22 rifle, hoping to bring home a rabbit for dinner. Whenever he took a shot, the crack reverberated again and again from the rocks of the Three Monkeys. When we went all the way to the top of the rock pile and leaned up against those gigantic blocks of sandstone, we looked out over the wide flat plain that stretched to the horizon. At the back of our house, that plateau appeared to be just a small hilltop. Nearby, the flatland was divided into square farm plots of green, yellow, and brown. Farther out, it looked to be bare desert punctuated by an occasional red rock eruption.

At night in the summer, before I drowsed off, my eyes roved over the great mound of rocks. I watched them change color with the sinking sun—the gold turned to rosy apricot, then mauve, then the sweet of milk chocolate. As the sky darkened, my eyelids drifted shut, and my summer lullabies began to sound from the hilltop. I heard the deep, slow, insistent beat of drums. Then began the chanting, the measured sound of men's voices, the high-pitched, wild ululations of the women. I wanted to go there, peek over the top of a rock or around a tree, to see what it was like.

⋆ ⋆ ⋆

We belonged too to the sandy-bottom arroyo beneath the Three Monkeys and to the great gnarled cottonwoods that rose from the arroyo bed. Perhaps it was the cottonwoods that gave their name to Teec Nos Pos, which means *A Circle of Trees.*

I often asked people, people who should know, "Where did the name come from?"

They tried to guess. "Maybe one of those cottonwoods in the arroyo was so twisted that it made a circle."

Or, "Maybe a bunch of cottonwoods grew in a circle." They mentioned *cottonwoods* because *T'iis* is not just any kind of tree. It is a *cottonwood tree.*

In the end, the answer was always, "I don't know."

Willow stands, whose stems turned scarlet in winter and whose leaves mingled their fragrance with the smell of the cottonwoods, lined the edges of the arroyo. The sand there was damp and cream-colored. All but the youngest of us met Sally and Carol Belone and sometimes the traders' children down there, and we used the damp sand to make miniature Navajo home sites. We mounded the soft earth into little round domes for hogans, the traditional Navajo dwellings. Twigs formed sheep corrals and breezy summer shelters. Other times, we dug out kid-sized rooms and played house in them. One summer, Dad helped us roof over a hollow in the rocky arroyo wall with leafy branches. When the monsoon rains came, flash floods filled the arroyo, and we put on swimsuits, and Dad came down with us to make sure it was safe to go in and wade in swirling brown water up to my waist.

⋆ ⋆ ⋆

We belonged to the juniper, sage, piñon, and rabbit brush on the hill behind the house. From the hillside, we called forth our Jamies in loud singsong voices, "Reddy Birdy, peesa sa-alt. Reddy Birdy, peesa sa-alt."

Dickie, when he was about three, had invented Jamies, and he granted them to all of us. They were small animals—rabbits, squirrels, chipmunks, sparrows. They could talk, and they had their own society, watched over by Reddy Birdy. Each of us had our own Jamies and our own Reddy Birdy.

We never saw cardinals in Teec Nos Pos, but my Reddy Birdy was that magical brilliant red I saw in picture books. "My Jamies are having a convention. It's a first aid convention. I'm teaching them how to bandage wings and legs. Do you want to send your Jamies?"

"Hmm. Nah. That sounds boring. My Jamies are going on a treasure hunt. We're going up to that little ledge on the Three Monkeys."

"Boring? They need to know how to take care of themselves."

Dickie looked askance at me and ran off. "You go ahead," he called over his shoulder.

Dickie and I had another game, this one my invention. In it we were twins who were born to a Dutch king and queen, then set afloat in wicker baskets that took us to Japan. It was an indication of our landlocked existence that a wicker basket voyage across oceans seemed plausible. When I was eight and Dickie was six, our parents bought us a bicycle to share. It was a red and black boy's Schwinn. We named it Amigo and called it our golden palomino. Amigo was our horse in Japan and shared in our adventures. In Japan, another king and queen raised us, but we were always trying to find a way to get back to the Netherlands.

⋆ ⋆ ⋆

Halfway up the hill, a clear spring bubbled, supplying water for the interpreter's nearby house and ours. There was also a free-standing spigot beside the road, and people from miles around loaded fifty-gallon barrels onto their wagons and drove up to get water.

Whenever he had the chance, Dad would catch them filling their barrels. "You know, Jesus said he would give you the Water of Life. If you drink the water he gives, you will never be thirsty again."

People must have thought, "This *bilagaana* [white person] must be crazy."

Dad told us, "If you want to catch a ride on the wagon, you say, *'Kingo deiya. T'aa shoodi?"*

People chuckled at our efforts to speak their language and said, *"Aoo' "*

So we hopped onto the wagon's tailgate and waited for them to finish filling their barrels, then rode off behind the horses that kicked up dust from the road. We clutched our nickels in sweaty fists and stood for long minutes in front of the glass case just inside the trading post's swinging doors. There were bright penny candies, Big Hunks, Paydays, Baby Ruths, and Hersheys with almonds to choose from.

Every Saturday, we lined up in the kitchen, holding out our hands for the ten pennies that were our allowance. Mom reminded us, "Be sure you put a penny in your Jesus bank," and we listened to them clink into our small round, brass-colored ointment tins.

"And four cents in your piggy banks," she added

None of our banks looked like pigs—they were Log Cabin syrup tins or cardboard boxes with slits cut in the tops.

⋆ ⋆ ⋆

One Sunday evening, Mom and Dad headed down the road toward the trading post.

"Can we come?"

"No. We never go anywhere just the two of us. We won't be gone very long."

We headed up the hill. I stopped at the swing while the others kept on a few feet higher to the spring. Suddenly, Dickie shouted, "Look!"

"Get it, get it."

"I got one. Two!"

"Me too."

I jumped off the swing and ran up the hill. Beside the concrete-covered spring was a round hole maybe a foot and a half across, thinly edged by moss. In the fading light, I saw Dickie, Trudy, and Danny scooping up something from the ground around the hole, cupping whatever it was in their hands, laughing and squealing.

"What is it?"

"Frogs. Little tiny gray frogs with red spots on their backs. Look!" Danny carefully uncupped his hands to show me a mass of wiggling, hopping creatures, no bigger than the end of my thumb.

"They tickle," Trudy giggled.

I joined in, and soon we had twenty or thirty little frogs. "What shall we do with them?"

"Let's take them down so we can show Mommy and Daddy when they get back."

Back in the house, we opened our hands and released the babies into the kitchen and chortled as the little gray and red things hopped all over the floor. When our parents got back, we shouted, "Look! Frogs!"

Mom looked like she didn't know whether to laugh or cry. Dad laughed and said, "Well, they're not frogs."

We gave him blank looks. "They're toads," he said, and started scooping them up. "Where did you find them?" He could hardly stop laughing.

"Up at the spring."

"Get them out of here! Now!" That was Mom. So we all started scooping. "That one just went under the stove. What's going to happen to it?" We scooped faster.

"We have to bring them back to the spring," Dad said. "Otherwise they'll die. It's too dry down here." We trudged up the hill with Dad, the little toads tickling our hands, and released them back to the waterhole.

~3~

The Sheep and the Goats

I STARTED HERDING SHEEP IN SHIPROCK BEFORE I TURNED FIVE. Eva Blackgoat came by the house in the evening when we were almost finished with supper. Dad was pleased because he could invite her to listen to the Bible story and prayer. She might even get some dessert if she timed it right. She asked if I could go with her to take the sheep for the last grazing of the day.

I felt special; Eva was probably eight or nine, practically a teenager in my eyes. Because of Eva, I learned about the difference between sheep and goats. The sheep stuck together in a nice clump, easy to follow, easy to round up and move where you wanted them to go. The goats ran all over the place—over rocks, behind trees, into arroyos. They kept us busy bringing them back to the herd. Mostly me. The goats were at least part of the reason Eva wanted me with her. "Look," she shouted. "There goes a goat."

I raced after it, got behind it with a rusty tin can that held a few pebbles. I shook the can, and the goat looked around at me and went on chewing. I rushed it, and it took off, not toward the herd but to another rock outcrop. Shaking the can and shouting, "Go on, go on," I got it back to the herd.

I felt important. I had a job to do—running after goats.

★ ★ ★

I learned about the difference between sheep and goats from the Bible too. Sheep in the Bible were just like sheep in real life, only they were people. People who followed Jesus and did what was right, caring for others. Goats were the people who didn't follow anyone. At the table, my father said, "When Jesus comes back, he will send the sheep to the right and the goats to the left. He'll say, 'Depart from me, you who are cursed, into the eternal fire prepared for the devil and his angels.'" That meant hell.

Sheep were believers, and goats were unbelievers. Our world was divided not into rich and poor or Navajo and white. It was divided into believers and unbelievers. Before going to sleep at night, I prayed:

Jesus, tender shepherd, hear me.
Bless thy little lamb tonight.
In the darkness, be thou near me.
Watch my sleep 'til morning light.

Lord, bless Daddy and Mommy, Dickie and Trudy, Danny and Bobby, the Christian people and the unbelievers. For Jesus's sake, Amen.

The distinction was clear and present in our everyday life. Thus our third circle of belonging was the community of believers, first in Shiprock, then in Teec Nos Pos and also in Beclabito, which was eight miles east of Teec Nos Pos. When we moved to Gallup later, our community of believers would be the people at Tohlakai. We lived in the Navajo Nation especially for the sake of the unbelievers.

"God is not willing that any should perish," my father quoted. "We are here to show them the way. So they can become believers. So they don't end up in the lake of eternal fire."

In some odd sense, we belonged even more to the unbelievers who surrounded us than to the believers. They were our purpose for being. In order to bring the unbelievers into the fold, Dad went out most days with his interpreter to visit people in their hogans, to talk to people while they herded sheep, to women while they wove rugs, to men as they made turquoise and silver jewelry.

"We tell them about Jesus, the Good Shepherd," he said. "They understand that. I talk about how they take the sheep for water and grazing, how they protect them at night in the corral, about coyotes coming for the sheep, like the Devil as a roaring lion comes after us, how Jesus will save them from that fearful end."

Sometimes Dad took me with him when he went out to evangelize. When he did that, I sat in the hogan or summer shelter and heard him speak words I could have said by heart. Then the interpreter talked in the Diné language, and I listened closely for words I knew. It was like an audible puzzle.

Most often when I went with my father, he dropped me off at the hogan of Mrs. Begay, a believer who lived in Beclabito. Mrs. Begay's daughter, Ilene, was my age. Ilene and I stayed in the hogan long enough to eat a puffy golden piece of fry bread. Then we scrambled down into the red rock canyon below the hogan.

"Lets pretend we're Pueblos," Ilene said. It was a way to be something neither of us was. We outlined the square rooms of our pueblo dwelling with stones and made stew from cow bones. Sometimes after the Sunday morning church service in Beclabito, Ilene came home with me for Sunday dinner. Afterward we went down into the arroyo, and once again, we became Pueblo Indians from long ago.

"Our name can be Pablo," I said, using the name of one of my classmates at the mission school. "It sounds more Pueblo, right? Not Navajo."

"Yes. Pablo," Ilene said.

When we pretended to be Pueblo Indians, we acted out traditional wifely roles. This reflected how I had begun to think of my future. I imagined I would marry a man and have children, just as everyone expected me to. The person who occupied my fantasies most fully, however, was whatever girl I had a crush on at the time. The man who was my husband in these daydreams was a shadowy, incidental character; the real object of my admiration and affection was the girl, and she played the starring role.

* * *

Once, Dad took me to Beclabito during a sheep dip. The dip was a long, narrow cement trough filled with chemically treated water for killing ticks that lodged in sheep and goats' wool. Dad dropped me off to play with Irma Ahasteen while he visited hogans.

People had herded their sheep and goats from miles around on foot, on horseback, by horse and wagon. It took some of them days to get there, pausing for the animals to eat sparse grass and salt weed, setting up camp each evening, and finally camping by the dip, visiting with others while they waited their flock's turn. Humans, dogs, sheep, goats, horses, and donkeys shouted, barked, bleated, brayed, and stirred up dust. When a flock was called, the herders got the animals into a corral and over to the chute that led into the dip. Workers wielded metal rods with crooks at the ends to take wide-eyed animals by the neck or prod them in their fat, wooly backs through the swirling brown water.

Irma and I pedaled our bikes around the seething life of the sheep dip. We smelled camp coffee brewing, fry bread browning in hot fat. We churned through the dust of shallow arroyos that branched away from the dip, and stopped to watch the animals get their baths. We watched women in long satin skirts and velveteen blouses with paisley scarves on their heads butcher a sheep, laying the glistening innards on the inside of the peeled-off sheepskin.

"*Ahehee'*, we said, thanking the ladies who offered us hot fry bread and cold, greasy mutton ribs. We shook plenty of salt on the ribs and stripped them shiny clean.

Every once in a while, we took a break from the sheep dip in the Ahasteens' cool stone house. A big chunk of Navajo cake, wrapped in Bluebird flour sacking, lay on the wooden kitchen table. Navajo cake is made only at the time of a girl's puberty ceremony, her *kinaalda*. First a big hole is dug in the earth and lined with cornhusks. Then a sweetened mixture of nutty-tasting, hand-ground Indian corn and raisins is poured in, covered with more husks and earth. A fire is built on top of it all and kept burning while the cake bakes for hours.

The Ahasteens offered me my first taste ever of Navajo cake. I took a lump of it and rolled its sweet grainy density on my tongue, pressing it to the roof of my mouth and slowly licking it down, feeling the raisins softly burst. I loved the satisfying heaviness it made in my throat with each swallow. I kept coming back for more. The Ahasteens laughed about how much I loved Navajo cake. They'd gotten it from someone else after a kinaalda.

"Because it's good luck," they said, "to give cake away to lots of people. When you give away a lot, the girl will have lots of babies. It's good luck to eat it too. You're going to be very lucky."

In the evening, as the dust settled, people cleaned out their cast iron fry pans, washed their bowls, and set their speckled enamel coffee pots on the embers for one last mug of camp coffee. Irma and I gathered with people tired from moving sheep through the trough all day. Dad opened the hood of the dark green mission pickup, started the motor, and hooked up a slide projector. He set up a portable screen, and people sat on blankets and folding camp stools to watch a Bible story narrated in the Diné language on a crank phonograph player. It was entertainment after a hard day's work. Dad hoped it would bring people to Christ.

* * *

With adults, I learned early on to shake hands Diné-style, a soft passing of palms with very light pressure. With them, I used my growing Diné vocabulary. The Diné understanding of belonging began with the hand pass, and then you never just used the greeting, *Ya'at'eeh*. You used a fitting kinship word—*shima* for a woman your mother's age, *shimasani* for a woman old enough to be her mother. This is the beginning of learning about *k'e*—how, in the Navajo universe, everything and everyone is in kinship with one another.

When people of Teec Nos Pos visited our home, my father loved for me to walk around and ask them, *"Gowheeh ninizin-ish? Abe' sha'? Ashii łikan ninizinish?"* Would you like some coffee? How about milk? Do you want sugar? They chuckled at the little white girl, but I heard pleasure, not derision.

These were the people with whom we worshipped in the Beclabito BIA school on Sunday mornings and in the tiny white clapboard chapel at Teec Nos Pos in the afternoons. These were the people with whom we had church picnics where the food was mutton ribs, mutton stew, grilled mutton innards, roasted sheep's head, and—best of all—fry bread. The women taught me to take a ball of dough, pat and stretch it into a flat circle, and flap it back and forth between my palms until it was almost as big around as the black iron skillet filled with an inch of bubbling hot lard. They threw it into the fat for me, and I watched it puff up. I didn't eat it then; I got another ball of dough. I was helping.

These were also the people for whom I watched my mother prepare the communion meal. She stood in our kitchen with me at her elbow, trimming the crusts from spongy white Rainbo Bread. Then she cut the slices into soft white cubes and heaped them onto a shallow silver plate. She laid a white cloth napkin over the bread, then took the deep silver container with its small, round holes for individual communion cups. She filled the cups with dark, sweet grape juice, placed them in the tray, and covered them with the silver lid that was topped by a tiny silver cross.

"When can I take communion?" I begged.

"You know the answer to that." My mother was impatient. No nonsense.

"But I believe. I believe Jesus died for me. I asked him to come into my heart. Isn't that enough?"

I knew the answer. I could belong in all sorts of ways—sitting on the slatted benches with everyone else, going up to the front to sing a special number while my mother accompanied me on the accordion, shaking hands with the grownups, later on even teaching Sunday school, but until I passed certain tests, I could not eat the bread and drink the juice, which stood in for wine and signified true belonging.

I could pass one test—I knew my catechism; I could answer any question posed by the elders. I would gladly stand in front of the church after I answered them and say, "I do," to the four questions followed by the big question, "What is your answer?" But I knew too that they wouldn't let me, not then, because the other test you had to pass was the age test. Answering the questions and standing in front of the church was called *profession of faith,* and you could not make profession of faith until you were at least seventeen or eighteen. I would be kicking against that restriction for some time to come.

With envy and longing, I watched my mother prepare this symbolic feast of togetherness. I wanted full belonging. The holiness of communion surrounded the meal with mystery that drew me in.

"Can I carry the bread plate over to the chapel?"

"No," my mother said. Even though it meant she had to make two trips—one for the bread and again for the juice tray—I couldn't be allowed to touch it. The sacredness was that jealously guarded. In fact, communion was so holy that my father, a lay missionary, was not allowed to speak the words for the service. The ordained minister had to drive out from Shiprock to do that. Dad could, however, carry the plates around to serve the people in the pews.

I followed my mother, laden with silver plates, over to the chapel and waited, sitting on one of those hard benches that left its marks on my bottom. Once the service started, we waited a long time for the actual serving of communion—singing and long prayers and a sermon in English, then in Navajo came first. When the minister finally spoke the words, "Take, eat, remember, and believe," I watched people lift the cubes to their mouths, yearning all over again to be included, to make that rite of passage. "Why not me?" I thought. "Why not now?"

★ ★ ★

The simplest form of communion, though no one thought of it as sacred, was allowed, even encouraged. "Whenever anyone offers you food, you take it and you tell them *ahehee'.* It's part of being friendly, of accepting people. Being accepted."

I can't say my parents were the most culturally sensitive people; after all, at the heart of their life purpose, although they didn't see it that way, lay the destruction of the very culture in which they encouraged us to partake.

Everyday Diné foods became commonplace to us. But if we were offered a chunk of fat wrapped in sheep's intestines and grilled to a sizzling golden brown at a church picnic, the unfamiliarity of this delicacy was no excuse not to take and eat it. The relatedness that comes from sharing food was obvious to me at an early age. When the little white kid chomped on this intestinal treat with gusto, adults laughed approvingly.

★ ★ ★

A sharp line was always drawn between those who belonged to the holy communion and those who stood outside it. I couldn't help peering over that line, intrigued by the shadows on the side that my parents said was dark and filled with evil. In late autumn, the Northern Navajo Fair took place in Shiprock. Afterward, when the grounds emptied, rings of upright juniper branches and black circles from enormous bonfires were left on the hard, pale earth. These were remnants of the *Yeibichai* dances, so sacred that they could only be celebrated after the first frost of autumn and before the first thunder of spring. Every year at this time, my father asked God to send rain to prevent these native, non-Christian dances from happening. Late autumn in New Mexico is the time for brilliant skies and crisp air, so rain seemed highly unlikely. I knew, of course, that if God wanted to, he could send a miracle of rain, though it never happened.

One evening, Dad and I walked across the road from the mission at Teec Nos Pos to feed our chickens. While we were scattering kernels of dried corn, I spotted a fan comprised of seven or eight large, rust-red feathers lying on the ground. They were bound together at the quill end by cream-colored suede that formed the handle. From that hung a fringe decorated with red and turquoise beads.

I picked up the fan and called, "Dad, look what I found."

He stepped over, carrying the red Hills Brothers coffee can filled with grain. "Wow! Those are peyote ceremony feathers, I'm pretty sure."

I'd heard him mention the dangers and sinfulness of peyote, so I was puzzled by his enthusiasm. "What are they for?"

"I'm not positive, but I think the roadman, the leader in peyote ceremonies, uses them to spread cedar or sage smoke. I'll ask around. See if I can find out more." Then he added unnecessarily, "Peyote ceremonies are wrong. They have Jesus in their ceremonies all mixed up with Navajo religion. And they think they need a drug so they can have visions."

"What's wrong with visions?" I asked. I was pretty sure I'd like to have visions. "The prophets and disciples had visions." I imagined my own burning bush or a blinding light on the road to Shiprock taking away my breath and giving me a divine command. I wanted more excitement and revelation than what was dished out in church. Why not? Why should people from two thousand years ago get those godly treats and not me?

"Yes," my father answered. "The prophets and disciples had visions so they could write the Bible. We don't need visions now because the Bible is complete."

While we talked, we shooed the hens into the coop and locked them up for the night. We headed back up the dirt road toward the house and supper.

"Why doesn't God want to give us visions anymore?" I asked.

"I just told you. Because he has already revealed himself completely in the Bible."

"But, Dad, the Bible says God never changes. Why would he change about giving us visions?"

"That's just the way it is." He quoted the Bible: " 'My ways are not your ways,' saith the Lord." I heard his exasperation.

When we got into conflict, there always came a point, if I wouldn't let go, when he summoned absolute authority.

The conversation was over. Much later, I realized that this exchange exemplified the contradictions in my father. On the one hand, he was intensely curious about Diné culture and language. On the other, he believed sincerely, even desperately, that he was obligated to replace that culture with Christianity—his brand of Christianity. He bridged this apparent contradiction with a neat form of denial: He considered Navajo religion and Navajo culture to be two separate things, whereas to traditional Diné, all of life is one sacred whole.

When we got back to the house, Dad put the peyote fan into a glass-fronted cabinet in his study, alongside Bible commentaries and books on hermeneutics and object lessons.

~4~

Missionaries

OUR FOURTH CIRCLE OF BELONGING WAS MADE UP OF CHRIStian Reformed Church (CRC) missionaries across the length and breadth of the Navajo Nation and the nearby Zuni Pueblo. The Navajo reservation is more than twenty-seven thousand square miles in size, about equal to the state of West Virginia. Zuni is around seven hundred square miles, about half the size of Rhode Island. The hub of the scattered missions was Rehoboth Mission, five miles and light years outside of Gallup, New Mexico.

Rehoboth had a grades one-through-twelve mission boarding school with three dormitories, a thirty-bed hospital, and a laundry to serve them. The Mission House had an institutional kitchen and dining hall downstairs and rooms for single women workers upstairs. There were houses for married workers—teachers, the doctor, the minister, and a crew of carpenters and maintenance men. This crew looked after the boiler that heated all the buildings on campus and traveled to the various mission posts to build new houses and chapels and maintain the existing ones.

CRC missionaries in the outposts were Native American, Dutch American, and Dutch Canadian. When we came together, I overheard the adults talk about things like the workings of the Mission Board in Grand Rapids or new developments at the Reformed Bible Institute (RBI), my father's alma mater. Often they talked about how to deal with people they called *backsliders.*

"We heard that Dennison Goldtooth went to a Yeibichai dance. He made profession of faith two years ago. It's so discouraging."

"How did you find out?"

"His sister-in-law told us."

"What did you do about it?"

"Nothing yet. We just found out. What would you do?"

"Well, it's pretty open-and-shut, isn't it? You go talk to him. Tell him the old way is of the Evil One. That he can't take communion unless he confesses his sin. Even after confessing, I would make sure he doesn't partake the next time you have it. Say that you're waiting to make sure his behavior changes. Being a Christian and going to ceremonies don't go together."

"What if it's not true? What if the sister-in-law has it in for him for some reason?"

"Revenge, you think?"

"It's possible."

"Well, you just have to ask. Your interpreter can probably find out the truth. He's from there, isn't he?"

"Yes, but that could make it hard for him in the community. You know?"

"He has to be prepared for that. Suffering for the sake of Christ. Counting all else loss."

Someone noticed me standing nearby, not saying anything. The man nodded in my direction and said, "Little pitchers have big ears." Everyone stopped talking, and I turned away. I felt ashamed for crossing a line.

We didn't see most of these fellow missionaries often; the adults were all busy with their soul-saving tasks. Great distances, often over dirt roads, separated us. When we met, we nearly always communed over food. Often we joined one or two other missionary families for Thanksgiving dinner. One year, when I was seven or eight, we drove all the way to Rehoboth from Teec Nos Pos, thirty miles over dirt and stone and another hundred over asphalt to be part of a Thanksgiving dinner for missionaries from all over the reservation. As we ate turkey and pumpkin pie, the wind began to whip up. It whistled around the corners of the Mission House and rattled the tall windows. At the end of the meal, we sang "God Be With You 'til We Meet Again." As we did, I felt that we cared deeply about each other, and a lump of emotion rose in my throat.

When we finished singing and walked out through the swinging doors of the Mission House, fat feathery flakes of snow floated around us. They began to stick to windshields and roads as the caravan of missionaries headed up what was then New Mexico Highway 666. At Tohatchi, Reverend and Mrs. Koolhaas turned off, and we waved. Slowly, with my stomach full of turkey and pie and my heart also full, I nodded off to sleep. Sometime later, I woke because my toes were so cold. I realized the car had stopped, and when I opened my eyes, I saw that my father was alone in the front seat.

"Where's Mommy? Why are we stopped?"

"There's an accident up ahead. Mommy went to see if she could help."

"Is it bad?"

"I don't know yet. The Yazzies drove back to Naschitti to use the Sietsmas' phone to call the police."

Just then, my mother came back and got in the car. She didn't have her coat on, and her teeth were chattering. "I'm going back out in a minute. Can you turn the heat on?"

She had laid her coat over some of the accident victims. She'd gone to help because she was a nurse.

"How bad is it?" Dad asked.

"Bad. The woman died before I got there. If an ambulance gets here soon, the man and kids will make it, I think."

My chest went chill, but I was grateful for the heat on my toes. "We should pray for them," I said, and of course, my parents agreed. Mom got ready to go back out into the thickly falling snow. Dad struggled out of his jacket and handed it to her. When she was gone, Dad prayed aloud. I added my own silent petition. I imagined what it would be like to waken and find my mother and father dead, and I felt like crying.

A little later, the snow turned pink and seemed to be revolving in slow motion. A heavy, white Cadillac ambulance was moving along the shoulder past our line of cars. My mother returned. The ambulance had gone on toward Shiprock, and our cars started up.

"The man died just before the ambulance got here," my mother said. Her voice was tight.

I faced a myriad of emotions—sorrow for the children whose parents were gone, fear that I could lose my parents, pride in us as a people, people who stopped to help, made the dangerous drive to call for the ambulance, waited with the injured and dying. And feelings I knew I shouldn't have—excitement at the drama of it and a sort of righteousness about who we were—people who helped others. The people I belonged to.

* * *

Our CRC circle of missionaries widened once a year, in August. All year I waited for our family trip across the northern part of the Navajo Nation to the Southwest Bible and Missionary Conference in Flagstaff. Missionaries and their families came from all over the Southwest—CRC missionaries and others from all sorts of Protestant denominations: Baptists, Assembly of God, Brethren in Christ, Mennonites, Methodists, Presbyterians, and Church of God in Christ. When we first arrived, we ran from campsite to cabin, finding friends from years before, getting shy because we hadn't seen each other for a year, then racing off to play together.

Some years we camped on the conference grounds in our green canvas umbrella tent. During the cold nights, I breathed in the slightly mildewed smell of the tent, the fragrance of the giant ponderosa pines, and the moist black earth. My parents made our meals on the two-burner Coleman stove. One year when we were camping, we got a letter from my grandmother, my mother's mother. It contained two momentous pieces of news. First, my mother's grandmother had died. Second—and far more memorable to me—my grandparents had gotten a TV. My mother was shocked and angry.

"They've always said television is wrong," she complained. "Now look what they've done. Gone and gotten one."

Other years, we got to stay in a thin-walled wooden cabin and eat in the dining hall because my father worked as the head cook. I liked camping, but I liked the dining hall years the best. The summer I was seven was one of those years. Dad let me help in the kitchen, peeling potatoes or setting tables, and that's how I got to know Marilyn, a Baptist teen-ager from Phoenix who was paying her way to the conference by working in the kitchen and waiting tables. Marilyn was tall and slim with a smooth brown pageboy and glasses, and I thought she was beautiful. More than that, she was kind.

At the end of every meal, someone read the Bible, and we prayed and sang gospel songs. "The Gospel Train" was my favorite because we added sound effects, tapping glass tumblers with spoons, shouting out "Woo woo" between lines:

I am traveling on the hallelujah line,
On the good old Gospel train,
I am on the right track and never will go back
To the station of sin again.

Marilyn told me every meal, "Tip the chair next to you up against the table. Then no one else can sit there." When she was done serving, she put the chair down and sat next to me during devotions, still wearing her apron.

Each morning, our family walked over a carpet of pine needles to the Tabernacle, the great wooden church that seated what seemed like hundreds of missionaries and other Christians, people we saw year after year. Every service began with

Blessed assurance, Jesus is mine!
Oh, what a foretaste of glory divine!

Heir of salvation, purchase of God,
Born of His Spirit, washed in His blood.

Marilyn sang in the choir behind the pulpit, and I didn't take my eyes off her even while we prayed, when my eyes were supposed to be shut. Then I had to part with the sight of her because the kids had our own classes where we heard Bible stories, learned new songs, made crafts, and practiced for the program we would perform in the Tabernacle on the last night of the two-week conference.

The year I was seven was also special for more than Marilyn. One evening during the end-of-meal prayer, my mind slipped away from what the adult was saying. "Lord Jesus," I prayed silently. "I know you stand at the door and knock. I am opening the door. Please come into my heart." My mind wandered from there to silently singing

Into my heart.
Into my heart.
Come into my heart, Lord Jesus.
Come in today, come in to stay.
Come into my heart, Lord Jesus.

I had sung that gospel chorus countless times, but, filled with emotion, I marked this prayer and song as my conversion moment, although it's hard to say what I was converted from. I just knew that there had to be a conscious moment when I made that decision. I told my mother afterward, and she, of course, was pleased.

I always felt sad saying good-bye to kids we knew as once-a-year friends, but the end of the conference that year was more poignant than any other. That last night, after our performance in the Tabernacle, I dreamed that Marilyn had shrunk to doll size so she could go home with me in my suitcase. On the way back to Teec Nos Pos, sitting in the back seat with my brothers pressed up against me, my mind was filled with that dream and feelings of loss and longing and imagining.

Marilyn's kindness went beyond the conference. She wrote me letters and sent pictures of herself in her cap and gown and a fancy white dress with red roses on it, and I sent letters back, up until the year I turned eleven.

Back at home I wrote another letter, this one to my grandmother, my mother's mother—she of the brand new television. I told her about asking Jesus to come into my heart and added, "Now I will have no fear when I cross the cold waters of the River Jordan into heaven."

I showed my mother the letter. "Erase that last sentence," she said.

"Why?"

"It's too melodramatic."

"But what about," and I started singing, "E'en death's cold wave I will not flee/For God through Jordan leadeth me"?

Mom's lips twitched for a second, like she was trying not to smile. She succeeded, and her command voice regained control: "Erase it."

Clearly it wasn't a choice.

* * *

Missionary stories were my earliest entrance into the wider world. I loved them as much for adventure in strange lands as for tales of people coming to Jesus. But the stories also got me thinking about a disturbing question. I followed my father into his vegetable garden one day when I was around seven or eight to ask, "What about the Indians in the Amazon?" I had read about the Huaorani in Rachel Saint's book—about them murdering her missionary brother in Ecuador. "Or the people in Tanganyika? What if they're alive now, but they die before they hear the Word? Will they go to hell?"

He gave me the only possible answer. "Yes."

"But why? That's not fair. Why would God send them to hell if they don't know about him? That's not right."

"We can't say that about God. It might not seem right to us, but the Bible tells us that God's ways are not our ways. We have to trust him. And we have to follow Jesus's command to teach the gospel to every nation. That's why our work is so important. So no one else dies without knowing."

"Still . . . ."

"No. That's how it is."

It was a lesson for me in accepting reality—the reality I was being taught as the Only Reality There Is.

~5~

The Outer Circle

We belonged to a fifth circle, though I was only dimly aware of its existence until the year I turned twelve. This was comprised of the CRC at large. Just as Rehoboth was the hub of the mission outposts in the Navajo Nation, Grand Rapids, Michigan, was the hub of the CRC in the U.S. and Canada. Somewhat sarcastically but also affectionately, we sometimes referred to Grand Rapids as *Jerusalem* or *The Holy City.*

My dad had grown up on a farm close enough to Grand Rapids that he and his brothers rode the wagon with their father to the Grand Rapids Farmers Market every week to sell milk, butter, eggs, and vegetables. Mom came from Everett, Washington, where her father worked in the Water Department. Once every year or two, we loaded ourselves into the car and drove to Grand Rapids or Everett for vacation. While we were in those places, we attended big, formal churches. After the services, Dad spoke about his work and showed slides of what was exotic to the people there, though normal to us. I got paraded up to the front of these churches to sing "Jesus Loves Me" or "Precious Jewels" in Navajo, feeling important and also different.

We moved around from relative to relative while we visited. Sometimes my brothers stayed on Uncle Fred and Aunt Betty's farm. I stayed with my cousin Mary Jo, who was three years older than I was. She listened to pop music, and although she was Christian Reformed, she lived in a world that was completely different from mine. These vacation trips and letters from family and friends were most of how I experienced that fifth and much larger circle of which I was only a tangential part.

The detachment I felt from our outer circle changed the year I turned twelve. That was when my sister Trudy, who was three and a half years younger than I was, was diagnosed with leukemia. Because of that, we moved to metropolitan Washington, D.C., so she could be part of a research program at the National Institutes of Health (NIH).

Enough years in age between us meant that I felt toward Trudy the way a lot of older sisters do toward a younger one—she was mostly a pest. We had shared a bed since she graduated from a crib; she snored, and I pinched her to make her turn over when she did. Sharing a bed meant we also shared a bedroom; she was a slob. To top that off, she had blonde hair and hazel eyes that people said made a beautiful color combination. She had a lovely child's voice, always on pitch, so she was given solo singing parts in school plays and concerts. Everyone expected her to grow up to do something wonderful in music. She was the pest of whom I was jealous. At twelve, I longed for a room of my own.

"Why can't we hang a curtain from the ceiling? We can run it down the middle of the bed. Then I can kind of have my own room."

"That wouldn't work," my mother said.

I could see how a curtain down the center of the bed would be problematic. "We could saw the bed in half and then put up a curtain. Please?"

"How would that work?"

"Daddy could build new legs under each side of the bed."

"She's your sister. You need to learn to get along. You need to stop talking about this."

A few months before Trudy's diagnosis, I had a dream that caused me to sleepwalk out to where my parents were getting ready for bed. "Trudy's gone," I said. I was upset, agitated. "She's not there."

Dad started to laugh. "Yes she is. She's there."

"No, she's gone," I insisted, now feeling bereft.

"Come on," he said. "I'll show you." And he brought me back to our room. "See, there she is." He was still chuckling.

I was angry. Angry with him for laughing. Angry about being wrong. Angry because I felt foolish. Dad laughed some more at my anger as I crawled back into bed.

When my mother told me about Trudy's illness and that she would die unless a cure could be found before then, I lay on my stomach every night, crying into my pillow. Trudy was in the hospital at Rehoboth, so it was all right for me to cry. We weren't supposed to tell her that she was going to die.

Mom and Dad told us how to pray for her. They sat us down in the living room, and Mom started, "We mustn't pray for God to heal her. That would be asking God for special treatment. We would be testing him if we prayed that way. Trudy has a fatal illness. We can ask God to keep her from suffering and to give us courage to deal with her sickness and her dying. We can ask that the doctors find a cure. But we mustn't ask God to make her well."

Dad cleared his throat and added, "Remember how Satan tempted Jesus in the wilderness?"

We nodded.

"And how Jesus said he would be tempting God if he asked for God to send his angels to save him if he jumped from a pinnacle of the temple?"

We nodded again.

"It's like that. We want to follow Jesus's example and not tempt God."

I accepted without questioning that we could rely on God for support, to grant us strength for this trial, and to ease Trudy's suffering. But we shouldn't test God by asking for a miracle.

Dad added, "I believe that God is giving us this trial so we are more able to feel with the Navajo people, feel what it's like when they lose a loved one."

I believed that must be right too.

Soon after her diagnosis, Trudy and my mother flew to Washington, and Trudy started receiving the experimental treatments that everyone hoped would prolong her life until a cure was found. She was about to come home to Gallup in her first remission, when she developed secondary spinal leukemia. That's when Mom and Dad decided the rest of us would move to Washington so we could be together.

The last Sunday before Dad and we kids took off into the unknown, we cried and hugged our friends at the chapel in Tohlakai, where we had moved by that time. We sang "God Be With You 'til We Meet Again" in the Diné language, our tears choking up the words.

A Navajo woman everyone called Grandma Havens, shorter than me, was round and soft with deep wrinkles. In her traditional velveteen blouse, long, full satin skirt, white anklets, and high-top tennis shoes, she rocked me back and forth after the service. Tears ran into her wrinkles, and over and over, she whispered, *"Shitsoi, shitsoi."* My granddaughter, my granddaughter. Then she reached up to a silver-and-turquoise butterfly brooch, unpinned it from her dark green blouse, and fastened it to my white one.

★ ★ ★

The CRC in D.C. was the only thing that was somewhat similar to our life before. It wasn't as big as the churches we'd gone to in Grand Rapids and Everett, but it was definitely more formal than what I was used to. Back at home, we had sat outdoors for our summertime services on a retaining wall outside the Beclabito School, where a goat kid once ran off with my dad's pocket watch in the middle of the service. Here we sat in matching rows of curving walnut benches, and the windows were made of stained glass. There we sang from the *Navajo Gospel Hymnal;* in D.C. we sang from the *Psalter,* the words of the Psalms set to music. But the English Apostles Creed was the same. The three-point Calvinist sermons and the catechism also were the same. Every single Sunday, in both places, the minister or missionary read out the Ten Commandments, in either English or Navajo.

Almost everyone at the church in D.C. had a Dutch surname. There was enough familiarity despite the differences that I eased into some level of comfort. However, there were no Diné.

These CRC people helped sustain us during a time when we were falling apart, not only from the devastation that was daily unfolding in Trudy's body but also from culture shock, and the fact that my father's Bible school training in no way prepared him to support a large family in one of the wealthiest urban areas in the country. He went from job to job.

One job was as a short-order cook in a government canteen. He came home exhausted, wearing the same brown wool sports jacket every day.

"Dad, what is that smell?" I asked after a few days.

He looked bewildered.

"It's your jacket. It smells kind of sweet but not in a good way."

He sniffed his armpits.

"No, it's not that kind of smell."

"No, I guess not," he said. "That's not a sweet smell." He tried to smile. He inhaled more deeply. "Oh, it's the grease from the deep fryers. My jacket hangs on a hook in a hallway by the kitchen. I can't do anything about it."

I tried not to let my face show how nauseating the cloying smell was.

Later he started selling *Encyclopedia Britannica* in the evenings to add to his cook's salary. He was enthusiastic at first, telling us what made *Britannica* unique. "It's the best, most complete encyclopedia in the world. The eleventh edition, published in 1911, was the first American edition." His voice grew more and more animated. "It's a collector's item now, but it's out of date, of course. Sometimes people trade them in for a new edition, and I can get a big commission if that happens." He sounded happy.

His zeal waned, though, as we asked every time he walked in the door, "Did you make a sale?"

Sometimes he got back his old grin. "Guess," he'd say. And we knew he wouldn't be teasing if the answer was no. Other times, his shoulders slumped, and he shook his head. Selling carpets at Montgomery Ward became his most stable job, but even that depended on commission.

The church softened that edge of poverty and worry. Women brought us casseroles. The deacons donated cash. People passed us their hand-me-downs. We children were parceled out among various families when Mom needed to be at the hospital with Trudy while Dad was working. The CRC network came through for us. We belonged, so it was there for us—a safety net, a group of people who automatically cared. Our family routines—prayer and Bible reading, meals eaten together, church and Sunday school—remained a foundation. They kept our lives from becoming utter chaos during the nine months of Trudy's illness.

When Mom and Dad were working or staying with the younger children, I spent hours with Trudy in the hospital. I massaged her legs because changes in her bone marrow caused intense pain. I played games with her and watched her sleep. When she came home on passes, we had a room with twin beds. When she was in the hospital, I essentially had my own room. I was sorry I had wished for it.

Things between us had changed. We talked more than we ever had, and I even started confiding in her. The rule that we weren't to talk about her dying was still in place, but clearly, I needed to find a way to talk about it. One evening when she was on a home pass from the hospital, I said, trying to sound casual, "If I die, I want to be buried in Teec Nos Pos. Where do you want to be buried?"

"I don't know. I don't think it matters," she said. She had grown old, older than I was.

* * *

While Trudy was hospitalized, I contracted rheumatic fever and had to stay home on bed rest for several months. Our minister, Reverend Jansma, visited me once a week to keep up my catechism instruction. I spent my daytime hours on the couch in the living room, and when he came, he pulled a kitchen chair up next to me. We started with the questions and answers from the *Heidelberg Catechism*. When I had recited, Reverend Jansma and I chatted about them. "What does this mean to you?" he might ask. Or, "What do you think about this answer?" Then we moved on, away from the catechism lesson. We talked about Trudy, about the fact that she was dying. We talked about what happens to us when we die, about heaven and hell. We talked about my own faith, catechism aside.

⋆ ⋆ ⋆

The people back home at Tohlakai, separated from us by so much distance, had also become part of our fifth circle of belonging. While we were gone, this little group of believers, poorer than us in our worst scarcity, took up a collection for us. Another time, we received a thin square package in the mail. We opened it to find a reel of magnetic tape. We all settled in the living room, and when my mother pressed play, we heard the whole congregation:

> *Nizhonigo jooba' diits'a'*
> *Yisdashiiltinigii,*
> *Lah yoo'iiya, k'ad shenahoosdzin,*
> *Doo eesh'ii da nt'ee'.*

We started to sing along to "Amazing Grace," grinning at each other. It was almost like being home. Then Charlie Becenti started to pray, *"Nihitaa' shidyin God. . ."* I knew we would be sitting quietly for a long time. One by one, people came to the microphone and said things to us, some in the Diné language, some in English. Everyone said they were praying for us. They sang more songs: "There'll Be No Dark Valley," "Precious Jewels." The last one was "The Great Physician" about Jesus healing us. Maybe the people at Tohlakai believed that Trudy could be healed. We sang along on all the hymns. Then we started the tape all over again. And again.

★ ★ ★

When Trudy died, we drove to Michigan. Her funeral took place in the little white clapboard church in Jamestown that my father had ridden to in a horse and buggy as a farm boy. The only other time I'd been there was for his mother's funeral. After the service, a black limo took us to Zutphen, a tiny hamlet named after a beloved town in the Netherlands, to bury Trudy next to my grandmother.

The gravesite stood on a small, windswept hillock. It was the middle of May, but a chilly breeze soughed around us. My long-sleeved blouse was made of thin cotton, and I shivered and closed my arms over my chest. I held on tight while the former missionary from Gallup read scripture, delivered a second sermon, and prayed. The group around the grave broke up, and people walked over to my parents to hug them and cry with them and talk to them.

Two weeks short of thirteen, I stood by, not knowing what to do. I held myself tighter. Although relatives and friends of our own ethnicity—more Dutch than American—surrounded us, they didn't truly know me, and I didn't know them. None of them came over to give my brothers or me a hug.

Then John Tsosie walked up to me. John had been my father's interpreter and, encouraged by Dad, was attending RBI in Grand Rapids. He was the only Diné at the funeral. We knew all the same people from the chapel at Tohlakai. John threw his arms around me and rocked me and sobbed. We looked deep into each other's eyes, and we didn't have to say anything. We cried together, and in that moment, I was comforted. We would go back to D.C. temporarily, but the people I deeply belonged with were the believers at Tohlakai.

~6~

Inheritance

EVEN THOUGH I WAS A GIRL AND WOULD EVENTUALLY have seven younger brothers, I was my father's heir apparent. My father's name was Richard, and he went by Rich. His parents hadn't had the inclination, or perhaps the time with eleven other children, to give him a middle name. He gave himself a middle initial. "P for Poor," he'd say. "No one should think because my name is Rich that I'm actually rich."

He'd laugh, his cheeks scrunched up to his slightly naughty eyes. Then he'd correct himself right away. "I'm rich in children. My quiver is full of arrows." He'd laugh again. I was the first arrow he planned to shoot forth. He planned and hoped and groomed me to become a Bible woman. He planned that for my inheritance, although I would not be aware of his goal for me until after I'd left home.

Early in 1952, before I turned four, my parents, Dickie, Trudy, and I boarded the train from Grand Rapids to the mission field in New Mexico. As the cars rumbled forward, my father gave me a stack of brightly colored, glossy papers folded like small books. "You go around our train car and ask people if they'd like one."

"What are they?"

"They're gospel tracts. They tell people about Jesus and how to be saved. People are just sitting looking out the windows. They have a lot of time for reading right now."

I took them without hesitation, filled with importance. I headed down the aisle and stopped at each seat: "Would you like a gospel tract?"

"What's a gospel tract?" a middle-aged man asked.

"It tells you about Jesus. Are you saved?"

The man stared at me.

"Do you know you have to believe that Jesus died to save you from your sins? You have to believe that to be saved."

"I don't have time for reading," he said gruffly.

"Daddy says that we have a lot of time on the train. You don't want one?"

He took one, no doubt in self-defense. Other people took them because they thought it was cute, this little girl acting the part of a missionary. Some refused.

One woman said when I asked the question, "Yes, I'm saved. It's wonderful that you're doing the Lord's work at such a young age."

I raced back to Dad, out of breath, and said, pointing, "That lady over there, she's a believer." My father and the woman smiled and nodded at each other.

Already, I knew how to divide up the world.

I've always believed that the CRC did not place a lot of emphasis on hellfire and damnation. Nevertheless, as I passed out tracts and talked with the passengers, I knew for certain that they would go to hell if they didn't accept Jesus as their savior. The hereafter was more important than how we lived our lives on Earth. Images of what hell would be like were seared upon my retina and my skin. I saw unsaved people—men, women, and children—immersed in a lake of fire. They burned and thirsted in constant pain for all eternity. Even at that tender age, I had some concept of eternity as something that would go on and on and never stop. I didn't believe I was destined for such everlasting torture, but I vividly imagined what being cast into that lake would be like. In moments of self-doubt, my imagination terrified me. And it gave me a passion to let everyone within my reach know that salvation was a prayer away, if they only believed.

★ ★ ★

In Shiprock, our home stood on the top of a hill covered by large, round river rocks. Not far from the imposing two-story house stood a white canvas tent, its walls reinforced with wood scraps from ammunition boxes. Rudy and Bobby Yellowhair lived in that tent with their mother year-round. In Shiprock, the average temperature ranges from fifteen to ninety-four degrees Fahrenheit.

Bobby and Rudy became my first playmates in the Navajo Nation. Every day, we built miniature Diné home sites in the shadow of our clapboard garage, like the ones I would later build with Ilene Begay. Bobby and Rudy were the ones who taught me this game. We chattered companionably, speaking for our imaginary families in Dummitawry English, the creole I'd picked up with ease. When Rudy and Bobby shifted to the Diné language, I stumbled on in our accented English with its modified syntax. Sometimes I recited the Apostles' Creed in Navajo under my breath because it had lots of sentences and made it sound like I was speaking the language I needed.

Without my father's recollection, that's all I would remember—the coziness, our games, and the mild subterfuge that enabled me to belong. Years later, my father continued to tell a different, though not contradictory, story. At first, he told it with pride. Later he would tell it to try to win me back.

As he told it, "One day, when you were playing with the Yellowhair boys, you ran to me. You said, 'Daddy, I told Bobby and Rudy about Jesus dying for their sins. They believe! Can you baptize them?' I had to explain that I was a lay missionary and that I couldn't baptize anyone."

My dad always ended his tale by saying, "At such a young age, you put me to shame with your simple faith and your courage to witness for Jesus to your friends." It didn't seem to count with him that every day, he went with his interpreter to people's hogans to preach the gospel, and he taught Sunday school and religious instruction in the surrounding BIA schools several times a week. Somehow, that wasn't enough.

"You set me an example," he would add. For years, his telling of this story could fill my chest with the warmth of his pride in me.

⋆ ⋆ ⋆

During meals my father asked me and often the rest of the kids too, questions about the Bible. I knew he cared about what we thought. He might ask, "What do you think Jesus meant when he said, 'Unless you become as a little child, you cannot enter the kingdom of heaven?'" Or, "What does it mean to not put new wine into old wineskins?"

One time, Dad and I had a conversation about a letter from Grandpa, his father. It was about one of Grandpa Kruis's cherished beliefs. Grandpa had been born within days after his family got off the boat from the Netherlands. Here in the U.S., he was raised in the cheerless Calvinist sect known as the *Nederduitsers.* No musical instruments, no stained glass windows, no imagery of any kind.

Dad started out with, "Grandpa says that it's wrong to have a cross hanging in church.

"What do you think?"

I could've given the quick and easy, the flippant response: "Grandpa thinks it's wrong to have a chair in church. He thinks it's wrong to be happy." But no, I was quite willing to work out a long answer. "He says so because of the second commandment. 'Thou shalt not make unto thee any graven image, or any likeness of anything that is in heaven above, on the earth beneath or in the water under the earth.' Grandpa thinks the cross is a graven image."

I paused to think through my dissection, and then went on. "God told Moses to raise the brass serpent when the Israelites were being bitten by snakes in the wilderness. If they looked at the brass serpent, they didn't die from the bites, right?"

My father nodded. "Go on."

I gained momentum. "The brass serpent stood for Jesus on the cross." This idea was not mine; I had been taught it and had seen pictures of the brass reptile on a cross-shaped pole. People on the ground were surrounded by snakes and gazed piteously up at the brass one.

My father nodded again.

Certain that I was on a praiseworthy track, I proceeded. "Since God told Moses to make the brass serpent, it couldn't have been wrong, even though it was a graven image. I think it's the same with the cross. It's a symbol of Jesus dying to save us from our sins. It's just there in the church to remind us of that."

My father smiled, and I went on. "The point of the commandment about graven images is that we mustn't worship things we make with our hands. It would be wrong to worship the cross." Here I could have earned a few more points by adding, "Like the Catholics do."

"But it's all right if the cross is just a reminder to be thankful for what Jesus did for us." I was finished. My father nodded again, and my inner glow mirrored the one on his face.

By the time I was twelve, my father considered me ready to put my knowledge and faith to good use. He gave me my own Sunday school class to teach. By then, he was serving the mission at Tohlakai, which was not as traditionally Navajo as Teec Nos Pos, where we'd lived before, because it was closer to Gallup. Teec Nos Pos was nearer the center of the Navajo Nation, with only dirt-road access. Because Tohlakai was closer to town, more people spoke English, and there was more alcoholism and less self-sufficiency. But some things were still traditional. I could herd sheep with my friends. Turquoise-and-silver jewelry was still a sign of wealth, as were livestock. Older women still dressed in brilliant long, satin skirts and velvet blouses. Middle-aged women, however, had assimilated to the extent that they wore long, full calico skirts and cotton blouses.

The chapel at Tohlakai nestled in a broad enclosure of apricot and cream-colored sandstone mesas. I would be hard pressed to call the room where we worshipped a sanctuary. When we first arrived there, the walls were Pepto Bismol pink. An insipid, popular reproduction of an angel guiding two blonde, curly-haired and rosy-cheeked tots over a decrepit bridge across a bottomless chasm hung behind the pulpit. Grandpa Kruis would have been appalled, because to him it would have represented a graven image.

My father didn't like it either. "It's not biblical," he said. "We don't know what angels look like. And they don't come down to us physically now anyway." He sounded a little grumpy.

"Also, the children are blonde and blue-eyed. The kids we serve have brown skin and black hair. How are they going to relate to that?" he said in a moment of cultural sensitivity that came and went.

The picture disappeared as soon as he felt he would not offend any of the members of the chapel. The walls were soon painted a soft, pastel peach, a choice my mother no doubt influenced.

A rickety old man whose son had been my father's interpreter at Teec Nos Pos lived near the chapel. Mr. Todacheenee came early every Sunday morning and on prayer meeting nights to light the propane heater in winter and to sweep the floor. Despite Mr. Todacheenee's efforts, whenever I think of Sundays at Tohlakai, my feet go chill because it was always cold down by the floor. The little trailer to the east of the church, where I taught my Sunday school class, was worse. It had no heat source at all, so we were forced to wear coats and jackets while we sang gospel choruses and I honed my skills as a storyteller.

Storytelling was what I loved best about teaching Sunday school. Each week, I had to recount the story selected by the church. My favorite stories were bound to come along at some point: Jacob wresting with God; Rahab brought into the fold; the woman at the well, an outsider who was the first to hear Jesus's biggest and best secret; the men on the road to Emmaus suddenly recognizing the resurrected Lord whom they'd been grieving. They were all stories of spiritual struggle, loss, redemption, and change.

I loved telling the stories just as much as I loved the stories themselves. I delighted in seeing children's eyes widen with suspense, watching them jump in their seats when the climax of a story startled them. I loved the power of making that happen. I thrilled when they asked penetrating questions like, "Why did God tell Abraham to kill his own son?" And I basked in the knowledge of my father's confidence that I was ready for this important task in God's kingdom.

By the time I was a junior in high school, someone other than Dad had recognized my Bible-teaching talents. I was marshaled into an army of religious instructors, mostly adults, who went on Wednesday evenings and Sunday mornings to the huge BIA school at Fort Wingate, fifteen miles east of Rehoboth. There, I taught second-graders about the characters who peopled the Bible and had been saved by God.

On Sundays, a group of us teens, along with a few adults from the mission, piled into vans and drove into Gallup to the county jail. The moment we stepped inside, the stink of pinto beans with lots of onions, farts they generated, filthy feet, dirty clothes, and stale alcohol assailed us. The jail had two large holding cells—drunk tanks—packed with men picked up from the streets of Gallup on Friday and Saturday nights. We sang hymns to them in English, Navajo, and Spanish. We took turns preaching. Women and girls were not allowed to preach in churches or even in chapels, which is what we called the fringy mission churches. But we could preach in the jail if we called it *bringing the message*, and I took my turn, first in front of the bars of one drunk tank, then the other. The tanks weren't soundproof, and while we preached at the second, men from the first tank, still half drunk and coping with hangovers, shouted and mocked the words we'd just spoken to them. Some of the boys in our group snickered. The catcalls of the men in the tanks humiliated me. The way the boys colluded with them made it even worse. The Bible says we are blessed if men revile us for the sake of the gospel, but I didn't feel blessed. I felt ashamed. I struggled to preach on, but I had no joy of it.

One evening a week, we got into the vans again and drove to the Gallup Rescue Mission on the north side of town. The pervasive beans-and-onion smell hit us again. But the men were showered and shaved and wearing clean second-hand clothes. They weren't allowed in if they'd been drinking. Some of them joined the hymn singing. We played our band instruments for them. And we preached. Girls and women could also preach at the Rescue Mission.

* * *

It's no wonder, given his own frame of reference and the pleasure he took in the exercise of my faith, that my father hoped I would become a Bible woman. Bible women attended Bible school, as my father had. They taught Sunday school, ran ladies' aid societies, and provided religious instruction in the schools. They might even visit people in their homes with a Bible and some of the pamphlets given to students in Sunday school tucked under one arm. But they could never, never deliver a sermon in church. They couldn't even pray aloud in a "real" church, only in chapels. They were, after all, just women.

I didn't know until a year after I taught religious instruction and spoke at the jail and rescue mission that this was my father's goal for me. He had never mentioned it, and in fact, my mother was the one who told me about his wishes when I came home for Christmas during my first year of college.

"Dad was disappointed that you're going to Calvin," she told me one evening when we were alone in the kitchen.

"What?" Calvin College was a rigorous liberal arts college, our church's flagship institution. There were two other church colleges, newer and not yet accredited but more conservative, so I could guess that his objection wasn't academic.

"*Ja*," she said. "He hoped you would go to RBI and become a Bible woman. He thinks you'd be so good at it." The focus at the Bible Institute was on training men to be lay missionaries and women to be what they euphemistically called *helpmeets* for the men. If they stayed single, they could be Bible women.

"But RBI isn't even a college," I protested.

Mom gave me a blank look, and I thought there was no point explaining anything.

"Why didn't he ever tell me that's what he wanted?" I asked in a gentler tone.

"I guess he hoped you would decide that on your own."

I nodded. Earlier on, I would have been thrilled by my dad's desire for me to follow in his footsteps. But even as I told Bible stories at the BIA school and brought messages to those men who were down and out, things were changing inside me. Years of being attracted to other girls were fulfilled when I fell in love with Grace my junior year of high school. Our relationship was a realization of my earlier dreams. I knew what I wanted, what made me happy. But my mother's pronouncement about Alice and Jennie had also showed me for the first time that what made me happy would mean losing the faith community I loved and wanted to serve.

The words, "RBI isn't even a college," said what I felt most strongly when my mother told me about my father's wishes. I thought, "He has no idea what I might really be able to do with my life. He has no idea what interests me." My relationship with Grace and my semester at Calvin had created a shift, so I felt a sort of contempt for the role of a Bible woman. Four classes of professional servants worked in the mission field: ordained minister, lay missionary, Diné interpreter, and Bible woman—in that order. What my father wanted for me was the lowest class in which the church was willing to let me serve.

~7~

The Test and the Prize

OUR TIME IN D.C. LENGTHENED FROM THE FEW MONTHS we'd first expected to nearly a year after Trudy's death. The long delay was because the Mission Board needed to arrange housing for us back in the Navajo Nation. Since my mother didn't need to spend time at the hospital with Trudy, she went to work as a nurse. Her salary took away some of our worry, but it was hard on my dad. Being of the "Greatest Generation," it shamed him to know that my mother could command better earnings than he could. Every time we asked if he had made a sale, whether it was *Encyclopedia Britannica* or carpets at Montgomery Ward, he looked grim when he'd been unsuccessful.

While we waited to go back home, I started to press my case for taking the big test, the one that would let me finally take communion—that ultimate symbol of kinship with other believers, of belonging and being nourished in my soul. Taking communion also meant something about being more grown up, an important rite of passage. This time, my relationship with the pastor made me feel I did not have to plead with my parents. They seemed, typically for my mother and atypically for my father, to be invested in maintaining the status quo. They believed I should wait four or five more years.

Although he always stayed safe within the stronghold of fundamentalist Christianity, my father did like to question authority and ideas. Despite his devotion to the fundamentals and within that simplistic frame of reference, Dad was capable of complexities that surfaced sometimes as contradictions, like the time when I found the peyote fan in the chicken yard, and he placed it in a cabinet with his books on preaching. My dad never questioned God's authority or the authority of the Bible, although he loved to explore different interpretations, asking questions such as, "What did Jesus mean when he said not to put new wine into old wineskins?" When it came, however, to my making profession of faith and taking communion earlier than our church's standard age of seventeen or eighteen, he held the orthodox line.

* * *

One evening when we were younger after we had moved to Gallup, Dad took Dickie and me to a small, storefront Baptist church. Communion was being served, and I listened closely to the minister's words, comparing them to what the preachers said in the CRC. One line leaped out at me: "If you believe that Jesus died to save you from your sins, you are welcome at the Lord's table. We will not turn anyone away."

I breathed in sharply and looked at Dad. "Can I?" I begged.

He hesitated for the briefest moment. Then he shook his head.

"Why not?" I whispered. "He just said if you believe. I believe."

"You haven't made profession of faith yet."

"But . . ."

"No."

I watched my father take the bread and the juice, and felt intensely that I was being left out.

After church, as we walked home, I asked again. "Why not? I believe. You know I believe."

"Even though we went to this Baptist church this one time, we're still Christian Reformed. We practice *close* communion. That means we make sure everyone is partaking in a worthy manner by first making profession of faith, by being old enough to understand the step they are taking, by not letting people take communion if they have been to a Navajo ceremony."

"That doesn't sound like *close* communion to me. It's *closed* communion."

"No, it's close. Close because when we all believe the same way, we are *close* with each other."

"Yeah. Closed. Closed to anyone who doesn't believe what we believe. It's closed to anyone who hasn't made profession of faith, like me. Even though I believe what's in the Bible. And the catechism. Closed."

★ ★ ★

Now, in D.C., I didn't consciously think I was outmaneuvering my parents, but instead of talking to them once more about making profession of faith, I went to Reverend Jansma. I had told him during one of our catechism sessions how much I wanted to make profession of faith. He hadn't seemed surprised, and he didn't mention that I wasn't the right age. In his non-reaction, I must have sensed openness, so one Sunday after Trudy's death, I waited until he was finished shaking hands with everyone as they left the sanctuary.

He shook my hand, and then I said, "Reverend Jansma?"

"Yes?"

"You know how I told you I wanted to make profession of faith?"

"Yes?"

"Well, I want to. May I?"

Perhaps Reverend Jansma didn't think I needed my parents' permission. Possibly he'd had a conversation with them about this very thing, based on knowing me so well. Maybe my parents just had no resistance left in them after the trauma of Trudy's death and the economic hardships we'd been through. There is a family snapshot that suggests that may have been the case. Taken a few days after Trudy's funeral, it shows every single one of us, even baby Ronnie, looking shell-shocked.

At any rate, without much more ado, it seemed that Mom and Dad had turned over the decision to the authority of the minister and the group of elders called the *consistory*.

Reverend Jansma arranged an evening for me to take the test that I had long known I would have to pass. My father drove me to the church. At thirteen, while I could have driven on the dirt roads back home on the reservation, I clearly couldn't drive myself to the church in D.C., and his taking me there signified his wordless consent. Dad left to run some errands, and I walked down the dimly lit steps into the church basement, pushed on the swinging doors, and faced thirteen middle-aged white men sitting around a large table under glaring fluorescent lights.

Reverend Jansma was the thirteenth man. For days I had been practicing the questions and answers of the catechism, because my mother told me that was what they would be asking me. That's what her examiners, one of whom was her taciturn, courtly father, had asked her.

I soon realized that my examination would be different from my mother's. Not one question came from the catechism. They started by asking for my testimony, the story of my faith. Testimonies are given in revival tents and mission chapels, not in the staid, by-the-book churches I had attended when we visited our relatives. Even though it was a more-formal church than the chapel at Tohlakai, the D.C. church also lay on a fringe of the denomination. Its location placed it far from the reach of the heartland, our church's own Bible Belt. Instead of congregations made up of Dutch immigrants, farmers, and factory workers, the men who were examining me were doctors, lawyers, and civil servants who sat in high places in the federal government. They were more educated than most people I'd known in the CRC, and later, I realized that this may have affected their mindset when they met with me. I had some sense, even at the time, that Trudy's death had played a role in my being allowed to take this step which folks in Grand Rapids and even in the Navajo Nation would have seen as premature.

I cleared my throat, and began. "When I was seven, we were at the Southwest Bible and Missionary Conference in Flagstaff. In the dining hall, during devotions after dinner, I asked Jesus to come into my heart. But I've believed that Jesus died to save me ever since I can remember." I didn't really know what else there was to say.

One of the men, whom I knew worked high up in the State Department because his daughter was my best friend, asked, "How has your sister's death affected your faith?"

"I think it made my faith stronger," I said. "God was my comfort. And I know that Trudy is in heaven now. Someday I'll see her again. And I'll see Jesus."

Mr. Bruinsma took it a bit further. "What do you think heaven will be like?"

I thought for a moment. "I don't think we'll just be standing around singing and playing harps all day," I said. "That would get boring, and heaven can't be boring or it wouldn't be heaven. I think it's a place where we'll be really creative."

The elders' smiles said, but I knew anyway, that it wasn't the answer they expected. I knew they liked it, and I was sinfully proud of that. I suppose my pride is why it's the question and answer I remember best.

The following Sunday, I sat in the front pew. When Reverend Jansma called on me, I stood up in my pale blue shirtwaist dress and white pumps and heard him read the form for profession of faith from the back of the *Psalter Hymnal,* the CRC songbook. At the end of the form were four basic questions about my adherence to the fundamentals of the faith. When the minister read, "What is your answer?" I proclaimed loudly, "I do." I had heard others mumble the two words so softly they could barely be heard, and I had decided beforehand that everyone in the congregation would hear me. Another moment of deadly pride.

The last words of the form were the ones I had longed to hear. "I now welcome you to full communion with the people of God. Rest assured that these privileges are now yours." To me, at that time, this meant one thing. I could now eat the bread and drink the wine or juice of communion.

⋆ ⋆ ⋆

While we lived in D.C., I had a heavy crush on the young woman who had hosted my mother and Trudy before our family moved there. At thirty-two, Ruth was nearly twenty years older than I was, but to me, she was young, cool, and funny. She lived with her handsome doctor husband in a split-level house with pink kitchen appliances. They had only two children instead of the seven my forty-year-old mother had borne by then, which was decidedly uncool.

A boy at church liked me, and I liked him, so I imagined that we grew up and married each other and had four children. I had all their names picked out, but in my daydreams, John was somewhere off to work, and in my fantasies, Ruth and I cared for the children together.

In real life, I babysat for Ruth and Jim's children and sometimes stayed overnight to keep her company while he was on duty at the Naval Hospital. Those evenings we talked nonstop, and she didn't seem to mind listening to me. When she got pregnant with her third child, I spent hours embroidering a set of baby nightgowns and kimonos and could hardly wait to present them to her.

The back of our *Psalter Hymnal* contained several liturgical forms. One was the form for the direct opposite of Profession of Faith: Excommunication. When I was bored during a sermon, I started reading it to myself with what may have been prescience. In each blank for the name of the excommunicant, I mentally inserted Ruth's name. She was always being expelled in my mind for some sexual wrong (what else?). According to the form, the sin must be persistent and without remorse. It was called *living in sin,* exactly how my mother would later refer to Alice and Jennie.

In my mind, Ruth committed adultery with some unknown man, because that was all I knew of sexual sin. I had just become a communicant, so certainly *I* could not be excommunicated. In fact, I was completely unaware that the communion I had joined would condemn my desires outright. My desires were for affection—physical to be sure, but they had not yet evolved into anything explicitly sexual.

* * *

I didn't get to partake of my first communion in D.C. because our church celebrated it seldom—only four times a year. I had asked my father once, "If it's so spiritually nourishing for us, how come we don't have it more often?"

He said, with no small amount of contempt, "We don't want it to be commonplace. It shouldn't become an empty ritual like it is with the Catholics. They can take communion every day if they want to."

If you wanted to take communion in any Christian Reformed church but the local one where you were a member, you had to get permission from an elder who would actually be serving the bread and wine or juice. The elders were the gatekeepers, though I don't know what they would've done if the plate with bread was going down a row and someone in the middle who wasn't preapproved took a piece. An elder could hardly scramble over several laps and snatch the cube from the person's hand before the minister told us to take, eat, remember, and believe.

Not many unknown or uninitiated people ever came to our churches, though, and the elders stood in the vestibule on communion Sunday to snag them and check their Christian, preferably CRC, credentials before the service ever started. I never heard one of those inspections, but I imagine they went something like this:

Elder: Welcome to our church. We're having the Lord's Supper this Sunday. Where do you usually attend?

Visitor: First Christian Reformed in Vriesland, Michigan.

Elder: Oh, you must know Reverend Boomsma.

Visitor: Yes!
Elder: You're welcome to partake.

Or:

Elder: Where do you usually attend church?
Visitor: First Baptist in Gallup.
Elder: Are you saved?
Visitor: Yes.
Elder: How do you believe you were saved?
Visitor: I believe that Jesus died to save me from my sins.
Elder: Were you baptized?
Visitor: Of course. I'm a Baptist.
Elder: You're welcome to partake then, if you're right with the Lord.

According to my father, the church was protecting the closeness of our communion. I imagine the elders also believed they were protecting unworthy partakers from damning themselves, since our church placed a lot of emphasis on St. Paul's words, "He that eateth or drinketh in an unworthy manner eateth and drinketh damnation unto himself."

By the time I got to take communion for the first time, we had returned from D.C. to the mission at Tohlakai. Since we didn't have an evening service there, my parents decided we would go to evening services at Rehoboth. Soon after our return, maybe even the first Sunday, communion was being served. At the evening service, people who had missed the morning service—nurses, mothers with small children, people who taught Sunday school at the BIA schools—sat in the front rows to partake.

My dad called the elder who would be serving to get permission for himself and my mom—ridiculous, since they were well known as part of the mission staff. I heard his end of the conversation.

"Ed, this is Rich Kruis. Mae and Anna and I will be coming to church at Rehoboth tonight."

. . .

"Yes, we knew that. That's why I'm calling. To get permission."

. . .

"There's something else. While we were in D.C., Anna made profession of faith."

. . .

"It'll be her first time."

. . .

"Yes. All right then. See you later." Off the phone he said, "Mr. Rienstra was glad I told him about you."

My first communion, at long last. I knew I should be appropriately solemn, but I tingled with excitement. I shouldn't be focused on what people would think—me being so young and entirely visible at the front of the church. But I was. So I felt self-conscious as the three of us walked up to the communicants' pew.

When the minister began reading the form for the Lord's Supper, I conjured myself into the upper room where Jesus held the Last Supper with his disciples. I felt the sorrow that I imagined Jesus felt, knowing what was about to happen to him. I didn't think that he might have been feeling fear. I imagined what it must have been like to be John, leaning into Jesus. Then the plate of bread came by, and in all the solemnity I had created for myself—but also nervousness—I took a cube between my thumb and forefinger. I heard several loud gasps behind me and was completely distracted from my sacred imaginings. I tried not to feel satisfaction at the stir I'd caused and to get back onto my holy track, but not with complete success.

Then the tray of tiny cups came by. They served real wine at Rehoboth, not the grape juice we used on the reservation. I'd never tasted any kind of alcohol before, and that single swallow gave me a shock—fire traveled like lightning from my throat to a spot between my legs—one more distraction. How could this be? Not at all the sanctity I'd anticipated. In a few seconds, the sensation was gone, and I was able to redirect my thoughts and feelings. I was thrilled that this privilege was now mine, even with its unexpected side effects and the fact that it was over so quickly.

~8~

Bliss

I WAS FIFTEEN AND A JUNIOR WHEN GRACE AND I BECAME GIRLfriends. We'd known each other since I was in fifth grade. That year, we saw each other in chapel, Reformed Doctrine, catechism, choir, chemistry, American History, and band. Our romance started in choir, where we stood next to each other in the alto section.

We started holding hands beneath the cover of our skirts. Then we played our fingers over each other's palms. We were partners in chemistry lab, looking so deeply into each other's eyes on one occasion that we nearly missed the titration point in our acid experiment. We played in a brass ensemble together. We rested our heads on one another's shoulders in the bus when the choir went to sing at mission posts on the reservation. Until then, my crushes had never amounted to more than fantasy. My relationship with Grace changed all that.

My junior year was also the only year, except when I was eight years old, that I stayed in a dormitory on campus. I was the first white student to integrate dorms that had previously been all Navajo with a few Zuni and Hopi students sprinkled in. These were the kids I felt most at home with, having started my life on a mission post deep in the Navajo Nation rather than at the main mission of Rehoboth, a place that always felt exclusive to me. It was the central mission where mostly white families who worked in the school or hospital and on the maintenance crew lived.

I hadn't gotten into the dorm without controversy, which would fuel my awakening consciousness of racism and other forms of oppression during my senior year. Before this time, there had been a missionary children's dorm, where I lived when I was a boarding student at eight. That dorm had closed a few years earlier, so when the principal suggested to my parents that I needed more of a social life at school, the high school dorm was the only place for me.

White missionaries got up in arms when they heard at the monthly mission council that I was already ensconced in the dorm without their approval. The rationale for separate dorms had always been about saving souls—to save spaces for unsaved or newly saved Native children. I wondered why, if that were the case, the Navajo missionaries' children had never lived in the missionary children's dorm.

The Diné missionaries on the council, men who had gone to the same Bible institute as my father and also worked as laymen, won the day. They believed that integration would be a valuable mission tool for saving souls by sending a message of welcome and equality. For once, the white missionaries' arguments paled next to the Navajos' line of reasoning. In fairness, I know that some white missionaries, including my father, agreed with the Native missionaries.

This was the mid-'60s, when the Red Power Movement was rumbling awake. In four years, Dennis Banks and several other Natives would found the American Indian Movement to fight for indigenous rights. A year later, Vine Deloria Jr. would publish *Custer Died for Your Sins: An Indian Manifesto.* Some of the more vocal Navajo missionaries seemed attracted to the movement, though I overheard my parents and other white missionaries talking about it in disparaging tones.

"Have you heard anybody talking about Red Power?"

"Oh, you mean those Plains Indians? Those Sioux? Something like those Black Panthers we've been hearing about."

"*Ja*. Well. Those Redhorse brothers. They're getting ideas about that kind of thing too. They seem to think they should have a bigger say than the rest of us about mission decisions."

"We better keep an eye on that. I hear that Preston Yazzie is kind of in with them."

I think the issue, small as it was, of my integrating the dorm was one way the Diné missionaries flexed their muscles, something that would happen more and more in the mission field as civil rights movements grew across the country. The white missionaries couldn't ignore what the Navajo missionaries were saying about desegregating the dorms, since the Diné had wisely couched their objective in soul-saving rhetoric.

Living in the dorm helped nurture my relationship with Grace. Had I lived at home in Gallup, we would have had fewer after-school opportunities to get together. We took walks arm-in-arm down the lane leading out to Route 66 and hiked through sagebrush fields to the canyons in the hogbacks. We joined each other in study hall after supper in the school library. Our first kiss on the lips happened through the screen of my dorm window.

But the blissfulness of my junior year quickly disintegrated at the start of my senior year. I moved back home so I could take a job as a cashier at Dandee Supermarket in town, starting in the summer and planning to continue part-time during the school year. Grace left on a summer mission trip and wrote me all those letters on onionskin paper. She was back for less than a week when her family took her to start her freshman year at Calvin College. A few weeks later, to everyone's surprise, Mr. Vander Laan returned by himself. "The family has decided to move to Grand Rapids," he told us. "I'm just back to pack up the house and tie up some loose ends."

I couldn't believe that Grace wouldn't have told me. Me, of all people. After all, she had pledged to love me forever. How did that fit with learning after the fact and secondhand that she wouldn't be coming back for Christmas vacation? I remembered her whispering when we'd hugged goodbye, "See you at Christmas." I was sure she'd known that the family was moving. In all those letters while she was on her mission, why had she left out this vital information about moving but told me just how many times some boy rubbed Coppertone on her back at the beach?

~9~

Villains

What I saw as Grace's betrayal initiated my senior year. Then came my mother's pronouncement, "They're living in sin," transforming my last year of high school into one of dread and growing withdrawal. The evening when Mr. Vander Laan came to the house for supper, I didn't dare ask him anything about Grace, fearful of another wound.

A couple of Sundays after that watershed day, Jennie, who had often sung solos in church, was asked to sing one last song. Call it her swan song, if you will. My mother told me, "Jennie and Alice have to leave the mission."

I went still.

"Jennie's parents are down from Grand Rapids. I hope someone talks to them."

Alarm bells rang. I forced my face to show nothing and thought, "What if someone noticed something about Grace and me? What if they talked to my parents?"

Oblivious to my fears, my mother plunged on. "Hopefully, Jennie's just under Alice's influence."

I stopped thinking about me and wondered, "Why only talk to Jennie's parents? Why not Alice's? It's because she's Navajo, and Jennie's white. It must not matter so much if

Alice is living a life of sin, even though we're here to save Navajos from sin."

Much later, I would recognize the homophobia in what my mother said. Alice, with her ducktail, leather Eisenhower jacket, pegged jeans, and down-to-earth stockiness, fit my mother's stereotype of a lesbian. Jennie, with her soft blonde wave and dresses didn't. So Alice was seen as the lesbian seductress and Jennie as her victim.

When Jennie went up to the front of the sanctuary to sing, I watched and listened with every fiber in me quivering. She wore a white shirtwaist dress and a hand-knit, cherry red cardigan. Even then, I saw her sartorial choices as a study in contrasts—purity covered over by sexual sin. Her face was pale, and she didn't smile. I was struck by how brave she was. Surely with all that my mother, who didn't even live at the mission, knew and judged, the other adults in church would also be writhing with condemnation. I pondered too why she'd been asked to sing one more time. Was it in hope that this would make her realize the error of her ways?

As I watched, I wondered whether anything in a gesture or expression would tell me I belonged up there with her. Not that I could sing like her. When she opened her mouth, the notes came out as melodious and true as ever. I wanted to cry for the beauty, the poignancy, the possibility that I was related to this woman, that I might at some point suffer a fate like hers. Would she be excommunicated, or was sending her away from the mission enough to cleanse the rest of us from the stink that stuck to her? And where was Alice? Already gone?

⋆ ⋆ ⋆

I met my new English teacher, who was fresh out of college, at senior registration. I carried my baby brother, Brian, on my hip and wondered what Miss Hartgerink thought of me—responsible like a little mother? She and Mom started to play Dutch bingo, the game that goes, "Who do you know that I know?" We always find out that in this relatively small world, we are not separated by six degrees but only one or two. And that all of us are Dutch.

"Are you related to Ann Hartgerink?" Mom asked.

"My father's sister."

"We knew her when Rich was the part-time evangelist in Ferrysburg."

"My dad is Otto Hartgerink. He's a pastor in Kalamazoo now."

On and on it went, and I kept my eyes on this blonde, blue-eyed woman—barely hearing her and my mother make their connections. Miss Hartgerink seemed bored with the bingo game, as if she were just being polite. I liked her for that. I was already on the verge of giving my heart away.

Miss Hartgerink turned out to be only four years older than I was—spirited, opinionated, and sure of herself. I quickly respected her, then admired her. I easily let my admiration for her fill the hole Grace had left—the sick feeling I had because she hadn't told me she was leaving permanently. I blamed my too-rapid shift in affection on Grace's desertion, hating the thought that I might be faithless.

As much because I loved Miss Hartgerink as for the subject itself, I became enamored of British literature. I loved the rawness of *Beowulf,* the whimsy and bawdy humor of Chaucer. Then we came to *Paradise Lost.* Miss Hartgerink had only to suggest that some scholars have proposed Satan as the sympathetic anti-hero in the epic for me to see it that way. From there it was a short leap to identify with the guy. Milton's poem begins with Lucifer cast from the "Ethereal Skie" into the "penal Fire." The second page in our anthology presented us with a woodcut of Satan, head and shoulders above the fiery pool, the rest of his body immersed, staring up toward heaven with a perfect visual rendition of words I can't forget:

. . . now the thought
Both of lost happiness and lasting pain
Torments him; round he throws his baleful eyes
That witness'd huge affliction and dismay

It was as if Satan's sorrow and pain were mine. I didn't think that I was the devil, or even demon-possessed or headed for hell. But I felt myself standing on the brink of an abyss, not knowing what lay ahead or beneath me but terrified that my slim edge was about to give way. I dreaded what Satan seemed in such eloquent language to be feeling—loss whose magnitude was unimaginable, separation from what once was.

From the day my mother spoke those fearsome words, I was certain that sooner or later, I was bound to forfeit what I prized most—home, family, and church. I started to think that it would be best to separate myself preemptively and permanently instead of being cast out by someone else. One night, not knowing anything about pharmacology, I took six giant red cold tablets. If size were an indicator, they should have been lethal. Then I went to bed, prepared to never wake up. But sleep didn't come, and I got more and more frightened that I could actually die, so I got up and told my mother what I'd done. I never told her why and she never asked. She called the mission hospital and was reassured that six Coricidin would not seriously hurt me.

"Give her a cup of strong black coffee, and she'll be all right," the duty nurse said.

My mother wanted me to confide in her. I couldn't because, since that Sunday of condemnation, I had been building the thickest, highest wall I could between us. I also sensed that she didn't want to hear why I wanted to end my life. So I said I'd talk to Miss Hartgerink, and Mom seemed relieved.

I didn't know how to broach the subject, so the next day I left an unsigned, hand-printed note on her desk: "Have you ever felt like killing yourself?"

When she saw it at the beginning of class, Miss Hartgerink ranted, "No, I never felt like killing myself." She went on in that vein for about a minute, while I bent my head low over my desk. In fact, I kept it down for the entire class. My stomach roiled. The one person I'd thought maybe I could talk to wasn't someone I could talk to after all.

At the end of class, she asked me to stay. "I'm so sorry," she said. "This note was from you, wasn't it?"

I nodded.

"The boys on the mission have been playing pranks on me. They took all the wheels off my car and put it up on blocks. Other practical jokes. So I thought this was just one more of those. I'm sorry. Would you like to talk about it?"

I nodded again. Later that week, we met at Denny's in Gallup for cokes. We sat at the counter, not at all conducive to spilling my guts. I probably couldn't have anyway. I left it to Miss Hartgerink to supply reasons for my distress. School wasn't challenging enough? There wasn't much of social life at Rehoboth? "Just wait for next year when you go to college. It'll be different: parties, concerts, people sharing ideas." I knew then that I couldn't tell her my reality either.

While she talked, I watched a waiter flit back and forth between the kitchen and the tables. His slim, swaying hips and bouffant pompadour told me I might be related to him somehow. His flamboyant flaunting of who he was made me queasy. At the same time, I couldn't help admiring him just a little.

Miss Hartgerink drove me home afterward, and I knew sitting in her white Mercury Comet that she couldn't possibly help me, even if I knew what help I needed. I was living in a vacuum. Four people in the world might be like me: Grace, who had precipitously disappeared from my life, and about whom I now felt guilty and disloyal as well as hurt; the boy at Denny's, who scared me; and Alice and Jennie, who had been tossed out of the mission.

That year, two things helped me hold on to a semblance of balance and normalcy: music and my work at Dandee Supermarket. It wasn't popular music because I rarely heard that. The Beatles had invaded the U.S., and Charlie Yazzie, already on his way to being a musician, mentioned them one day at lunch in the Mission House.

"What are you talking about?" I asked. "Some kind of bug?"

"Are you kidding? They're a band. They're touring all over the U.S. They're changing music as we know it. You are really out of it. Spending too much time thinking about Grace?"

I felt my face flush. Charlie was the only one who had ever commented on our relationship. The year before, he'd asked Grace, "Is Anna your male substitute?"

Pushing canned peas around on my plate, I mumbled, "I don't listen to the radio much."

"I guess not." Charlie turned to talk to someone else.

The music that saved me arrived on the great swells of Bach, a torrent of organ music propelling us out of the church on a Sunday evening under starlight. It was being in the All-State Girls' Chorus, stopping singing in pure awe when our voices lifted on the first notes of the "Miserere" from Beethoven's *Missa Solemnis*. It was community concerts in Gallup, to which I'd bought a season ticket, sitting alone in the Methodist church and being carried a world away by a string quartet, a solo pianist, or madrigal singers. It was lying on my belly in front of the console record player, listening with my eyes closed to the thick, 78-rpm Columbia records playing Tchaikovsky, Rachmaninoff, Mozart. It was playing my trombone in the school quartet, our brassy majesty earning us a "First" at the New Mexico State Music Festival. All of this, being part of this beauty, became one tenuous thread of salvation from the depths of depression.

Working at the supermarket quite simply put me into a frame of reference outside the mission and the church. Customers and co-workers came from all walks of life: traditional people who spoke only the Diné language; shoppers whose surnames told me their families had come from Italy or the Slavic countries; nuns and priests from the Catholic school; cowboys and sheepherders. Very few of them knew that I was Dutch American, Christian Reformed, and certainly not that I was in such a deep struggle to discover who I was. Little is more basic than food and supplying it to others, and working after school and on Saturdays grounded me in the larger world.

But one night, the supermarket evoked sharply the issue that would drive me from the cradle of my faith. It was near closing time when Jennie and Alice arrived at my check stand. Mine was the only stand still open, or they might have seen me and chosen someone else. I longed to have them to know I was on their side, since it seemed pretty clear that there were sides. The only thing I could think of was to be friendly and try engaging them in small talk. But they were both closed off, barely talking, unsmiling. Their unresponsiveness left me feeling bereft. When the sack boy came back from their truck, he laughed as he loudly told the other boys how the two women had sat right next to each other in the cab. I turned sick, realizing that even in the larger world, there was no safe place for me. I already knew that the church offered no refuge.

Back at school, we began reading *Macbeth*. Like *Paradise Lost,* it became another reflection of my fears and incipient self-loathing. Miss Hartgerink played some of the dark, high drama for us on a scratchy LP—the witches over their cauldron, Lady Macbeth's torment, Macbeth's final soliloquy. It was Lady Macbeth who was me, crying, groaning, "Out, out damn spot." It was not that I believed I had committed some great crime—and yet . . . and yet. My very being threatened to cut me off from humanity. This one spot was my doom. Satan and Lady Macbeth. To identify with such villains was to expect to be cut off—from God, the community of believers, my family.

It wasn't all Satan and Lady Macbeth, though. I also encountered the sublime poetry of Gerard Manley Hopkins, a Catholic mystic who was profoundly in touch with God in nature. First came the poems in our anthology, "Pied Beauty" and "The Windhover" (dedicated "To Christ our Lord"). In "The Windhover," I thrilled that the poet could address Christ so intimately as, "ah my dear" and "O my chevalier!" To be in love with Christ our Lord. Then Miss Hartgerink took me past those two most famous poems to Hopkins' collected works. The first stanza of "The Wreck of the Deutschland" became a symbol of hope for me. Hopkins was grappling with the death by drowning of five Franciscan nuns, friends of his. I was grappling with why God had made me the way he had:

Thou mastering me
God! giver of breath and bread;
World's strand, sway of the sea;
Lord of living and dead;
Thou has bound bones and veins in me, fastened me flesh
And after it almost unmade, what with dread
Thy doing: and dost thou touch me afresh?
Over again I feel thy finger and find thee.

★ ★ ★

In our Church History class, the minister assigned a research paper. He expected us to choose a topic like the creation of the Nicene Creed, Martin Luther's ninety-five theses, or John Calvin's Kingdom of God in Geneva. I got permission to write about Rehoboth Mission. But I did not write about its history. I wrote a critique under the unwieldy but descriptive title, "How the Gospel is Not Presented at Rehoboth Mission." I wrote about what I saw and felt, and what my Navajo friends underwent and told me about. I wrote about how single women missionaries were treated as second- or third-class citizens. I didn't have the words *sexism* or *racism,* but that was what I wrote about, replete with concrete examples. I did not, however, in any way, question our right or obligation as Christians to proselytize. Nor did it occur to me to write about the unfairness of what had happened to Jennie and Alice.

Satan, Lady Macbeth, the oppressiveness of a mission that I saw operating contrary to the command to live and work from love—all conspired to make me question my faith. The big question—Is there really a God?—was definitely on my mind, but I don't think I would have felt compelled on a particular Sunday afternoon to talk about it with anyone except that I didn't want to miss communion. And I wanted to talk with Miss Hartgerink.

The impetus came from the fact that communion, which, remember, was only served four times a year, was being served that evening to those who had missed it in the morning. Although I was afraid I might be losing my faith, I hated to miss this sacrament that seemed to have the power, even if only for a moment, to draw me back into the fellowship that was slipping away. I didn't want a few doubts to stop me. The choice of *whom* I would talk with was all about my crush on Miss Hartgerink.

I was genuinely worried about those words, "He that eateth or drinketh in an unworthy manner eateth and drinketh damnation unto himself." Just what might make me unworthy? Living in sin? Had I lived in sin with Grace? Not preparing for communion ahead of time by reading assigned scriptures during the week? Of course, not believing in God—or even just wondering—must constitute a pretty big unworthiness. So on that afternoon, I sat in Miss Hartgerink's living room, which just happened to be the living room in what used to be Grace's house, and hashed out my doubts.

I plunged in with, "I don't know if I believe in God anymore."

Miss Hartgerink didn't seem surprised. "Why not?"

As we talked, I realized I was fabricating reasons, that I probably didn't truly doubt God's existence. My questions felt so much bigger, far more worrisome, and completely unmentionable than any anxiety I might have about the reality of God. I floundered through with ideas I'd read or heard, when what I really wanted to know was if I was loveable. My question wasn't, "Is God real?" It was, "Does God love me the way I am or the way I might be? Even if the Church doesn't?"

Finally I asked the question most pertinent to the moment. "Do you think I should take communion tonight?"

First Miss Hartgerink gave me the right answer, "That's between you and God." Then she gave her opinion, which I had counted on her to do. "I don't see why not."

I sat in the front row with the few others who hadn't been at the morning service. That meant the minister was standing practically nose-to-nose with me during the communion portion of the service. I hadn't voiced my questions to him, but whatever I might have written in my Church History paper made me certain that when he read the part about "unworthy manner" and "damnation," he looked directly at me with an icy stare. I felt fear, guilt, and, yes, rebellion. "It's between God and me," I thought. "You don't know what's in my heart." And I took the soft white yeasty cube and turned my thoughts to Jesus.

Afterward, I drank the little cup of wine. I let communion pull me back into the circle of belief for the time being.

~ 10 ~
Glimpses

IT IS MY CONVICTION THAT ONLY THOSE WHO ENTERTAIN DOUBTS have need of faith. I questioned our beliefs from an early age. When I look back, I see two facts about my probing. The first is that, until I made a break with the Church, I always posed my questions within the framework of our beliefs. I did not ever truly doubt the fundamental assumptions. Second, questioning with lively persistence only served to deepen my faith. Doubt is to faith as darkness is to candlelight—essential if the light is to be visible.

Despite the fact that I remained within the basic confines of the faith, my explorations hinted that I was peering outward, catching glimpses of other ways of looking at things. Living in the Navajo Nation, I couldn't help seeing and hearing evidence of the Navajo Way from time to time, although my parents made sure that I had the right perspective on it. I had heard those summer lullabies from the ceremonies on the hill behind the mission. I had seen the circles of juniper branches left behind after the Yeibichai dances. I had found the peyote feathers down by the chicken coop.

Living in Washington, D.C., also provided me with a broadened vista. For the first time in my life, I knew Jews who lived not in the pages of the Bible but in real life, and they became some of my closest friends. I noticed when they were absent from school for holidays we didn't celebrate. I argued vehemently against the vocal anti-Semitism and racism of a girl whose family flew the Confederate flag from their front porch. One of the kindest people at NIH was the nutritionist on Trudy's floor. She showed an interest in our family, coming over to make spaghetti for the whole crew. Once, after Trudy's death, Miss Charest and a friend took me and another teen to the beach in her convertible. She was Catholic, and according to my parents, Catholics weren't Christians. I had to look at Catholics in a slightly different light after Miss Charest. I met other CRC people, like those in the youth group, who were open-minded enough to discuss evolution and the possibility that it was a fact, albeit under God's guidance.

★ ★ ★

During my difficult final year of high school, I was not only trying to understand where I fit (or didn't) in the scheme of my world but was also grappling with how I, as a Christian, fit into the wider world. I was developing a social conscience, which I expressed, however concretely, in that paper I wrote for Church History class. It came up in discussions with my father too—a man who believed firmly in the trickle-down theory of economics despite the fact that he'd been born into abject poverty and would never get beyond scraping by.

One Sunday afternoon, he and I were talking about the poor and solutions to poverty. In my naiveté, I was certain that education was the answer to that and a good many other of life's ills. My father favored prisons and Christian witness. I inserted the word *love* into my education argument.

"Ach!" he exploded. "You talk too much about love."

In a fever of righteousness, I shot back, "How can I talk too much about love when the Bible says that God is love?" I stalked off on the high heels of Sunday.

★ ★ ★

Mercifully, that school year came to an end. Our church had three colleges, all in the Midwest. I didn't want to go to any of them, but I was afraid no other schools would accept me because I had gotten an inferior education at the mission school. (This turned out to be far from the truth.) The church colleges had to take me because I was a member (one of the "privileges" that were now mine after making profession of faith). I enrolled at the most established and academically rigorous of the three: Calvin College, also considered the most liberal college within our circles.

However, in 1965, these rules were still operative there: Women students had a ten o'clock curfew on weekdays, twelve on weekends; men had none. Women students were allowed to wear pants in one public building—the cafeteria—for Saturday breakfast and lunch only. By sit-down dinner in the evening and at all other times on campus, we were to be wearing skirts or dresses in public. Dinner was family-style at round tables for eight. Four girls stood at alternate seats and painfully waited for boys to claim a seat on either side of them, then pull out the chair for the girls to their left. We attended compulsory chapel three mornings a week. Incremental consequences for missing chapel included letters home and the potential for academic suspension. A common saying was, "Know your chapel checker," the person who marked and turned in a grid to show whether you had been in your assigned seat. Anonymity had its benefits, though; if your checker didn't know you, you could bribe someone to sit in your place. The student handbook included the description—rather than a rule—"Calvin women do not smoke." It was liberal all right.

I started smoking at Calvin partly in defiance but mostly because my new friends did. I hung out with a group of girls who thought of ourselves as the In-Out Group—in with ourselves, cool in a James Dean sort of way. We favored chambray work shirts and cords whenever we were outside public buildings on campus.

Most rules other than the non-smoking one, I accepted without question. The dress code rankled the most. I simply preferred wearing jeans, and they made the most sense during Michigan winters. The curfew, although I disliked the unfairness of the different rules for men and women, offered relief when I was dating guys because there was a time by which the date had to end.

Homosexuality was not mentioned in the student handbook. I dated boys, had crushes on girls, and was afraid to talk to anyone about my feelings. Sometime during my freshman year, two boys were discovered in bed together. They were ridiculed all over campus and threatened with expulsion. When others gossiped about them, I kept silent. My fear grew, and I contained it.

In addition to smoking behind the cafeteria in freezing Michigan weather and wearing our uniforms of rebellion, my friends pushed the limits in other ways. None of them had made profession of faith. They had come to Calvin because it was expected of them, not because they wanted to attend a Christian college. Only one among the seven of us would complete more than two years at Calvin.

One Saturday, we lingered after eating at a cafeteria table that had a few scraps of bread and half-full tumblers of orange soda left on it. We knew that the next day, the Christian Reformed churches around campus would be celebrating communion. I mentioned to my friends my irritation with our church's practice of *close* communion, which I considered *closed* communion. Although they had not made profession of faith, they had all been raised in our church, so they knew what I was talking about. Calvin students who wanted to take communion had to fill out cards naming our home congregation before the service.

"I'm just going to do it," my roommate said. "How will they ever find out I haven't made profession of faith? Do you think those elders write to every home church to find out? Who has time for that?"

She was probably right, that filling out the cards was just a formality. I wondered on her behalf about the "eateth and drinketh damnation" part. Then I did something I still don't fully understand. I took a leftover roll from Becky's plate, after raising my eyebrows for permission. I began to break it, first in half, then in quarters, then eighths, saying as I broke it, "This is my body, broken for you. Take, eat, remember, and believe."

I passed the plate, and each of us took a piece. I heard some nervous giggling and felt some uneasiness, but I proceeded. I lifted my glass of orange soda and said, "This is my blood, shed for you unto a complete remission of all your sins. Take, drink ye all of it." And we drank. Truly feeling guilty then, I said, "I shouldn't be doing this." I paused, then picked up where our earlier discussion had left off. "But isn't this what *close* communion should be? Close friends communing with each other?"

I had confirmed a role as the group priest, the only one who professed to have any faith. In that moment, I had negated my faith by making a mockery of what was to me the most meaningful and holy ritual of being a Christian. I rationalized to myself in the same way I'd just done with my friends—that communion was about belonging and fellowship. Yet it was also about something more—about shared belief and sacredness. We Dutch had a word for what I had just done—*spotten*—to mock or defy. In our CRC circle, we used it more specifically, to mean the mockery of something sacred. As I look back, I see that it was also a way that I stepped outside the bounds I had accepted until then, even if only for a few moments. In a sense, it represented one more glimpse outside the walls of our church.

⋆ ⋆ ⋆

Two classroom assignments at Calvin also indicated that I was edging out, exploring other realities than the Only Reality. Early in the first semester, my English professor assigned a one-paragraph essay in which we were to define religion. Mine began with examples: a Navajo *hataałi* (called a *medicine man* by white folks) singing the Red Ant Chant; a Muslim family reading the Quran; monks chanting Gregorian hymns. It ended by drawing the examples together as ways of approaching God. The professor read my essay to the class and commented that religion was much broader than the Christian belief about what we must to do be saved. That was apparently how most of my classmates had defined the subject. "That's Christianity," she said, "not religion." I was gratified.

My Western Civilization professor was not quite so broad-minded. Our textbook had a single chapter on Asian history as it related to Western society, and the professor decided we wouldn't cover it in class. Instead, we were to read the chapter independently and write a related research paper. Intrigued by the influence of Buddhism on Asian culture, I decided to compare Buddha's teachings to those of Jesus. This was probably the first time I'd even heard of Buddha. I had no idea that I was entering the field of comparative religion. I had no idea such a discipline existed.

From the Hekman Library, I checked out a thin fifty-cent Dell paperback titled *The Teachings of the Compassionate Buddha* and spent the next few days reading it. I found, to my satisfaction, many similarities with Jesus's words, which I knew so well. I needed the Bible only to be sure I referenced chapters and verses accurately. I typed into the night on my light green, portable Hermes and turned in my work.

I got an A on the paper and one comment, a question: "Are these your own ideas or someone else's?"

I was irritated. "How could he be so obtuse?" I wondered. After all, I had referenced only two primary sources: the Buddhist scriptures and the Bible. Of course the comparisons were my own. He was questioning my academic integrity. Only later did I realize that the professor, who was also a CRC elder, might have been uncomfortable with the idea of my comparing religions, which was definitely not an orthodox way of thinking.

⋆ ⋆ ⋆

My sophomore and final year at Calvin presented me with one more window through which to look out from the CRC onto the wider world. It began one day at the end of my freshman year when a distant relative who was graduating from the college offered me a chance to take her place in an off-campus position that provided room and board. Since I was barely holding things together financially, I was eager to explore the money-saving opportunity. The family was Jewish, and, as with all similar situations, had been approved by the college.

Katherine picked me up in a snappy black sports car, and we drove to posh East Grand Rapids for dinner, which was really a job interview. On the way, she talked a bit about the work expectations, then added, "Don't ever try to proselytize them." Also raised in the CRC, Katherine knew well the requirement to try to bring people to Christ.

"Okay. I won't," I said, realizing with some surprise that I felt relieved, as though a burden had been lifted. Something had shifted in me, perhaps beginning with the humiliation I'd suffered preaching in the jail. Whereas witnessing to others had once been a joy, it had begun to feel taxing at times.

The next fall, I moved in with the Krissoffs. In many ways, though they were active in the local Reform temple, they were assimilated. Far from keeping kosher, they included bacon and ham in their diet. Mrs. Krissoff had even graduated from Calvin College after a long hiatus in her post-secondary education and would later teach at Aquinas, the Catholic liberal arts college in town.

I watched with interest what their religious life was like. On Friday evenings, candles were lit, and Abe, not Sylvia as would be more traditional, said the Hebrew blessing that begins, *Baruch atah Adonai elohaynu melech ha'olam.* I loved the prayer and still say it at times. The name *Adonai* felt to me like an adoration of God, although it means simply *Lord.*

Abe told me he often gave Christians tours of the temple. "They always ask, 'Where is your altar for burnt offerings?'" He laughed. "We don't make animal sacrifices any more than you do."

The Krissoffs went to temple every Friday night, and occasionally asked if I wanted to go along. I always did. The first time, Sylvia's diminutive, silver-haired mother, Ruth, sat next to me. Early in the service, everyone turned to greet each other with, "Good Shabbos." Ruth turned to me and said it. I hesitated. She said, "Come on, you can do it."

It wasn't that I couldn't. I was afraid of being presumptuous, acting as if I belonged. At Ruth's urging, I said the words, and felt that I did belong.

I became aware of the roles of Rosh Hashanah, Yom Kippur, and Hanukkah in the Jewish faith. But the holy day that touched me most deeply was Passover. Christian tradition says that Jesus initiated the ritual of communion during a Passover feast, so I was eager to join in my first Seder—to see, hear, and taste from the table that was the antecedent to the meal that meant ultimate belonging to me.

I helped Sylvia prepare the dinner, getting down the platter for the lamb shank bone, the egg, and the parsley. I watched her make the *haroset* from chopped apples, nuts, honey, and spices. I wanted to know what it was for. "You'll see at the meal," she said and seemed to enjoy making my anticipation grow. I spooned fat white discs of gefilte fish into a bowl and put horseradish into a smaller dish. I set the big dining room table with purple and blue placemats and napkins and good china and silver. I put matzohs into a napkin-lined basket and made a tossed salad, one of my routine tasks.

The meal itself, full of ritual and symbolism, went deep into my soul. I grasped it as a celebration of liberation. I felt grief when I tasted the salt water that represented the tears of the Israelites in bondage in Egypt. I tasted the irony of the haroset, symbolizing both the mortar used by the slaves to build the pyramids and God's sweet mercy. I loved singing *"Dayenu,"* the fifteen-verse explosion of gratitude for the mercy of God's deliverance.

~ 11 ~

The Tie That Binds

There is a place in New Mexico where enormous red rock formations are shaped like great, splendorous rolling waves. After rain, the rocks are the deep maroon of a Cabernet. In the evening sun, they glow the gold of amber. On a winter day, they are flat pink, sometimes topped by snow. At the base of the rocks are salmon-colored sand dunes. It is across from these high desert waves that Rehoboth Mission lies. The Navajo name for Rehoboth is *Tse Yaniichii',* meaning *Where the Red Rocks End.* In the summer between my junior and senior years of high school, these imposing rocks were separated from the mission compound only by fields of sage and the narrow asphalt strip that was Route 66. That summer, my father's alma mater, the Reformed Bible Institute, held a reunion picnic at the base of the giant red waves.

Those who attended were all missionaries, Navajo and white, and their families. We ate the odd mix of foods typical of missionary potlucks in the Navajo Nation: mutton ribs, Jell-O salads, fry bread, hot dogs, macaroni and cheese, mutton stew, baked beans, roasted Indian corn, tossed salad, and, if we were lucky, kneel-down bread—the sweet, moist, dense, nutty-flavored treat made of coarsely ground Indian corn, wrapped in husks and baked in an earthen pit.

When the leftovers had been shared around and packed away in station wagons and pickups, we gathered in a circle around the extinguished picnic fire and sang:

Blest be the tie that binds
Our hearts in Christian love.
The fellowship of kindred minds
Is like to that above.

When we asunder part,
It gives us inward pain.
But we shall still be joined in heart
And hope to meet again.

My throat filled with a tender ache whenever we sang that song. I didn't need to think about what it meant; I felt it. I looked around me and saw Ella Descheeny who had given me my Navajo name when I was a baby; the Hamstras and Bazuins with whom we often ate our Thanksgiving dinner; Preston Yazzie, who had worked with my dad in Shiprock and shared his mannerism of pulling a comb out of his back pocket and slicking back his hair whenever he got out of the pickup. These were my people, people with whom I was safely and deeply tied.

Short weeks later, my mother proclaimed her denunciation of Jennie and Alice. After those shattering words, I knew on a deep level that there would no longer be room for me in the only place I'd ever belonged. But that knowledge would lie like a hidden fault, far beneath the surface, for the next nine years. I struggled privately for those years, trying to hold myself together and in place. I stayed in the church, taught Sunday school, and directed a youth choir. After two years at Calvin, I transferred to the University of New Mexico in Albuquerque to study English and linguistics, returning to the land I loved. I still attended a Christian Reformed church every Sunday.

During my first semester at UNM, I received a call from two missionaries from the Navajo Nation who were in town to attend a meeting. They were guys I knew well, the ones we had often celebrated Thanksgiving with and afterward played chess and picture charades, our homegrown version of Pictionary, with. They asked if they could take me out to dinner. I got the feeling they knew I was having a tough time with my faith, but they never brought it up. We just ate and chatted and laughed together. Times like this bound me closer to our community, making me hope there might still a place where I belonged.

* * *

Near the end, before I took leave of the church, and eight years after the day that marked my dividing line, I did something I could never have predicted. I returned to Rehoboth Mission as a teacher. The return represented my last-ditch attempt to be a part of what I knew in my heart I would eventually leave. While I taught there, I did everything I could to stay attached. I memorized and quoted more Bible verses than ever before. From a clutching heart, I recounted Bible stories so passionately that my former students still talk about my storytelling more than forty years later. I struggled to remain an integral part of all that I had questioned, because I couldn't imagine any other life.

The struggle included ways in which I tried to hide from myself what the Bible could be saying about who I might be. In my personal Bible study, as I read Romans 1, I underlined in red all the verses but the one that was thought to refer to homosexuality, the very one my father had mentioned to Grace's father when they talked about that transgender man in Denver.

One day, during recess, I stood in the school office with the other teachers who didn't have outdoor duty. Miss Douma came in with visitors from the Midwest. She had been the girls' dormitory matron for thirty-six years, including all my years as a student. Now she was retired but continued to live at the mission to guide visitors around the campus. She introduced those of us who stood around sipping coffee. When she got to me she said, with pride in her voice, "And this is one of our own. Her parents are missionaries on the field, and she's a Rehoboth graduate."

I smiled as expected and greeted the visitors while a charge of guilt ran through me because of what was going on inside me. Shame would enshroud me as it had Jennie and Alice if anyone at the mission knew. Besides, I had thought of myself as a maverick at best, ever since I wrote that critical paper in Church History class.

Now I heard "one of our own" from the voice of the establishment. Her words created dissonance in me—pride on one hand at being called "one of our own," but on the other hand, I was pretty sure I wouldn't last much longer. Nevertheless, Miss Douma's words became one more knot in the tie that had bound me so close, so tight—the tie that would, in some sense, always connect me with these people.

Part II

Exile

no one leaves home unless home chases you
fire under feet
hot blood in your belly
it's not something you ever thought of doing
until the blade burnt threats into
your neck
and even then you carried the anthem under
your breath

—Warsan Shire, "Home"

~ 12 ~

Out and In Again

I STILL GET CHILLS AND A LUMP IN MY THROAT WHENEVER I HEAR Aretha sing "Young, Gifted and Black." I don't hear it that often anymore, but at one time, it frequently resonated through our home on a weekend morning or late at night when we were worn out from the day. Neale's and my home. Neale was all of those things: Young. Gifted. Black.

Ironically, my mother was the one who told me, with a surprising amount of enthusiasm, about Neale. I was teaching at the mission, and my salary was so minuscule that I moved back into our family home in Gallup. I was helping my mother in the kitchen when she said, "Ted and Evie have a black girl staying with them. She just became a Christian." When I think about it, she probably actually said, "a colored girl." I'm basing this on a later conversation with my mother about What Black People Want to Be Called. Mom's enthusiasm was not about Neale's race or gender, but about her recent conversion.

"She's from Brooklyn and just graduated from Hope College."

That got my attention. "Why did a black woman from Brooklyn go to Hope, of all places?" I asked. "And now she's living at the mission with Ted and Evie?" Hope was the premier college of the Reformed Church in America, and Calvin College's archrival, located in the small, very Dutch town of

Holland, Michigan. The series of events my mother described seemed pretty far-fetched.

"Oh. Well, she attended a Reformed church in Brooklyn, and her pastor recommended Hope. A few Sundays ago, she came forward at the Fort Wingate Church. She has the most beautiful voice. Sings solos sometimes in church. You'll meet her today."

"Well, this will at least be interesting," I thought.

Neale was nearly six feet tall, more like six-three with her Angela Davis Afro. She had smooth caffè latte skin and a soft, full mouth. She was indeed interesting. We quickly found out that we had both majored in English, were both teaching, and knew a lot about each other's colleges. We also had enough different interests to make what became a growing friendship intriguing.

Neale's family on one side had been in the U.S. for generations. On the other side, they were immigrants from Barbados. She had both the sophistication and the street smarts of someone who had grown up in New York. Neale's knowledge of black literature, history, and culture was formidable. She introduced me to Lorraine Hansberry, Nina Simone, Miles Davis, Countee Cullen, Lucille Clifton, Nikki Giovanni, Alice Walker, Billie Holiday. And Aretha. I brought to the relationship my familiarity with Navajo ways, my study of languages and linguistics, and my love of the baroque masters. We both loved traveling, cooking, and camping.

Six months into our friendship, we became lovers.

Neale not only acquainted me with black America but also took me by the hand and led the way to learning about my own people. She embodied the consciousness and habits of someone who had fought oppression as a black child and adolescent. In recent years, she had been involved in the feminist movement. I knew how to do research with the best of them, but the little I'd read about homosexuals and homosexuality was either downright or slyly negative. Neale, from her years of experience, despite the fact that she'd never considered being with a woman before meeting me, pointed us both in a liberating direction.

She found us *Lesbian/Woman,* published in 1972, the year we met, by longtime partners and activists Del Martin and Phyllis Lyon. I hungrily read the first literature that celebrated me, that spoke of possibility instead of condemnation. Together we learned about the Stonewall Riots, which launched what now has become the LGBTQ movement, in New York in 1969. Twenty-one when Stonewall happened, I was then grieving the end of a guilt-ridden, clandestine affair with one of the nurses at the mission hospital.

In my high school romance with Grace, in my painful affair with the nurse, in all my fantasies, I had not considered what it would mean to commit to living my life with another woman, for us to create a home together. Neale didn't seem to have any doubt that we would, but she did understand to some extent from attending Hope College the conflicts I would have as I began to weigh my faith against the joys of our relationship.

There was sweet, soft comfort in spending the night in each other's arms. There was joy in the intensity of getting to know each other, in hearing one another's stories for the first time. We loved sharing books—books we'd read, books that had just come out, books we hoped to read. Even more than that, we delighted in sitting next to each other in bed or in the car and sharing a book aloud. There was satisfaction in cooking and eating West Indian and traditional Dutch foods, with some Navajo and traditional New Mexican meals thrown in, and in preparing a meal of any other ethnicity together.

Alongside these ordinary but satisfying pleasures, I was forced to take spiritual stock. My mother's disgust when she condemned Jennie and Alice sprang forcefully to body memory. I couldn't help thinking of that chapter in Romans where I'd underlined all but that one verse in red. Now I reconsidered the verse and sought out other interpretations. I thought about the soul-feeding communion that was such a vital part of my life in the Church. I remembered the conversation when my father accused me, *"Ach!* You talk too much about love." And how I'd shot back, "How can I talk too much about love if God is love?" The idea of God As Love began to take on even deeper meaning.

I could not imagine giving up the joys, the comfort, the friendship, the exchange of ideas, the sensual pleasure, and the communion I shared with Neale. How could I relinquish loving and being loved? How could I give up the potential freedom of being myself?

In 1973, our church said I had to choose between being myself openly and honestly and being in the church. The CRC made that abundantly clear in its *Acts of Synod* that year. That summer, I stood in the dining room of the house where Neale was living—once again, as serendipity would have it, the house that Grace's family had lived in. That dining room was full of memories of my first love, the one my mother had so vocally condemned by association.

I started reading the *Acts of Synod* while standing next to the table. Then I had to sit. My stomach twisted on itself as the church's position became clear:

> Homosexuality is a condition of disordered sexuality that reflects the brokenness of our sinful world. . . . Homosexualism [that is, explicit homosexual practice] . . . is incompatible with obedience to the will of God as revealed in Scripture. . . . The church should do everything in its power to help persons with homosexual orientation and give them support toward healing and wholeness. A synodical report titled Pastoral Care for Homosexual Members is available.

Until then, the church's official position had never been stated. All I'd heard was "They're living in sin. They should see a doctor." Now I was reading that I should see my pastor. I knew there would be no parallel synodical report titled "Pastoral Care for Heterosexual Members." The statement didn't say I had to leave the church; in fact, it said that the church should support me in healing from my disorder.

I spent weeks in anguish, coming to terms with the fact that I didn't want to be healed from loving Neale. Since the first day of condemnation when I was sixteen, I had clung to the sacred communion of church and family for nine years. Now the choice was no longer a choice. I had to be myself, and I needed to love and be loved.

★ ★ ★

I didn't get to tell my parents about Neale and me, and I probably would not have chosen to do so for a long time to come. Near the end of my first year of teaching, I took my third graders on a fourteen-hour field trip. I had barely stepped into the house through the kitchen entrance, entirely spent, when my mother and father came in from the living room, closed the door and said, "We want to talk to you."

I knew what was coming, and exhaustion had taken down all my defenses.

"We want to know about your relationship with Neale," my mother said.

"We want to know before something funny happens," my father added in a testament to the vacuum that most LGBTQ people lived in then.

When he said it, my mind went to the nights Neale had spent with me in my twin bed in this very house, even though there was a second bed in the room. They'd assumed that was the bed she slept in.

Too exhausted for words, it took Mom saying, "We'll pay for you to see a psychiatrist so you can change" to restore my voice.

For years I had been praying that my desires would change. Now something *had* changed, but it was not my desires. "I don't want to change. I love Neale," I said, quietly but firmly. "I *want* to love her." Then I asked, "What made you ask me about this?"

"Dorothy told us." A friend of Neale's and mine who was struggling with her own sexuality had confided in an older nurse at the mission. Marie later admitted that she'd told

Dorothy about Neale and me in order to take some of the focus off herself. Dorothy felt it was her Christian duty to tell my parents, in much the same way my mother had hoped someone would talk to Jennie's parents.

I barely heard whatever else they had to say. No doubt that verse in Romans was part of it. Finally I said, "I need to go. I'm going to Rehoboth to talk to Neale." By this time, nausea and fear had penetrated my numbness. I drove Old Highway 66 in the dark, strategizing as I avoided potholes. In those few miles, I decided that I would wait enough weeks to make it sound realistic, then tell my parents I had decided to change my relationship with Neale. "We're going to just be friends," I'd tell them. I sought consolation from Neale in her room at Rehoboth.

My parents' confrontation had taken me off-guard because, despite the publication of the *Acts of Synod,* homosexuality was not an everyday topic in our world. If people in the CRC even had TV, it offered no programs featuring LGBTQ characters. Gayness had not become the hot topic that it is in churches today, and if anyone thought about it, they neither wanted to discuss it nor knew what homosexuality would look like. Although Alice and Jennie had been found out nine years earlier, I had thought that if we were careful, people around me, including my parents, simply would not be attuned to anything but their heterosexual, evangelical reality.

* * *

I went on to teach for a second year at the mission as Neale and I began our life together. We set up our first home in Allison, a tiny settlement nestled among gold sandstone mesas two miles west of Gallup. In 1973, Allison was listed as a New Mexico ghost town. Like many others in the Southwest, it had been a company-owned mining town. Despite its ghostly status, though, flesh-and-blood people inhabited most of the wood frame houses along the single dirt street.

Slightly above the rest of the town stood two identical clapboard houses. Below them, an abandoned stone-and-stucco building that had once held the company offices and clinic was slowly crumbling back into the earth. We rented one of the two clapboards that had probably been built for Victor American Coal Company officials, one of them possibly the eponymous Fletcher J. Allison.

We found a certain level of safety in Allison. We were eight miles from my parents' eyes and fifteen miles from Rehoboth. We had a room that we never used and referred to as my bedroom. We never showed any sign of affection in public. We kept up the ruse of being "just friends" around my family. Today the irony of hiding out in a ghost town is not lost on me, for Neale and I were living a phantom life that could not thrive where we were.

~ 13 ~

Emptying

As I continued teaching at Rehoboth, I gradually became aware that an inner change was taking place. I still loved telling the children Bible stories because I loved storytelling, but the stories had just become good yarns, little different from a morality tale about an ugly duckling or a foolish Navajo coyote.

I didn't find it so easy anymore to give pat answers to the children's penetrating questions. One day I told the story of the Israelite spies being helped by Rahab the harlot. Interestingly, no one asked what a harlot was. Neither had I as a child; harlot just seemed to be part of Rahab's name. In the story, Rahab hides the spies, and when the Jericho police come looking for them, she says she hasn't seen them. When the story was done, a boy raised his hand, "Wasn't it wrong for Rahab to lie?"

Had I been a more experienced teacher, I'd have asked the rest of the class what they thought about Jacky's question—good teaching, plus a way to get myself off an uncomfortable hook. But I hemmed and hawed, finally saying I didn't know. So many shades of gray had entered my life.

Neale and I stopped attending the Fort Wingate CRC and started going to the Episcopal Church in Gallup, not because it had an open and affirming policy toward gays (it didn't), but simply because it was more liberal. More and more often, we just didn't go to church at all. Every once in a while, I was struck by the fact that I didn't feel guilty and didn't miss church. Instead, I enjoyed an unexpected, pleasurable freedom. Church had seldom seemed an onerous obligation before, but now, on the days I didn't go to church, I could sleep late, eat a full, relaxed breakfast, walk among the mesas, read, write, and do projects. A Sunday when I didn't go to church became a true day of rest.

While I didn't feel guilty, I did undergo twinges of fear. Not about hell or heaven, but I worried, "What if the mission school board should question me about my church attendance?" I could say I was attending the Episcopal Church, a partial truth, but that was not an approved church by any means. More worrisome was the possibility that someone would guess the reality of my relationship with Neale. I imagined my mother going to the school board in a fit of righteous zeal and telling them about Neale and me. I need not have worried. I learned later that she was so ashamed that she didn't want anyone to know. When she met up with friends of mine in town, she could barely look them in the eye because she assumed that they knew about us.

After the school year ended without incident, Neale and I packed up a yellow Ryder truck with the household we'd begun accumulating along with Lavender, the pregnant cat we'd inherited from my youngest brother. I felt as if I'd been holding my breath all year. My dad and brothers helped us load the truck, and my family too seemed to let out a breath. Mine was a breath of freedom, theirs a breath of relief. They wanted to go on believing that Neale and I were friends and roommates.

I've never been drawn to Albuquerque, but we moved there in 1973 after I got a job teaching in what was then called Cañoncito, a small Navajo reservation thirty-five miles west of the city. Neale decided to take pre-med courses at the University of New Mexico. At last we had found the space and anonymity that allowed us to breathe.

To my surprise, whenever I happened to notice, all things religious and spiritual seemed to be pouring out of me. It was as if I were a bowl that someone had tipped over, and, through no effort of mine, my spiritual past poured easily and fluidly out.

My Uncle Chinua helped to tip the spiritual bowl that was me. Of course, with a name like *Chinua,* he's not my real uncle, but that is the affection and admiration I have for him, and that is how profoundly the late Chinua Achebe, the renowned Nigerian writer, influenced me. It was Neale who introduced me to his classic novel, *Things Fall Apart.* She was teaching literature for UNM at Crownpoint in the Navajo Nation to a class full of Diné women who worked in the BIA school as educational assistants. They were taking courses to get a teaching credential, so at last Diné children would have teachers from among their own people—role models and instructors who knew from experience where they were coming from.

Every Tuesday evening, Neale and I ate sandwiches in our little blue bug and tooled out to Crownpoint. While she taught, I sat in the school office grading papers, planning lessons, doing homework for the Teaching of Reading class I was taking. And I read the books that Neale was teaching.

Achebe's seminal book, *Things Fall Apart,* is the story of a village of the author's own Ibo tribe. It begins with scenes that describe daily life, customs, and the system of justice before the arrival of the British missionaries, who operated hand-in-hand with the colonial government. The story goes on to show how that life falls apart in a deeply tragic way, particularly for one man. It is clear that the old way of life, even with its fears of the supernatural and evident flaws—such as the casting of infant twins into the Evil Forest to die—is a social system that functions well for the tribe and its people.

Neale's students identified profoundly with what happens to a colonialized people who are grossly misunderstood by the occupiers. They related more to Uncle Chinua's tale than to *The Man Who Killed a Deer,* about a Taos Indian who comes into conflict with Anglo laws, possibly because the author of that book, however sympathetic, is still writing as a white man.

In *Things Fall Apart,* the parallels between what happened to the Ibo and what had happened among the Diné I grew up with were starkly obvious to me. But what affected me most deeply was a conversation in the novel between a white missionary and an Ibo shaman. Mr. Brown was a missionary who, in spite of his orthodox beliefs, was exceptionally tolerant and genuinely interested in hearing what the shaman had to say.

The shaman explained to him that Chukwu, their big god, was the same as the missionary's god. He said that the people prayed first to their personal gods in order to spare Chukwu their small everyday complaints and needs. This seemed to me not unlike Catholics praying to the saints, and some Protestants who call on angels for help.

Most Protestants, though, and Missionary Brown as well, are reluctant to do this. He emphasized, "There is only one god, and you mustn't pray to all these others."

The shaman agreed, "Yes, there is only one god." However, Missionary Brown's openness went only so far. He insisted that the one god was *his* God.

I thought, "This shaman shows greater generosity and wisdom than Mr. Brown is capable of giving or receiving." I recognized that the Navajo religion had worked as well for the Diné as the Ibo religion worked for the Nigerians. I also saw that the Christian religion worked for my father and Missionary Brown.

My adherence to the Christian faith was falling apart. Uncle Chinua, whose own father had taught the Christian catechism at a mission school in Ogibi, made me feel it was okay that my faith was spilling out as so much of my former life fell apart.

In the process, my worldview turned upside down. The change I felt in the meaning of the first lines of the old gospel hymn, "Out of My Bondage," said it all:

Out of my bondage, sorrow and night,
Jesus I come, Jesus I come.
Into thy freedom, gladness and light,
Jesus I come to thee.

Before, I had thought of myself as being in bondage to sin. I was certain that believing that Jesus died for me had saved me, bringing me freedom and gladness. Now I saw the Church as the purveyor of bondage to a system that denied an important part of who I was. Leaving the Church had brought freedom, gladness and light; the words, "Jesus, I come to thee," could not, however, be twisted to fit into this upside-down schematic.

~ 14 ~
The Family Hold

THE EMPTYING PROCESS HAD BEEN PAINLESS AND FREEING, except for one thing—my family. I didn't miss the Church. But our family had been a tightly knit unit, and spirituality was how we did intimacy. Having been emptied of all things spiritual, I had nothing left to share with them beyond the superficial.

My family never outright rejected me. If I was in the area during a family gathering, they accepted that I would participate. Sometimes my partners even came to family events. There was always an awkwardness when they were present, so it was easier for me to go alone. As Neale once said, "They can never decide whether they want to hug me or not." And I always had to prepare myself for the chill I felt, the judgments that I knew were ever-present. I learned over time that for years, when the family got together, if I wasn't there, they discussed homosexuality and the Bible and what should be done about me. They did it so persistently that some of my sisters-in-law finally said, "Enough." Not that they didn't agree that I was living in sin; they were just sick of talking about it.

Four of my seven brothers felt it incumbent upon themselves at one time or another to write letters chastising me, quoting scripture and freely sharing their prejudices.

After one discussion, Ron, a minister and dean of students at a small Reformed seminary, wrote, "God has turned you over to the devil." It just so happened that Ron and his family had been hurting financially a few years earlier. When I heard about it, I sent them what was a significant amount of money for me and undoubtedly for them at the time. I didn't send the money in order to be thanked, but they never did thank me. A paragraph after claiming that I was now in the hands of the devil, Ron wrote, "By the way, I never thanked you for the money you sent us. Thanks."

My brother Ed knew many gay people because he was in theater. One summer while he was still in college, I helped him get a job with the Albuquerque Civic Light Opera, and he lived with Neale and me. He was such an easy housemate, and I felt his absence for days after he went back to school. I was stunned when I was later living in Denmark to get a condemning letter from him. After his offering of Bible verses against homosexuality, he wrote, "Romans sixteen says that I should shun you. But I love you too dearly to do that." I lay on the bed in my apartment in Copenhagen and wept.

Many years later, my brother Bob had a change of heart regarding the acceptability of homosexuality. Feeling remorse about how I had been alienated from the family, Bob once said to Phil, another brother who was a minister, "We abandoned Anna."

"No. She abandoned us," Phil said.

My father became the most difficult for me to deal with. Whenever I was around him, I was on guard. He leaped at me with verbal martial arts, stealth attacks that could come at any time, any place. One afternoon when I was visiting, he asked me to go for a ride with him. We chatted about things of little consequence. Then he cleared his throat. "In the Ten Commandments, it says that God visits the sins of the fathers upon the children. I've been wondering if your homosexuality is God visiting my sins on you."

My stomach took a dive, and I was silent.

"Before I married Mom, when I was in Alaska in the service," he said, "I had a girlfriend. I had sex with her." He then went into detail that would have made me extremely uncomfortable even if he weren't tying his event to my sexuality.

He pulled the car into the driveway, and I thought I might escape. But he wasn't finished. "Come into the bedroom," he said. "I want to read you some scripture."

The early training to obey my parents ran deep, and instead of cutting him off, I followed.

He pulled down a Bible and turned to the story of David and Bathsheba. "God took the life of their child because they sinned together. He visited the sins of the father upon the child. I think God may be punishing me for my sins by allowing you to go your way and live a homosexual lifestyle."

I felt squeezed—squeezed near to death, and I left the room vowing never to be alone with my dad again. After that, I didn't ever get into the car with him or go into a room with him if no one else was present. But avoiding him took all my awareness. Once as I got ready to head back to Albuquerque, he caught up with me in the hallway.

"Judgment Day is coming," he started in. "When that day comes, you will be crying out for the rocks to fall upon you."

As usual, I was speechless. I chose to visit my parents less and less often. Several times, I moved away from them across the U.S. and then twice to other continents, but each time, I'd come back to my New Mexico roots. I had gone from being my father's heir apparent to being one of the goats that would be cast out on Judgment Day. The place where I had felt safe, important, nurtured, and loved had shut me out. I wasn't thrown out; I was shut out. What happened was a form of bullying; you're still there, but you are the butt, the unlovely, the less-than, verbally attacked or left out. I went from feeling secure about how to be in this family to hiding, downplaying, and disguising myself. I had left the closet, but around my family, I was trying to drag the clothes out with me, trying to stay covered.

My mother's harsh judgment had been the first to send me spinning away from all that had once cradled me. But her love—and no doubt also her guilt, thinking she had created my "disorder"—made her try hard to understand. She asked me once to get something for her from her closet. On a shelf, I saw a shoebox labeled *Homosexuality,* full of tapes from various Christian ministers and psychologists. When I saw it, I felt sick. Later I realized that the information she gleaned, even from those biased sources, enabled her to stretch herself for me as far as she could, given her beliefs. Eventually, she got over her shame and guilt enough that she would even correct other people's stereotypes about LGBTQ people, such as seeing them as pedophiles.

My mother still thought that choosing to live gay was wrong. But she wanted a relationship with me, and one of the ministries she turned to advised her to love me rather than judge me. Called *Spatula Ministries,* a name I found ridiculous and reprehensible, it helped my mother and restored us to a relationship, albeit an uneasy one. The evangelical woman who had founded it felt when her son came out to her that she had to be scraped off the floor with a spatula. The letterhead and envelopes even displayed a red line drawing of a woman draped over a spatula like a Raggedy Ann doll.

Besides letters and tapes, my mother received a round stone from Spatula Ministries on which someone had hand-painted the words, "Mae's First Stone," flanked by yellow daisies. This ministry was an industry. The stone was inspired by Jesus's words to the people that had wanted to stone the woman apprehended in adultery: "Let him who is without sin cast the first stone." Living gay was still a sin, but it wasn't up to my mother to judge me. I think the stone helped her, and I saw her become a milder, more accepting person in general because she was willing to change as much as she could.

I tried to help my family find a way to reconcile their beliefs with their love for me. My daughter now says that this is what makes who I am so hard for them—that their beliefs are held with such conviction and yet they actually do love and even admire me. In my own efforts to come to some sort of reconciliation, even though I could no longer call myself a believer, I had read *Is the Homosexual My Neighbor: Another Christian View* by Virginia Mollenkott and Letha Scanzoni, two evangelical biblical scholars who specialize in the intersection of theological and social issues.

These women focused on interpreting the seven passages in the Bible that have been used to condemn homosexuality and on the biblical command to love our neighbors as ourselves. Their elucidation presented the seven verses in a completely different light from what I'd been taught, resulting in an unqualified "yes" to the title's question about neighborliness. I had changed too much to go back, and the Church, with very few exceptions, had not changed at all. I did think that if anything might help my family open their minds and hearts, it would be this book. I bought and mailed copies to all of them. Forty-plus years later, I learned that many of them had never read it, despite their obsession with discussing homosexuality and me. I began to realize that—barring some catalyst that had nothing to do with me, perhaps only something cataclysmic in their own lives—my parents and most of my brothers were probably incapable of change. As I accepted that, I thickened my armor in order to survive.

* * *

For our first Thanksgiving together, Neale and I drove up to Denver. Reverend Holbrook, who had been her pastor in Brooklyn and had recommended Hope College to her, had taken a new church there. We drove up to visit him and his family. At one time, the Reformed Church of America and the CRC had been one church, but in 1857, they split over what had always seemed like fine hairs to me. The Reformed Church was more liberal than the Christian Reformed by a bit, and Pastor Holbrook was perhaps more liberal than most.

Neale had a long talk with him and told him about our relationship. He said something that, although I only heard it through Neale, has stuck with me. "If you leave the CRC," he told her, "you lose everything—family, culture (the church being mainly made up at that time of Dutch immigrants and their descendants), community, maybe even your faith."

I breathed a deep sigh, feeling that this man I barely knew had truly seen my situation. It would be many years, though, before I would recognize and be able to say to a few select people that losing the Church was the greatest loss of my life. It also meant the loss of the deep intimacy I had once shared with my family.

In *Going Clear: Scientology, Hollywood, and the Prison of Belief,* Lawrence Wright tells how people who leave that religion are stalked and hounded in an attempt to bring them back and maintain damage control, in case the escapees might divulge secrets to the media. No one stalked me or tried to prevent me from exercising my civil rights, other than the civil right of marriage equality. But disapproval, verbal harassment, and marginalization were tools my family employed powerfully to try to get me to return to the fold.

~ 15 ~

Refuge in the Wilderness

A WILDERNESS MAY BE A LUSH FOREST, UNTRAMMELED BY human industry and protected from invasive activity by government regulation. For me, though, the word *wilderness* conjures up vast tracts of barren land, merciless, void of vegetation and without human comfort. I think of the first seven years after I left the mission as my wilderness years, emptied as they were of all things spiritual and of my deepest connections with family and community through spirituality and religion. Those years are the most remote, as though spent in some far-off desert, nearly the definition of *exile.*

Exile is not an easy story to tell. A level of shame arises from exile—shame at being unwanted in the homeland. Pain too, because there is no home to go to, pain over connections severed. As I try to recall those years, I realize that long ago, even while they were occurring, I encased them in an opaque carapace, walling off my pain until I could pretend it didn't exist.

It is human to seek belonging and intimacy. Many southern and eastern African tribes embrace a worldview known as *Ubuntu.* One translation of the word is, *People are people through people.* A healthy response from those who have, for whatever reason, lost family and/or community, is to create family, to find new community, in order to satisfy that basic peopling need. And yet what we create, while it may in some ways be better than what we lost because we have chosen it, can never exactly replace what is gone.

As Neale and I settled into our new life in Albuquerque, I didn't say to myself, "Now I'm going out to find a substitute community." The need to be linked is so strong that most often we seek it automatically. As Church and family slipped away, I found community in two places.

Not all ties with the mission had been severed. Carol Adakai, a year ahead of me at Rehoboth, had been offered a teaching job at Cañoncito, today known by its Navajo name, *Tohajiilee.* Carol had other commitments, and called me one afternoon to suggest that I take the job instead of her. Besides being Rehoboth alumni, we had both graduated from UNM and had just taken a graduate language assessment class together. So I had the Rehoboth Good Old Girls' Network to thank for allowing Neale and me to leave Allison and Rehoboth for Albuquerque.

In 1868, when the surviving Diné were released from the four years of captivity that decimated their numbers at Fort Sumner, New Mexico, they retraced the Long Walk back to their homeland. Three bands of Diné stopped and settled along the way, forming three small Navajo reservations separated from what is known as the Big Navajo. I had always known of the Ramah Navajo Reservation, which is relatively close to the Big Navajo. In fact, until my contact with Cañoncito, I didn't realize that Ramah was a separate reservation. I had never heard of the Cañoncito and Alamo bands.

My new job was as an English teacher, but in fact, I became more of a community organizer. Four teachers and a principal had been hired to start an alternative high school in this community, which had never had a high school before. Most students, in part because of the long round-trip commute to Albuquerque, dropped out of school before or during their freshman year.

Ironically, the new school would be housed in an abandoned, one-room, cinder-block jailhouse with broken windows and no doors. When the five of us walked in for the first time, we found a bare concrete floor piled thick with bird waste and chunks of shattered glass. The director of education for the entire Navajo Nation hailed from Cañoncito, and the new school was to be a gift from him to his home community. But the community, motivated by internal politics and a resistance to change, didn't want the gift, and the Albuquerque Public Schools (APS) administration fought it every step of the way. If the school became a success, it would mean a loss of state and federal revenue for APS. No one seemed to care that we might be graduating kids who had never had a real chance before.

Cañoncito, despite the fact that we had to sell the school and ourselves to the community, was a taste of home for me—literally and figuratively. It might be far from the Big Rez, but I still greeted people with, "Ya'at'eeh," and the soft, palm-stroking handshake I'd learned as a child. I slipped into Rez humor and unconsciously went back to speaking with a slight accent, a mild form of Dummitawry English. To promote the school and try to sign up students, I visited hogans and rectangular homes that could have been placed in Teec Nos Pos or Tohlakai. I sat through hours of chapter meetings, sifting out familiar Diné words and phrases to grasp the gist of what was being said. We put on a community feed of roast mutton, mutton stew, fry bread, and watermelon to entice people to come and hear about the school.

While we tried to interest students and parents, the jail slowly became a large open classroom—windows were glazed, doors hung, walls stuccoed, carpet laid, books ordered, classes scheduled. We began to teach—or, in fact, because of the small numbers, tutor—kids for high school credit. I wrote a successful grant proposal for a child-care center that would teach child development and parenting skills for high school credit to pregnant and parenting teens. I became part of a community that felt like a slice of home. Of course, I existed only on its fringe, but that was where I had always lived in Diné society.

A year and a half later, I left that job when I was hired as one of the few whites to work in a small educational Native American publishing house. The organization would become a magnet for some of the most creative people I've known. I rubbed elbows every day with educators, artists, writers, poets, shamans, linguists, and the Diné half of the team that had written the *Navajo Language Dictionary.* I learned things about Navajo cosmology, about the interconnectedness of life that Diné had known for centuries, ideas that physicists were just beginning to "discover." The Native American Materials Development Center (NAMDC) continued to replace a part of the community I had lost, and kept me tied to a segment of the world that welcomed me. At the same time, what went on there blew my mind in ways that the culture never had while I was growing up, simply because so many parts of the Diné worldview were forbidden me by the Church. I thrilled to be on the forefront of an educational movement that honored Navajo children and communities and their language and traditions.

At NAMDC, our director was a woman who came from Shiprock and had attended Rehoboth several years before me. She held a graduate degree from the Harvard School of Education and was an accomplished poet and painter. More than that, she was possessed of far-reaching vision and was quick to see and draw talent to the center and create out-of-the-ordinary possibilities.

Some of the other staff members were graduates of Rehoboth. One of them was Ilene, the girl with whom I had played Pueblo Indian "house" all those years ago in Beclabito. Ilene had gone to BIA schools for her first few years of education and then joined my class at Rehoboth when we were in sixth grade. We graduated together from high school, and later both of us took linguistics and Diné language classes at UNM. At NAMDC, we shared an office, sometimes slipping into talk about our childhood games and our families. We had a lot of shared history that made our friendship feel sisterly to me at times. Once she made up a story with a Navajo character named Beila Weila to introduce a particular activity, and when she told me the story, I saw that floppy person down in the red canyon where we'd played all those years earlier.

I was not far from my missionary kid roots. In our first year, in a staff pep talk, our director invoked the missionary zeal some of us knew all too well. We had just completed a collaborative effort with the National Geographic Society and needed to distribute thousands of glossy, four-color copies of *Nashdoi Yaazh* (*Lion Cubs*), the most professional children's book published in the Diné language up to that time.

The bilingual education movement was in its infancy. You might think that parents and grandparents who had been harshly punished for speaking their language would be eager to have their children learn to read and write and study school subjects in Navajo. But the pain and humiliation accompanying their lessons had gone deep—Navajo was not the language of success. Many parents had avoided speaking the Diné language with their children, which often meant communication was fractured at best. I knew families where parents spoke only Navajo and their children only English. Most Navajo Nation educators were opposed to bilingual education too, as was American society at large.

Our director gathered us for our pep talk as we prepared to sell *Nashdoi Yaazh* to people attending the Intertribal Indian Ceremonial in Gallup. She said, "I went to a mission school. We've all had contact with missionaries at some time or other. One thing we can say for them is that they are full of enthusiasm for their message. And they are persistent. They don't let anything stop them. We need to adopt their methods, their idealism, their fervor. We are the missionaries for bilingual education. Go out and spread the word. Spread the books."

We looked at each other. Some of us chuckled and nodded. My arms were covered in goose bumps. We were the NAMDC missionaries for bilingual education and had just been given our *Great Commission,* the name given to Jesus's command to spread the gospel.

Guilt by association was part of what inspired my zeal. Bilingual-bicultural education, profoundly integrated with Navajo traditions, was a way to repair some of the damage done by missionaries' attempts to stamp out anything they thought smacked of traditional religion. Of course, that included my mother and father and the many missionaries in whose circle I had been nurtured. In fact, when I taught religious instruction in the BIA school at Fort Wingate while I was in high school, I participated in the damage too.

Ilene once told me I could give up feeling guilty. In the ultimate benison, she said, "You have something to offer that no one else here has. You know things about our culture from inside and outside."

No one on the staff knew better than I how to be a missionary for reversing the cultural genocide perpetrated by people to whom I was still bound by love, ambivalence, and deep-seated training.

Thus it was that Navajo communities continued to offer me communion when I had lost so much of the communion I once had with believers and family.

~ 16 ~

Mission in the Wilderness

In 1974, despite the beginnings of gay pride at Stonewall five years earlier, finding the LGBTQ community in Albuquerque was like embarking on a treasure hunt in which we had to create the clues ourselves and then draw the map as we went. Happily, I did not have to hunt on my own. While Neale and I were still living in Allison, the first thing we knew to do from our reading was to try to find a gay or lesbian bar. I was teaching for the second year at Rehoboth and moonlighting at the Gallup branch of UNM, teaching freshman composition. From her essays, I recognized one of my students, a nurse at the Indian Health Service Hospital, as a lesbian. A generation older than Neale and I, she had done her own treasure hunt in Albuquerque with more skill and background knowledge than either of us possessed. She told us about a private women's club in the North Valley.

We drove up and down Fourth Street a few times before we found the unmarked building. The interior was dark and smoky. One offering from the jukebox was Patti LaBelle and the Bluebelles singing "Lady Marmalade." Dancing was wrong in the CRC, but Patti's, "You wanna give it a go?" and Neale's insistence seduced me onto the floor despite my self-consciousness. We hadn't gone there to dance or to drink but to find community. As a first attempt, it was disappointing. Everyone else seemed to know each other. They *were* there to dance and drink, not to meet two women who were obviously together.

We kept looking for clues and putting out feelers after we moved to Albuquerque, and gradually we met people who shared our values, especially a commitment to social justice. Ken was a gay man, a political activist, and a handyman who had done some work on our house. One evening, he invited us over for roast lamb and couscous. I could tell that we weren't there just to eat a delicious dinner or talk about the skylight we wanted him to build. He got to the point over dessert. "There's a building at Girard and Central that used to house medical offices. It's been bought by a group that wants to use it for alternative organizations. There's going to be a natural food co-op for one. There'll be massage therapy, acupuncture. What if we started a gay and lesbian hotline and walk-in center and speakers' bureau there? One of the small offices will rent for $35 a month. We could pool resources to pay for it."

That dinner conversation developed into the Lesbian and Gay Co-op. We'd met Ken at a similar organization on the UNM campus, but it was a group that was fraught with problems. This would be a fresh start. Having an off-campus location would make us more available to non-students, and being close to the university would keep our center easily accessible to students.

We staffed both a hotline and walk-in peer counseling. Over and over, I heard my own story from people who stepped through our door or called in pain and loneliness—different details, similar losses. To claim ourselves as the people we were, most of us had paid a steep price. I couldn't help thinking of Jesus's words about losing your life in order to find it.

Perhaps most important, my life was greatly enriched by the act of reaching out to offer encouragement to people in need. I met teachers, carpenters, architects, scientists, lawyers, car saleswomen, radio announcers, social workers, writers, and doctors. I knew guys in their teens and twenties, kicked out of their homes for being gay and supporting themselves the only way they knew—through prostitution. I met IV drug users who were like me in the other ways and would later fall prey to HIV and AIDS. I got to know a woman who had shot her lover and sat with her body all night before turning herself in. I met a man who wanted to be a cross-dresser and had no sense of style but a big heart. I talked with a blind woman in her sixties who had never told anyone about her love for other women.

Many stories are forever seared on my memory—like that of the man who'd spent his whole life living alone as the respected, unmarried postmaster of a small Iowa town. Once a year, when he went on vacation, he was gay. He fell in love with New Mexico on one of those vacations and promised himself that when he retired, he would move there and come out. His decency, stamina, and the courage to make the choices he had made, to change so radically at his age, affected me and other co-op members profoundly. He became a volunteer with us within months of showing up as a walk-in.

When I write of prostitution and addiction and other painful exigencies for members of the LGBTQ community, I hasten to say that these things are not intrinsic to being LGBTQ but are instead due in large part to loss of social support. In *Religion for Atheists: A Non-believer's Guide to the Uses of Religion,* philosopher-writer Alain de Botton writes about how

> . . . religions . . . know that to sustain goodness, it helps to have an audience. The faiths hence provide us with a gallery of witnesses at the ceremonial beginnings of our marriages and thereafter they entrust a vigilant role to their deities. However sinister the idea of such surveillance may at first seem, it can in truth be reassuring to live as though someone else were continually watching and hoping for the best from us. It is gratifying to feel that our conduct is not simply our own business; it makes the momentous effort of acting nicely seem a little easier.

Exile from one's faith community and the social community at large denies us much-needed support, not only for relationships but also for coping with life in general. As de Botton acknowledges, the support of a faith community can have its disturbing side, and it is that ominous side that so many LGBTQ people have found it necessary to forsake. But there is also loss when you walk away, when you enter exile. The loss is broader than just the absence of the support of a religious community; it is also the loss of support from other conventional social structures. That is the cost that comes with the freedom. But as society has changed in its level of acceptance and support, many of these painful side effects fortunately have lessened.

Besides staffing the hotline and walk-in center, where we began receiving referrals from therapists, pastors, and other professionals, the Lesbian and Gay Co-op started a speakers' bureau. Our purpose was to educate the community at large, to destroy myths and raise consciousness. We spoke to medical school, college, and high school classes; we participated in training workshops for educators and counselors; we were even asked to talk to a few church groups.

Once I spoke to a class at the UNM School of Medicine. As soon as the panel had seated itself before the tiers of future doctors, I recognized the older brother of one of my former students at the mission school, himself a missionary kid. For a moment my heart leaped to my throat. I wondered how he would see me, whether he would come at me from an evangelical perspective.

But I forgot about him when I launched into a story that I wanted these prospective physicians to hear. "A few weeks ago," I told them, "I woke up with a painful lump under my jaw. I came to the clinic here at UNM, where notes in my patient record told the resident who was going to see me that I was in a lesbian relationship. I waited in a treatment room, and through the closed door, I could hear the attending physician and the resident talking.

" 'This patient has a painful swelling under her left jaw,' the resident told him. 'Oh, and by the way, she's a lesbian.'

" 'Well,' the physician said to her, 'the lump is probably psychosomatic then. Homosexuals are rarely happy people.' "

I looked out at the class and said, "I felt completely discounted as a human being. This doctor had decided without even seeing me, let alone examining me or talking with me, that I was unhappy because of my sexuality and that my unhappiness was the cause of the swelling under my jaw."

One of the students raised her hand. "What did you do?"

"When they entered the room, I told the physician that I had overheard what he said. I told him that what he had said was unprofessional and unscientific, that in fact, I was probably as happy as most people, and that he had discounted me by stereotyping me.

"The point of my story," I added, "is not that you have prejudiced professors teaching you, although that possibility is something for you to be aware of. The point is that as health practitioners, you shouldn't make assumptions based on preconceptions. Prejudice can keep you from providing the best possible care for your patients."

The brother of my student raised his hand, and I thought, "Here it comes."

He started by saying, "I know you. You were my little sister's teacher."

I nodded. "How is Kerry?" I asked.

For a couple of seconds, he looked nonplussed. "She's fine. Graduating from high school this year." Then he asked, "But shouldn't we take into account when we're treating someone, that homosexuality is a disorder and . . ."

The instructor interrupted him. "You've just missed the point. Our speaker is saying that your prejudices can get in the way of you seeing the person and what they're presenting with. Besides, homosexuality is no longer considered a disorder by the AMA or the APA." In that moment, our speakers' group had an ally. And I felt proud that things were changing, that I was helping to change them.

It wasn't all pain and suffering by any means. We at the co-op celebrated the freedom we'd earned to be ourselves. We joined in exuberant humor that only we understood. We gave and got each other's support through difficult events. We marched together in Albuquerque's first Pride Parade with about twenty-five participants. We held potlucks and holiday parties. All our events were alcohol-free, in an attempt to offer an alternative to the gay bar scene.

Neale and I also had a group we socialized with on a regular basis—another lesbian couple and a gay male couple. We broke bread together, discussed books and movies, and laughed a lot. One of the men was part Laguna native, and his cousin had a crepe restaurant in Cubero, a Spanish land grant village adjacent to Laguna Pueblo. One Sunday evening, we all drove the 108-mile round-trip to eat dinner in that incongruous setting where we were feted as the only customers. During the meal, we noticed an ancient wooden pump organ standing in a dusty corner, and afterward, we gathered around with me at the keyboard, pumping away, and sang gospel hymns. The moment was poignant; I felt as if I was my mother, playing the pump organ for one of my dad's services when I was sixteen. It was also a joy-filled moment, singing songs I loved and missed more than anything else about church, except perhaps for communion.

★ ★ ★

Just as I had in the Navajo bilingual education movement, I drew on my missionary training within the LGBTQ community. I couldn't forget how isolated I'd felt in small-town Gallup and at the mission. At one point, I put an ad in the Gallup paper. I had gotten permission to use the lobby of the community health center. I wanted to reach out to others who might be feeling lonely and afraid in that small town. So one afternoon after work, two other co-op members and I headed west on I-40. In Gallup, as darkness pressed against the building's large glass panels, we waited. We began to wonder if anyone would show up. Statistics said there should be at least fourteen hundred LGBTQ people among the town's fourteen thousand residents. Were they still too afraid to come out to a gathering like this? Or had they formed their own hidden networks and didn't need this kind of support? Finally one young man showed up, a teacher in the tiny, mostly Mormon hamlet of Ramah, adjacent to the Ramah reservation. His isolation was a match for mine in the early days, and his relief at finding someone to talk to was palpable.

I thought of the gospel hymn about the ninety-nine sheep who "safely lay in the shelter of the fold" and of the shepherd who went out to find the single one that was lost. We had driven a total of 272 miles, and I had dreamed that we would be instrumental in starting an organization in Gallup like the Albuquerque co-op. Gallup wasn't ready, but Randall was. Maybe others had read the ad, and a seed was planted, the idea that community could exist. Oh, yes, my missionary upbringing stood me in good stead—just not in the ways my father had hoped.

* * *

Once, when I was riding the Southwest Chief from Los Angeles to Gallup, the train passed a small puddle in the midst of cracked red earth between Winslow and Holbrook, Arizona. Five little black ducks were swimming away in that tiny pond that would also soon turn to cracked earth. I loved those little black ducks, taking from the wilderness every drop of precious water they could find and reveling in it. They were my kin, my *k'e,* for I too took from the wilderness everything I could to sustain me during those years.

~ 17 ~

Drawn

EVEN BEFORE THAT GREAT EMPTYING, WHEN I WAS ENGAGED in the great battle between who I was and who the Church said I must be, my spirit was nurtured by nature. I took pleasure in the small and large sights, sounds, and smells around me: the freshness of rain on desert earth and sagebrush; the rattle of golden seed pods on mimosa trees; the striped racer streaking across someone's yard, switching its brilliant turquoise tail and taking me back to the inevitable presence of lizards in my childhood; grackles wheeling across the evening sky by the hundreds; the heavens changing at sunset from gold to orange to purple to indigo. Even at the darkest of times, ever-present feasts for the senses brought a swelling of joy to my chest and often tears of gratitude.

I had learned the Bible so thoroughly that at times, verses just came to me. When the Sandia Mountains turned pink in the evening, I often sang the Psalm, "To the hills I lift mine eyes, to the hills whence cometh my help." At sunset, I couldn't help thinking, "The heavens declare the glory of God, the firmament sheweth his handiwork." Those moments were filled with particular joy.

I had been drawn to mysticism since childhood when I talked to my father about wanting God to talk to me. I just didn't know that what I wanted was called *mysticism*. Miss Hartgerink provided my first encounter with modern mystics, people who listened for the voice of God, often in nature. At times, I would recall Gerard Manley Hopkins' words: "Glory be to God for dappled things—/. . . For rose-moles all in stipple upon trout that swim/. . . All things counter, original, spare, strange;/Whatever is fickle, freckled . . ." I sensed that Hopkins' connection with nature connected him with God.

For high school graduation, Miss Hartgerink gave me a thin red Dell paperback, Thomas Merton's *Seeds of Contemplation*. It carried me into a new spiritual world that appealed to my imagination, to my dreaminess. I romanticized the narrow cell of the contemplative. I imagined myself in a cloistered life. I tried to emulate Merton in my prayers. Because I loved Miss Hartgerink, I was even more taken with Merton and Hopkins than I might otherwise have been. Love is the great opener.

* * *

When I left Calvin College in 1967 after only two years, I joined several of my friends from our In-Out Group in Boston, where I planned to finish my degree. Five of us, with assorted hangers-on, lived in a tiny flat on the backside of Beacon Hill, but instead of going to school, I ended up working a series of odd jobs.

It happened one night that I was alone in the apartment. I had been reading the Bible, the book of Jeremiah. I was taken at the time with the romantic idea of becoming one of God's prophets, and I loved the imagery Jeremiah used: the flowering almond branch, God the Potter forming and reforming the jug he was making, the wind in the wilderness.

In the darkness after reading, I began to beg God, "Use me, Lord. Use me. Use me." All the while as I prayed, I was nearly certain that I was too sinful to be used for holy purposes. Nevertheless, I prayed over and over. I had never heard the word *mantra,* but that was what those words became. Then it seemed that someone or something that was not me took over my breath. I breathed in and in and in and then, my chest hugely full, I held all that air inside. A brilliant white light exploded in my inner vision, and out of that light, I saw Jesus walking toward me from a distance, coming closer and closer. My heart filled with love for him. At last I had to breathe out, and with that, the light and the vision were extinguished.

The next day, I told some of my roommates and their friends about it. One guy who attended Boston University told me I'd had a white light experience, something I had never heard of. He said that many mystics spent a lifetime seeking the white light. I didn't know what to make of it.

I told an older friend from the CRC about it. Far from being impressed as the guy from B.U. had been, she said with pragmatic Dutch asperity, "I don't think it's of much value unless it affects your daily life in some way."

The Church had not in any way prepared me to make use of my vision, if that was what it was. I wondered if the occurrence was simply a product of an overly active imagination. Now, I know that the imagination is of use in mystical communion. I let the event fade, though at times it returned to my consciousness.

⋆ ⋆ ⋆

Neale's and my relationship was no different from any other intimate relationship when it came to the stressors that crop up as the honeymoon wears off. In the absence of societal backing, pressure grew. At times, I wanted to go home, to talk with family about what was going on, to get some encouragement. I knew that our problems would only be viewed as evidence of the disordered nature of homosexuality, as the result of its sinfulness.

People in the LGBTQ community did lend their support. During my third year of spiritual wilderness, as things between Neale and me became more difficult, I went to stay with some lesbian friends for a few days. One night while I was there, I woke from a dream so vivid and extraordinary that it seemed to be more a vision than a dream.

In it, I was driving a VW bus through snow-covered flats and mildly rolling hills with an unfamiliar woman. As we drove, a brilliant, flashing silver light began to cross our path. It happened again and again. We came to a place where people dressed in flowing orange robes were playing catch. It became clear where the flashes of light had come from because the people were tossing around a softball-sized ball of light. I pulled the van off the road, and my passenger and I joined them. The group tossed the silver-white ball to me many times, and in the dream, that was significant. A sense of fun and purpose and camaraderie permeated our play.

I woke to a feeling of wonder, joy, and anticipation. I believed that the dream was in some way prophetic, and I was intensely curious as to when and how it would be fulfilled.

* * *

For something new to be born, something old must often die. What died for me at the end of the seven spiritually hollow years was my relationship with Neale. What was born was a desire, a hunger, to once more have a spiritual life. Like Oliver Twist, I held up my spiritual bowl and said, "Please, sir, I want more."

During Neale's and my time together, I had continued to read works that I hoped might allow me to return to Christianity. When Elaine Pagels' *The Gnostic Gospels* came out in 1979, it became the precursor to my reopening to spirituality. I had been taught that the Bible was God's inerrant word and unquestionable guide for our lives. But even before I left the Church, I had seen that many inconsistencies existed in scripture. But I had also been well tutored in the exercise of mental gymnastics to explain them away. We could always fall back on, "God moves in mysterious ways."

When I left the Church under my own steam, I left the Bible behind with the rest of what had poured out of me. *The Gnostic Gospels* allowed me to see that I could view the Bible in new ways. I learned that many gospel accounts about Jesus had been lost or hidden to prevent zealous Church fathers from destroying them. The fathers were men who wanted the Church to go their way, and saw those gospels as a threat.

I went on to read Evelyn Underhill's *Practical Mysticism* and Anne Freemantle's *The Protestant Mystics*. Freemantle's book shed some light on my father's firm contention that God didn't need to talk to us directly anymore. She wrote that a distinguished Protestant theologian had claimed, "There are *no* Protestant mystics." On the contrary, as Freemantle's book ably documents, there certainly have been and are Protestant mystics. However, she also noted that when she had set out to demonstrate their existence, the Calvinists, *en masse* "thought that even if there were mystics, there shouldn't be any." My Calvinist father apparently came by his stance honestly.

I used the information and suggestions in these books to try to meditate, without much satisfaction. Nevertheless, I continued to be drawn to mystical practice.

~ 18 ~

The Mystical Way in Scandinavia

My relationship with Neale ended painfully, but the growing dysfunction in our home combined with the lack of societal support made ending it necessary. Raw and grieving, I left Albuquerque in my orange VW station wagon for San Francisco with $80 in my pocket. A few months later, the Bay Area became the jumping-off place for travel to Europe. I'd longed to travel abroad for years, so after I met Irene, a Danish woman who had made world travel her life's work, I joined her a few months later in Copenhagen.

One of the greatest gifts I received in Scandinavia came as a surprise. On a dark, rainy summer afternoon, Irene and I sat beside a window over coffee in the Klaptreet Cafe. We'd been to see a film in the attached art theater, and as we chatted, I mentioned that I had a headache.

"You have a lot of headaches," Irene observed.

"Yeah. All my life since I was about five."

"You need yoga."

"I've tried yoga. I didn't like it that much, and it certainly didn't help with my headaches."

"You didn't do this yoga. This is different. You need to try it."

I was dubious, but on the way home, just a few doors down from Klaptreet, Irene pointed out the entrance to the Scandinavian Yoga and Meditation School. "Try it," she said again. "You won't be sorry."

I was skeptical until I walked into the school's reception area a few days later. The peach-colored walls and simple wood-frame Danish furniture seemed to have been chosen and arranged with consciousness. *Consciousness.* I'd never thought much about that before, but it was what I sensed. And calm. I was in the right place in a way that I'd never felt before.

I signed up for a morning class that met for four hours a day for ten days. The class introduced me to *asana* (poses), concentration practices, meditation, and yogic hygiene, such as the use of a neti pot. My headaches didn't improve, but I loved the yoga and meditation. My body and soul stilled and joined together, which was deeply satisfying. That is what *yoga* means: *oneness.*

A few months later, I took the train and then a bus from Copenhagen to a three-month intensive yoga and meditation course at the school's international course center in Håå, in rural southern Sweden. As the bus rolled through snow-covered farmland and stands of bare trees into the early Swedish twilight, I sat alone among strangers and felt some apprehension about what might lie in store.

By the time we reached the large, two-story red farmhouse with white trim, darkness had descended. The New Year was just past, and a single small fir tree in the yard was still strung with twinkling white lights. The snow was crisp underfoot, and our breath hung in the air. Inside, we piled our luggage in a corner and went in to settle our accounts and get room assignments. After that, the forty or so of us trooped into the dining room for steaming bowls of vegetable soup, yeasty homemade rolls, and nettle tea.

After supper, we had some time to settle in, then went to meet in the large yoga room with its deep blue walls, sanded pine floors, and orange yoga mats. These were not the thin rubbery mats used today in yoga studios all over the U.S. They were two-inch-thick cotton mattresses with washable covers, ones that could be folded or rolled for different meditation poses and laid flat for asana practice.

On the first evening, Swami Janakananda presented the course expectations and rules. For example, we could walk the roads through the nearby forests and among the farms, but we were not to go into the tiny village of Hamneda. The chief draw there was a kiosk where one could buy candy or cigarettes. Or cheese not made from Norwegian goats' milk. Meals were to be taken in silence. Silence would always be observed in the yoga room, except to ask a question. Janakananda told us that it was better to have come alone to these courses, so as not to be distracted from our inner work—from the dragons (my word) we would be confronting. After talking about rules and expectations, he led us in our first brief meditation of the course, and then we left for bed.

The course was divided into three sections. In the first few weeks, we got up at 5:30, did asana and *pranayama* (breathing exercises). We then ate breakfast, consisting of a glass of grain tea with a few spoonsful of kernels in it. Afterward, we spent around an hour doing karma yoga. This is work done with one's whole attention—attention to the task, attention to body and mind while performing it. It is work done for the sake of the work.

When we were called back to the yoga room, we learned *ajapa japa,* a chakra-cleansing meditation. Then we ate lunch, did voluntary karma yoga, or had free time, followed by yogic health practices. Before supper, we learned and practiced *Antar Mouna,* the meditation of Inner Silence. After supper we could do more voluntary karma yoga or choose free time. Finally, we participated in an evening program until nine or ten.

Evening programs might be *satsang,* a talk by Janakananda including questions and answers from us students. Or we might engage in Sufi dancing, *khirtan,* (chanting accompanied by a harmonium), freeform dancing and singing to contemporary instruments, or meditation.

During the second part of the course, we got up earlier and earlier until finally, the bell ringer came for us at three in the morning. We were learning *kriya* yoga meditation, and spent the entire instruction time, more than a month, in complete silence. Eventually, the silence grew so deep that more than thirty years later, as I write about it, if I say something aloud to myself, I'm startled by the sound. In that moment, I feel certain that I have broken the silence. As we learned kriya practice, the meditation lasted longer and longer until it was about three and a half hours long. We did shorter and shorter asana programs during this time and more and more karma yoga to keep us grounded as our energy from the kriyas built. Even when we rose at three, which proved grueling in the cold and dark, we continued to meet until nine or ten at night.

During the last third of the course, we continued to rise early and practice kriya meditation for three hours. We started to do more asana again and a little less karma yoga. We also spent time learning a healing meditation, *prana vidya.*

Learning to meditate was a process: It was one thing to be taught a meditation practice, another to go through the steps of the practice, and still another to actually meditate. When I did a particular mediation for the first time, or if I hadn't meditated for a while, I slipped easily into a meditative state. Highly aware, my body and mind were altered, present in the moment. This might last only for seconds or for minutes. The state ended when I said to myself, "Oh, look at this. Look what I'm experiencing. I'm meditating." Then I was no longer meditating. After that first time when it came so easily came the time to work at it. To just practice. And practice.

Janakananda told us, "Don't have expectations when you're meditating. Don't want this meditation to be like the last time you practiced it. If you look for a certain experience, you will miss the one you are having or the one you could be having."

More than once, Janakananda told us that yoga is not a religion. I was ready to accept that. I began to see yoga and meditation as a spiritual tool, one that could be used for personal growth by anyone from an atheist to a Christian or Muslim or Jew or follower of traditional Native American practices. The more I practiced meditation and the union of body and soul in asana, the more I found awareness through karma yoga and the buildup of energy in pranayama, the more I knew that these practices were a pathway to experiencing the Divine in everyday life.

My early spiritual training and my love for it predisposed me to sometimes color my meditation experiences in Christian hues. Two meditations were especially powerful for me in this respect. One of them ended with a visualization of a flame on top of my head. That flame could be envisaged rising through the roof, into the sky, and beyond the confines of Earth. The similarity between this meditation and the flames descending upon the heads of the early Christians at Pentecost is obvious. Pentecost had meant the powerful, mystical arrival of God in the person of the Holy Spirit, and I naturally made that connection. Because of it and a remarkable vibration I felt in my body, this became a favorite meditation, connecting me with what I had lost, with spiritual home.

In another meditation, Janakananda directed us to feel a hand placed lightly on our heads. I had not yet let God back into my life. Yet to me, in a sort of existential contradiction, the hand on my head was the hand of God, large enough to cover the whole top of my head, loving and protective, blessing me. Yoga and meditation would later become the tools that gave me a direct experience of God, the direct communication, most often wordless, that my Calvinist father had told me not to even want, much less expect.

* * *

Karma yoga is a great teacher. I got it, the thing about work for its own sake, one morning after asana practice. I was assigned to sweep and mop a large tract of tiled basement floor. I had just finished mopping when one of the yoga teachers came in from outside where others were digging a trench in the frozen Swedish ground. He sauntered onto my shining wet floor, trailing mud the entire length of my work. We were in silence, so I could not say anything, but I was furious.

"These yoga teachers are supposed to be aware," I thought. "Consciousness is what yoga and meditation are all about. This is the height of unawareness!"

Right away, I laughed at myself. Some karma yogi or yogini would mop the floor again tomorrow and the next day and the day after that. Perhaps it would be me again. And again. Each one, whoever it was, would be doing the mopping, or trying to, for the sake of the work. Even for the love of the work. Not for the end result. Not to be praised for gleaming tiles or a job well done. I could not mop over the teacher's tracks because the bell ringer called us to meditation. I had to live with the knowledge that the karma yoga leader might well think I'd done a lousy job. I reminded myself that karma yoga is work done in the present. In that moment, I would do my best, but I couldn't be attached to lasting results.

Often in karma yoga, a new understanding of life came to me, because karma yoga is about engaging in life fully. If I could be present in every waking moment, I would be doing karma yoga all the time, and karma yoga is part of the spiritual life in many traditions—cloistered Christian nuns and monks engage in it without calling it that, as do Buddhist monks and nuns. In other walks of life, it could be called community service. But it can also be part of everyday life in any home or job, depending on the attitude and the wholeheartedness with which it is done. When I wash dishes or water plants with awareness, I benefit from karma yoga.

* * *

We never knew until we entered the yoga room after supper and dishwashing, kneading the next day's bread, and toasting grain for breakfast tea what the evening program would be. I was always delighted when the yoga mats had been placed in a circle, and Hari Prem, asana instructor without parallel, came in and lit an incense stick beside Janakananda's mat. It meant we would be having satsang. I love little better than being taught, especially through storytelling. Listening to Janakananda's wisdom, hearing stories from all walks of life and traditions was a soul-reminder of listening to Bible stories after dinner at home. Even today, certain pithy statements or stories from those nights in Sweden come back to reinstruct me, to offer new meaning, just as a Bible verse will at times.

One that came back to the seeker in me again and again was, "Yes, all roads lead to Rome. But to get to Rome, you must choose a road."

* * *

The three-month course begins in the dark of winter, which in southern Sweden, means many hours of darkness. During that deep dark, during the weeks when we rose at three in the morning, while we were learning physically and mentally challenging practices, while we kept silent, we were forced to confront the darkness within as well. Our dragons.

I had brought with me a purple cotton blouse I'd gotten for Christmas. It wasn't a rule, but we were severely encouraged not to read or write during the course. I decided to embroider a scene on the back of my blouse during some of my free time rather than read or write. I appliqued a circular frame of blue and white batik onto it, then filled the circle with a stream banked by wildflowers and spanned by an orange bridge. Beyond the stream stood snow-capped mountains, and above it all flew a red dragon.

I wasn't conscious of it then, but that dragon was significant because during the course, I was powerfully confronted by the dark roiling of my own dragons. I faced loneliness, feeling as I had when I was sent to boarding school at age eight—wanting to go home. I encountered the hopelessness of ever finding a spiritual home to go back to. I looked into the ugly face of the addictions I had used to try to assuage my longings and hopelessness. I felt the heaviness of the depression that had been with me since high school. Several times, I wanted to run away from it all, and once I nearly left for Copenhagen. But there was something there for me, something I needed, and I stayed to the end.

On our first night at Håå, Janakananda had mentioned that we would quite likely have vivid dreams, especially after we entered the silence. It may have been during this time that I first had what would become a significant recurring dream. In it, I was back in the church at Rehoboth. The sanctuary was clothed in darkness. Objects and people appeared as shadows. Three enormous black boxes stood on the platform, and I stood in front of them, behind the pulpit to lead the service. The organist kept losing her place, and the singing would stop. With a gesture, I indicated we should go on, and the organist and people followed my direction. This kept happening, and the stops and starts felt awkward. Yet I continued to lead, and the people seemed committed to following. As we went along in our halting way, the room began to lighten, gradually at first, then more and more quickly, until we were bathed in a golden glow. The music grew fluid and harmonious. I now recognized people I'd sat with in childhood and adolescence. Their faces shone with love and joy. We all saw that the boxes behind me had been transformed into great golden thrones.

This dream did not have quite the visionary quality of that earlier dream in which the orange-robed people and I played catch with the silvery ball of light. But the content reminded me of it. It seemed to me that I might one day be called upon to shed some light on the darkness that existed within the church of my youth. I felt that I might know what the darkness and the light could be.

* * *

Near the end of every course at Håå, students have an opportunity to talk privately with the course instructor. In my talk with Janakananda, I told him that for a time during the course, I hadn't had headaches but that they'd come back. I thought he might tell me to do certain yoga poses or hygiene practices. Instead he asked, "Did you have headaches during the silence?"

I thought, then answered, "No."

He said, "Have you been talking a lot since the silence ended?"

"Yes."

"When you talk, you have to take responsibility for what you say. That causes stress."

What a simple idea. That thought and the effects of having been silent for so long had an impact, causing me to be more judicious than before about using my words. Silence is a powerful practice in itself.

* * *

With the coming of spring, everything brightened in Håå and in me. The days promised the energy that comes with the long sun of summer in the far north. The silence ended, and we were now simply practicing what we had learned. One afternoon, I took one of the school's bicycles and rode and rode, delighting in the crocuses and hyacinths poking their heads into the light. At one point, I lost my way and was relieved that the silence was over so I could stop at a farmhouse and ask directions.

I got back just in time for supper. Daffodils graced the tables in the dining room, and we were served miso soup with homemade tofu and soft rolls. A quiet rain had begun outside. I realized I'd grown to love the seven other people at my round table, and my eyes filled with tears. My heart opened to spring, to nourishing food, and to communion with people who shared, in the days we were there and perhaps beyond, a common purpose.

~ 19 ~

God Again

DURING COLLEGE, I WORKED IN HOSPITALS AS AN OPERATING room technician, which I'd been trained to do at the mission hospital. When a patient is lying on the table and the surgeon discovers a deep infection in the wound, the operating room moves into crisis mode. The room and staff are treated as contaminated, so everything used during surgery gets special handling. Intravenous antibiotics are started. Sometimes the surgeon elects not to close the wound, to let it heal from the bottom up so an abscess won't form in a closed cavity.

It was that kind of deep healing I found, healing from the bottom up, when I surrendered to a Twelve Step program. Addiction is endemic to Western society, perhaps to the human condition. It is complex, to say the least, but I believe it is accurate to say that the basic drive into addiction is a misguided attempt to heal our most painful wounds; most often this ends instead in partially numbing our pain. The specific addiction that brought me into one of the Alcoholics Anonymous spin-off programs is not important here; what is important is that dire consequences finally made me willing to feel my pain instead of seeking to deaden it.

Unexpectedly, it wasn't only my heartache that started to heal when I entered the program. In the rooms where I listened to the stories of others and shared my own story, I got back something vital that I had lost.

The Third Step of Alcoholics Anonymous and its many derivative programs states that we "made a decision to turn our will and our lives over to the care of God as we understood God." With those words, my Twelve Step program gave God back to me. Not only did I receive the gift of having God in my life again, but I was also given the utter freedom to have this be God as I *experienced* God. I had read scientific evidence in physicist Fritjof Capra's *The Tao of Physics* that pointed me back in the direction of God, but the Twelve Step program granted me the gift.

At the yoga school, spirituality, never referred to as such but always there for the recognition and the taking, was all about experience, not about rules to be followed or beliefs to be held. Meditation was to be experienced. The body was to be experienced. Life decisions were to be experienced. *All* of life was about experience. And now God was about experience, direct experience. I began to see that this was what I had longed for as a child when I wanted God to speak to me. I wanted to *experience* God, not just think *about* God.

Addiction is stubborn, and I held onto it as the hope, the thing that could mute my deepest anguish. Most of the time, we have to plumb the depths of our pain to realize that the substance or process to which we are addicted is not as anesthetizing as we had hoped it would be. Many people describe their entry to a Twelve Step program as "crawling in on my hands and knees." I had left Scandinavia, and spent ten months living in New Zealand where I gave birth to my daughter, Cheyenne. Returning to the United States, we settled in the San Francisco Bay Area. On the evening, about a year later, when I walked into the basement room of Berkeley's Finnish Brotherhood Hall, I felt exactly as if I were crawling in on my hands and knees.

I stumbled down cement steps into a dark, wood-paneled space. I found a seat in the outer ring of folding chairs, hoping to remain unseen. Along one wall stood a table with the obligatory coffee service, one of the hallmarks of Twelve Step meetings, and the more or less optional hot water and bags for tea. A table along another wall held program literature. I felt as if blood and guts were pouring out of me, and I couldn't stop crying.

I had confronted some of the dragons of my addiction during the three-month yoga course, but that was only a beginning. Making a deal with myself to focus on my destructive thought processes and behavior was hard-core. I met up with my darkest, most needy, most manipulative self. I had to face the fact that I'd expected the addiction to meet my deepest needs and it would not.

The program taught me to care for myself in a basic, easy-to-remember way. Among other things, I learned the acronym HALT, which stood for "Hungry, Angry, Lonely, Tired." The admonition was to not get too hungry, too angry, too lonely, or too tired, any of which could lead to behavior that didn't serve me. I needed to take care of all these seemingly simple things, and not let them get out of control.

At the time, Cheyenne had just turned two. Sometimes I wished I didn't have the responsibility of caring for her because I wanted to place all my attention on this new task of taking care of myself. There had been other times in recent years when I'd felt the pull to devote myself to self-care, but I had always put work, romance, travel, and everything else first.

In Twelve Step programs, newcomers are encouraged to attend ninety meetings in ninety days. I heard people around me talk of doing that. As a single mother, I was able to commit to only one meeting a week. Sometimes I resented that. I wanted more for me, now that I was paying attention to taking care of myself. One evening, Cheyenne was in bed, and I was doing laundry. I started thinking about how completely absorbed in their recovery some folks in the program were. It seemed that their whole life revolved around their recovery, that there was nothing else. These were usually people who were responsible only for themselves. As I folded Cheyenne's small shirts and jeans, I realized that she and my responsibility for her were a gift. They kept one foot in the tasks of everyday life—making a living to support us, preparing food, getting her to day care, and yes, even washing and folding her clothes. She had become the karma yoga that taught me about real living and helped me stay balanced.

I saw how the Twelve Step program could easily have become like the religion that had poured out of me when I left the Church. In itself, the program wasn't a bad thing. In fact, it was good for me. But had it not been for Cheyenne and a sort of wariness of any all-consuming system—as Christianity had been for me, my family, and my church—the program could well have become an obsessive distraction from life, just as my addiction had been before. I saw it happen around me.

I got to know people in the program who had been hurt by the religions of their early years, much as I had. In the first weeks, I gravitated to what they had to say about the Third Step and also the Second, which reads, "Came to believe that a Power greater than ourselves could restore us to sanity." Some people had been too hurt or come too far to be able or to want to have anyone called God, or even Goddess, in their lives. (This being Berkeley, lots of members said "Goddess" when they prayed the serenity prayer.)

Twelve Step programs are founded on spiritual principles with surrender to a Higher Power at their heart. I listened hungrily to how people negotiated the "God" steps. One woman talked about how she made the group her Higher Power. "The Second Step just says 'a Power greater than ourselves,'" she said. "I figure the group is bigger and greater than me. Using the collective wisdom of the group could help me get back some sanity in my life." For her, this had been an early step on the way to having a Higher Power, which many referred to affectionately as *HP,* as in "HP told me . . . ." or "HP helped me realize . . . ."

Others turned "GOD" into an acronym for "Good Orderly Direction," knowing their chaotic lives needed exactly that; it was what they could relate to at the time, helping bring some order to their lives. Some had a more-conventional

Christian or Jewish God who had stepped into our meetings along with them.

One reason the program worked well for me was that it was all about stories. A friend called it "showing each other our owies." In fact, we seemed so young and vulnerable when we told our stories that one evening, as one of our number drove out of the parking lot, the same friend said she wanted to cry out to him, "No! You're too little to be driving!"

It was important that our stories not only be about the pain we had tried to numb with our addiction. We also were encouraged to share our strength and hope. Now I realize that those were our resurrection stories, the stories about newness of life and a new way of experiencing God.

The Third Step became a favorite of mine, the one about turning our will and our lives over to the care of God. When I took this step, I felt it almost physically as a free fall into an enormous safety net that would always be there for me. The feeling was sublime. The idea of surrender is often connected with defeat. But we also talk of sweet surrender, as in the joy and pleasure that come with complete surrender in lovemaking. Surrender was like that in my return to God.

I admired how people who desperately needed and wanted healing went to great lengths to make the program work for them. The flexibility that was built into the Twelve Steps, the way it gave me back the gift of God, reminded me of a character in Chaim Potok's *The Promise.* The man is a Jewish scholar whom Orthodox Jews consider apostate because of how he interprets the Bible. But another scholar says of him, "To develop a theology for those who can no longer believe literally in God's revelation and who still wish to remain observant and not abandon the tradition—that is a remarkable achievement."

The scholar who spoke those words was himself an Orthodox Jew. For years, I mistakenly thought he had used the word *mitzvah,* meaning *good deed* or *blessing,* rather than *achievement.* Perhaps that was because the freedom to have the God of my own understanding was the program's greatest *blessing* to me.

I longed to be able to share my faith, such as it was, with my own family, to return to the intimacy of spiritual give and take with them. I deeply desired for them to be able, despite their own orthodoxy, to see beyond their narrowness and know that my faith also was of value. I longed for them to have the generosity of spirit that Potok's Orthodox scholar had shown.

At about this time, my brother Rick, a physician, was working as the medical director of substance abuse programs for the Navajo Nation. As he worked with traditional Diné health practitioners and roadmen who lead the Native American Church peyote ceremonies, he was able to differentiate between Christianity and spirituality.

Once when I visited Rick's home, one of my three minister brothers referred to a Navajo shaman as a Christian.

After a thoughtful pause, Rick said, "I wouldn't say he's a Christian. But he is a very spiritual person."

I was both surprised and gratified. Rick's response told me he could see the existence of spiritual realities other than his own, something uncommon among evangelicals. His openness gave the two of us a window through which we began sharing spiritually—a gift to both of us.

★ ★ ★

The windows into Diné and Jewish traditions, along with Uncle Chinua, had taught me that relationship with God was not limited to Christianity. The Twelve Step program reaffirmed what I had learned from sitting in on that literary nighttime conversation in the shaman's hut in Nigeria. Still, Christianity had been planted deep within me, and the drive to reconcile what I'd been taught with other spiritual traditions remained strong.

"Who would you like to spend an evening with, living or dead?" has become a popular question, and a popular answer is, "Jesus." That would also be my answer, mostly because I would like to see if I could understand what it was about him that had such an impact on the people who met him. Why was his influence so powerful that millennia later, so many people respond so strongly to stories told by people who were touched by him?

My spiritual recovery in the Twelve Step program was accompanied by work with a gifted therapist. One afternoon, soon after I'd started with Susan, I felt as though a sheet of warm water was cascading softly over my shoulders and down my back. I knew deep within me that I was receiving love in its purest form, that Susan was simply a conduit for that love. At forty-one, this was the first time in my life that I had *felt* loved. I told Susan I knew my parents had loved me, and she said, "There's a difference between *knowing* you are loved and *feeling* loved."

Susan's greatest gift was a conscious ability to be present with me, and, I'm sure, with her other clients. To me, being present is what love is. I think that is why God is described in the Bible both as *I am* (which is presence) and as *Love. Being Present* and *being Love* are interchangeable. As my experience of feeling loved grew, it happened one day in a therapy session that I had the overwhelming urge to fall on my knees, face to the floor, before Susan as she sat in her rocking chair. I wanted to exclaim, "My Lord and my God."

Afterward, I thought, "This must be what Jesus's disciples felt when they were with him on the Mount of Transfiguration—that Presence, that Love expressed through him. Those were the words they spoke. My wanting to say this to Susan would be considered blasphemy among most evangelicals and fundamentalists, but the feeling gave me a visceral comprehension of Jesus and how his disciples had experienced the Presence of God in him.

Experiencing being loved as a soft sheet of water was kinesthetic. In Sweden during an evening meditation, Janakananda gave an instruction that led to my feeling completely present in my body. Shortly afterward, he got up and walked inside the circle of meditators. As he walked past me, he said, "Meditation is an experience of the mind, not the body." For me, however, the body experience was important, just as the sensation of being gently washed by a warm waterfall was. I am first and foremost a kinesthetic learner, even when it comes to spiritual learning. Perhaps this is part of the reason I missed the corporeality of communion so much.

~20~

Forays

FROM THE TIME THAT I LEFT THE CHURCH AND UNDERWENT that great outpouring of all things religious, I made small forays into churches, always hoping for reunion. The first of those was Neale's and my attendance at the Episcopal Church of the Holy Spirit in Gallup while I was still teaching at the mission. Mostly I went there to keep up some semblance of meeting the school's expectations in order to keep my job. But I held onto a thin slice of hope that a more liberal church would enable me to stay connected, even as every tie seemed to be breaking.

In Albuquerque, Neale and I attended the Metropolitan Community Church for a time. An evangelical church that ministers largely to the LGBTQ community, it got us in touch with a certain segment of the population, but ultimately, neither of us found it satisfying or necessary.

The longer I was away from church, the harder it became to give up Sundays, which I had come to regard as my time for journaling, meditating, walking or hiking, listening to music, and, much later, taking Cheyenne to a park. I reveled in the relaxation of doing things at my pace, as they suggested themselves to me. I didn't have to think about what to wear or be ready to be somewhere at a certain time.

But I didn't mind giving up that spontaneity for a few hours when I found a church that nurtured me. I moved to Watsonville, fifteen minutes south of Santa Cruz on the California central coast, to take a teaching job when Cheyenne started kindergarten. The minister of the Unity Church in Santa Cruz was a wise old crone with a wicked chuckle. Unity is a metaphysical Christian church influenced by the Transcendental and New Thought movements, by people like Ralph Waldo Emerson, Bronson and Louisa May Alcott, and Walt Whitman. They believed that people are inherently good, as opposed to the Calvinist idea that we are born totally depraved. They interpreted the Bible metaphysically; that is to say, they took meaning from stories and teachings in a way that was not detectable through the senses, definitely not literal. For example, Jesus's death and resurrection were thought of not as atonement for our sins but as symbolizing death of the self followed by spiritual renewal. This was a Christianity I could live with.

Every week, I came away with some nugget of learning that I could use for my growth. A guided meditation always took me to a higher plane. Receiving a spiritual takeaway was important to me. There was no communion in the sense of bread and wine, which seemed logical, since communion in traditional churches symbolizes the body and blood of Christ given for remission of sins. I did miss it, though. And I found no communion in the sense of community either. I was there for what Emily Sanford could teach me. Plus I also liked the fact that Cheyenne was getting some form of spiritual teaching in Sunday school.

⋆ ⋆ ⋆

Eventually, I decided to move back to New Mexico. As far as my family was concerned, I still lived on the edges. Despite that, when my mother had a heart attack during our second year in Watsonville, I went home for Thanksgiving a month later and began thinking of moving back to live closer to my family. I also felt it was important for Cheyenne to connect with her extended family, even though they marginalized me and, by extension, her.

Less consciously, I also relocated to reconnect with my roots in the Navajo Nation. We moved to the tiny town of Cuba, near both Navajo and Apache reservations, where I began working as a clinical counselor. Cuba is two and a half hours from Gallup, where my parents and three of my brothers lived—close enough but not too close.

My father assumed that I didn't attend church. (I'd never told my family about Unity, knowing they would hardly consider it a church.) One of his first questions when he knew I was moving to Cuba was, "What churches do they have there?"

I was only certain of two: Catholic and Jehovah's Witness.

He shocked me by saying, "Well, you better go to the Jehovah's Witnesses then. At least they believe in the resurrection."

"What?" I thought. "And the Catholics don't?" He'd always taught us that Catholics weren't Christians, but I was sure they were closer to our church than the Jehovah's Witnesses were. The CRC regarded the Witnesses as a cult, along with Mormons and Seventh-day Adventists. They were all included in *The Chaos of Cults,* a book well known within our circle.

I didn't plan to go to any church in Cuba, though I soon learned that Baptists, Mormons, Presbyterians, Church of God in Christ, and several nondenominational fundamentalist churches, as well as a plethora of mission churches, had a presence there. As it happened, I entered the Catholic Church twice—once for the First Holy Communion of one of Cheyenne's playmates and again for the rosary of the great-grandfather of another of her friends.

Although I only went twice to the Presbyterian Church for services, the first time presented me with a meaningful encounter. A friend had told me that the new interim Presbyterian minister was one half of a lesbian couple. These were lovely women, and despite the Presbyterian Church's policy at the time, allowing only celibate gays to be active in ministry, Elaine had been open with the local church's governing body.

One elder had asked another when Elaine used the word *lesbian,* "What does that mean?" His friend took him outside and explained.

The first man's response brought tears to my eyes. "God made them that way. We don't know why. It's not up to us to decide."

Thus, Elaine and her partner were accepted for as long as they would be there.

I shared my own story with Elaine and Joan, particularly as it related to the Church. I felt deeply seen and understood by these women—a great gift. One evening, not long before Christmas, we shared a meal, and Elaine mentioned that the church's ancient pianist was ill. It seemed quite likely that she wouldn't be able to play at the Christmas Eve service. The congregation had been struggling along without accompaniment for regular Sunday services. "But it would be so nice to have the piano on Christmas Eve," Elaine said.

I hesitated for a few moments, then offered, "I haven't played for ages—especially not for a service. I was never very good at accompaniment. But if you choose the songs ahead of time, and I can get into the church to practice, I guess I could do it." Elaine had no reservations, and together, we chose carols that I could play. More or less.

The Presbyterian Church in Cuba was more than a hundred years old, a white stucco adobe with a blue metal roof. It was a short, wide structure with pine board flooring. The days I practiced, with no one else in there, reminded me of going by myself into the tiny chapel at Teec Nos Pos to practice my piano lessons every afternoon.

A couple of days before the service, Elaine came in while I was practicing to make some preparations. She mentioned that they would celebrate communion at the service. My heart picked up. I told her how much I missed communion and what it had meant to me. "Do you think, knowing what you know about me, knowing what I believe and don't believe or what I doubt, do you think it would be all right for me to take communion?" I'm sure she heard the longing in my voice. "I mean, I don't believe Jesus had to die for our sins. You know that. For me, communion has to do with spiritual nurture, with community."

Elaine smiled and said, "It's your decision. I think if you want to, you should." I heard an echo of Miss Hartgerink's words when I had wondered about taking communion way back then.

I thought about it several times over the next couple of days. Such a big thing had been made of who could and couldn't take communion in the CRC, and human permission was so important there. I hadn't rooted all that out. I didn't believe or even feel that I would eat and drink damnation to myself if I partook unworthily (whatever that meant). But almost as if it were imprinted on my cells, it seemed that certain standards must be met and that human approval from an external source was required. It had been more than twenty years since I'd taken communion. I considered the elder who hadn't known what a lesbian was but who was so guileless, knowing it was not for him to judge. Who better to share the table with?

Christmas Eve arrived. I practiced one more time before the service, then went home for supper. The night was cold and crisp, the sky filled with shimmering stars but only frost, not snow, on the ground. As we drove into the church parking lot, we could see a single candle shining from each window. Inside, the small sanctuary glowed golden.

We sang, and I played, sometimes with my fingers stumbling over each other. It reminded me of the times I had played for services at Tohlakai when my mother couldn't make it. At times when I lost my fingering, I would keep up with the congregation by just playing the right hand until I could pick up the tenor and bass chords again. Accompanying the singing never lost its stressfulness, that feeling of having to keep up, of struggling nervously not to let people down. And not to seem foolish for thinking I was up to the task.

Elaine called the worshippers up to the altar to take communion, and that was when I finally decided; I got up from the piano bench to join them. On the table lay a square golden loaf of homemade bread. I happened to know its secret ingredient—beer—which we had chuckled about before the service. A chunk of bread would be dipped into a large ceramic goblet filled with grape juice. As I neared the altar, my heart speeded up again. I could hear Elaine, as people broke off their chunks of bread, saying different things to different people. Sometimes she said, "The body and blood of our Lord." Other times, "Take, eat, remember, and believe" or "The body of Christ, broken for you."

When I took my piece of bread, Elaine said softly, "The bread of life." She could not have found more perfect, meaningful words for my need. What a mix of emotions ran through me. I felt completely seen and heard by her and felt the greatness of the gift of life. I felt the grace that could include me in the family of God, regardless of what I did or did not believe. I walked back to the piano, blinking back tears, and played the introductory notes to "Oh Come, All Ye Faithful."

After the service, we all went down to the church basement for a traditional northern New Mexico Christmas Eve meal of *posole* with red chile, tortillas, and *bizcochitos,* the little cookies sprinkled with sugar and cinnamon. I sat at a long table with people I knew from counseling their children, buying food in their stores, attending community meetings with them. We chatted quietly over the savory and sweet food, laughing now and then, and this was another kind of communion.

Months later, I went to the Presbyterian Church one more time. Elaine and Joan had moved to Denver, and a guest minister stood in the pulpit. I hadn't known it, but communion was once again being served. The preacher said, "This is God's table. No human can turn anyone away from a table that belongs to God." The words were right, but something—I don't know what—held me in my pew when the time came to go forward.

That second visit marked the new beginning of a search to satisfy a longing for something I needed, or at least wanted. Something about my search had changed: I no longer especially wanted to meet my family's expectations or to have my expectations of them met. In fact, for quite some time, I had given up having any hopes at all where family was concerned. That way, if I got nothing, I wasn't disappointed. "If I get something good from them," I told friends, "it's like whipped cream on my cake." When Rick, for example, could acknowledge that someone could be spiritual without being a Christian—that was whipped cream.

My forays in search of spiritual community were brief, tentative, and sporadic—months and sometimes years apart. I tried Unitarian services. Believing as I do that I can learn from all spiritual paths, and having a commitment to social justice, I would seem to be a good fit for the Unitarians. I had left a church that was intellectual in its approach, but the Unitarian services, intellectual in a much different way, did not touch my heart. At Unity of Albuquerque, I found no spiritual meat.

I tried the United Church of Christ, a mainstream church that announced it was open and affirming—code for its acceptance of LGBTQ people. That was my longest attempt—a whole eight weeks. The fact that I sensed coolness among the people there had something to do with why I stopped going. But also, although something deep within me longed for reconciliation, I wasn't yet ready for it.

I tried the Metropolitan Community Church again, the denomination that ministers mainly to LGBTQ congregations. As it happened, they were having communion. The communion portion of the service may have been the most deeply moving of any I have partaken of as an adult. When I went up for bread and grape juice, two older gay men stood to the side of the table. One of them placed his hands on my shoulders and welcomed me and prayed for me. I started crying. The feeling that I belonged was unmistakable. The sermon, however, did not offer me anything that nurtured my soul. I did get a mug with a rainbow and the words "MCC of Albuquerque welcomes you" printed on it. Not enough to keep me coming back.

I had read many books over time, always with the goal of finding my way back to the Church. Instead, the knowledge I gained from them introduced obstacles to believing in the Bible as the authoritative Word of God and in Jesus as the blood sacrifice for my sins. I studied about how portions of the Bible were written for their times and then often rewritten to fit the next period in which they would be read. I knew some of how the Bible had been tampered with purposefully, as well as by mistake, in later years. I saw the writers as people who had had a profound encounter with God or been part of a culturally prescribed event. They had written about their meeting with the Divine, often to the benefit of posterity. I could use what the Bible offered for my growth, but I couldn't take it literally. It was not an authority but more of a guide and inspiration. That limited the pool of churches where I might feel comfortable. It also restricted the number of people who might be comfortable with me, if I were to be open about my ideas.

I had a hard time thinking of myself as a Christian. In part that was because of how I'd been rejected by the Christians I knew best, the ones who had once cradled me. It was also hard to identify as Christian because of others who have been rejected, because of atrocities committed in Christianity's name, and because of unscientific thinking. I can't imagine identifying myself with Christians who think God put dinosaur bones into the earth to test their faith; they can't acknowledge the existence of real dinosaurs so long ago because it would call into question the age of the Earth in their literal interpretation of the Bible.

Beyond church, I visited a Zen *sangha* once. The meditation practices I learned in Sweden have a lot in common with Zen sitting practice. I was comfortable with the proceedings there until the chanting after the Dharma talk. One line went, "The Buddha way is the best way." It ended for me right there. I'd had more than enough of the "best way" and the "only way" to last me a lifetime.

~21~

A Good Stranger

I MADE ONE MORE EXPLORATORY ATTEMPT TO FIND SPIRITUAL community. It would not be until this foray came to an end that I would realize just how deeply Judaism had been embedded in my soul from my earliest days, sometimes in a peculiar way. Our church placed as much emphasis on the Old Testament as it did on the New, if not more.

At home on Sundays, we followed strict rules, and we called the collection of them *Sabbath observance,* as the Orthodox Jews do. On Saturday nights, my mother peeled potatoes for Sunday dinner and bathed us. My father cut the boys' hair, made coffee cake for Sunday breakfast, and polished our good shoes, in order to do as little work as possible on the Sabbath. On the day itself, we went to church twice and sometimes three times.

In the afternoon, when we weren't in church, there were many things we weren't allowed to do, and a few things we could do. We were not allowed to play with the neighbor children because they were Catholic, which in our world meant they were not Christian. We couldn't ride bikes. Recently I learned that Justice Ruth Bader Ginsberg's father destroyed her brother's prized bicycle for riding it on the Sabbath when they were children in an Orthodox Jewish home. We would never buy anything on Sunday because that would cause someone else to break the Sabbath.

We were allowed to play with our siblings, whose Christian status we were pretty sure of. We could play catch with a baseball but not baseball with a bat—go figure. We could read *The Banner,* our church's weekly magazine. We could write letters. We could go for walks. Sometimes we went on long walks with our father, who was a sensual man and would pluck a pinch of sagebrush, rub it between his fingers, hold it out to us and say, "Smell!" He showed us many wonders of nature and passed on to us a love for all things bright and beautiful.

We could take naps too, something my parents did more often than we did until we reached our teen years. I doubt if they knew of the Jewish commandment to enjoy conjugal bliss on the Sabbath, but I'm pretty sure they lived up to it quite often. One Sunday afternoon I opened their bedroom door without knocking, and they were upset enough for me to surmise later that that is what they were about to do, or were doing.

Our deep devotion to the Bible was evident in the fact that the Word was considered the most important sacrament, rising far above communion and baptism in the church's estimation. This dedication was evident in our daily reading and memorization and in long, drawn-out sermons. We, as well as the Jews, could have been called People of the Book. My own love for the Book was reflected in my delight in parsing scripture for its meaning and significance with my father, in my ability to name a verse for any argument. Some time would pass before I realized that scripture could be used to support almost any point that I or anyone else wanted to make.

I loved Bible stories, and the characters in them were as real to me as people I knew in the flesh. I was especially drawn to the people God called and spoke to, as I wished he would call to me. Moses at the burning bush, Jeremiah at the potter's wheel, Daniel with his gift for interpreting dreams all appealed to me. I took pride in the few women heroes—Esther who saved her people, Rahab who rescued the Israeli spies, Ruth who cast her lot with a foreign people and a foreign God.

Because of the similarities to Orthodox Judaism in our upbringing and my ensuing deep connections with this path, I wondered for years if I might be able to find a spiritual home within Judaism. After that first Seder I shared with Abe and Sylvia while I was attending Calvin College, I was invited to many more Passover celebrations, including others with the Krissoffs, some in Albuquerque, and a lesbian one in Santa Cruz, California.

But the most unusual one occurred when Cheyenne and I lived in Cuba, New Mexico, which, with its few surrounding settlements and countryside, numbered around 3,000 souls. That Seder was unusual in part because of its location, where practitioners of traditional Diné religion and the Native American Church flourished; where numerous Protestant fundamentalist churches and sects were represented; where the greatest percentage of people belonged to the Catholic Church; and where, until recently, the Roman Catholic sect of *Penitentes* had reenacted Jesus's crucifixion, including cross-bearing and self-flagellation at the little stone and clay *Oratorio de Jesus Nazareno.*

I was quite surprised when our postmistress casually mentioned one morning something about "our rabbi." I would learn later that she came from an old family of New Mexico crypto-Jews.

"Rabbi? You're joking, right?"

"No, we have a rabbi living here. He and his wife just had a baby."

Not long after that, I met Gershon and Lakme at a New Year's Eve dinner, and we became friends. In the spring, they invited Cheyenne, who was then eight, and me to Seder. This would be the first time I attended Seder where a rabbi was present—the second thing that made it unusual.

As we went through the *Haggadah,* Gershon sprinkled in his own teachings, evoking times around our family table when I had deconstructed the Bible with my father. At one point, Gershon said, "The Hebrew name for Egypt is *Mitzrayim.* Mitzrayim means *The Narrows* or *The Narrow Place.*

When the people of Israel left The Narrows, they entered the wide-open place, the wilderness. The wilderness belongs to no one; hence, it belongs to everyone. This signifies to us that spiritual teachings are for everyone. No one group can lay claim to any one teaching."

My inner eye opened wide as Gershon's words about wilderness struck me deep inside. The Church had been my narrows, and I had entered a wilderness when everything religious and spiritual poured out of me. When Gershon said that no group could lay claim to any one teaching, I sensed that there might be an opening for me in Judaism, particularly in the Jewish Renewal Movement to which Gershon and Lakme belonged.

By this time, I had read a lot of Jewish literature, identifying powerfully with much of it. I'd gone beyond fiction to read the works of rabbis like Abraham Joshua Heschel whose book *The Sabbath* put the purpose of the Sabbath into a new light. In some ways, he echoed words of Jesus I'd been fond of quoting to my parents: "The Sabbath is made for man, not man for the Sabbath." I read Leo Baeck, a hero to me because he had remained with his Berlin congregation in the Theresienstadt Camp during the Holocaust when the Nazis offered him safe transport to Britain. I was especially fascinated by his openness, even promotion of Gentile conversion to Judaism. I read Harold Kushner on suffering and living with disappointment, especially later in life. And I read Michael Lerner, the founder of *Tikkun* magazine, on healing the world through social justice. One of the most profoundly affecting books I read was Tirzah Firestone's memoir, *With Roots in Heaven,* about leaving Orthodox Judaism, exploring other spiritual paths, returning to her faith in a renewed form, and ultimately becoming a rabbi.

With no small amount of trepidation, I invited Lakme, who is herself a teacher of the sacred, to dinner. She is also a convert to Judaism, which is why I invited her rather than Gershon. Perhaps the fact that she is a woman also had something to do with it.

Near the end of the meal, I asked Lakme about her conversion. Knowing that some Jews do not welcome converts with enthusiasm, I was a bit nervous that I might give offense by asking. On the contrary, she was delighted to talk about it. Then, with my stomach quivering as it used to when I came out as a lesbian, I did another sort of coming out.

"I've been thinking of converting for a long time," I said.

"Really?" She said it with excitement, not skepticism.

"Yes. Gershon's and your teachings—well, they touched my hunger for studying the Bible deeply. It reminded me a lot of discussions I used to have with my dad—something satisfying that I've been missing."

"I come to Albuquerque every Tuesday," Lakme said. "We could get together on Tuesday evenings."

I was living in Albuquerque by then. "I would love that. I'd be happy to make dinner for us on Tuesdays." We struck an agreement for every other Tuesday, since Lakme had to make the hour and a half drive back to Cuba afterward.

"To convert," she said, "you need to complete five areas of study: Jewish theology, rituals, history, culture, and customs."

"Let's start with history," I said. Two weeks later, Lakme showed up with an armful of books and a box of Shabbat candles, a pre-conversion gift.

A few short weeks later, seeking deeper understanding, I asked, "Can we also do Torah study together?" Lakme was the ideal teacher, always pleased with my suggestions, and the idea of Torah study was no exception. So we began reading and discussing the *parasha,* the portion of Torah to be read each week at Shabbat services.

Despite my early feeling of belonging when I went to temple with the Krissoffs and the fact that I was seeking spiritual community, in the several months that I studied with Lakme, I only went to Shabbat services once. That time, I met Lakme at Nahalat Shalom, the Renewal synagogue in Albuquerque. It happened to be Succoth, the harvest feast, replete with ritual and ending with a potluck. The sense of community was overwhelming, more intimate than I was ready for. People were welcoming, but I was self-conscious, acutely aware of my otherness.

A few weeks later, the Torah portion was about the Jews' exodus from Egypt. As I read in preparation for our study, a remarkable, almost physical inner shift took place. Deep within me, I felt that I was reading this story as a Jew.

When we got together on Tuesday, I told Lakme about it. She said, "Yes, because you feel God is protecting you as a Jew."

"I don't know if that's it," I said. "I didn't analyze it. I don't think I can. It was more a core feeling, a deep knowing that that was me, standing in a hut, sandals on, eating the meal, ready to leave."

There is a story about the family name I was born with: Kruis. It's a Dutch name, though not a common one. It means *cross.* In fact, it's so uncommon that most people in the U.S. who have that surname are related to us. Sometime in the '70s, friends of mine met people in the Virgin Islands named Kruis. Those Kruises knew the history of their name. Their ancestors had been Sephardic Jews living in Spain. As the Inquisition heated up, they converted to Catholicism and took the Spanish name *Cruz,* meaning *cross.* When things got too horrific to continue in Spain, these Cruzes fled to Holland, where their name transformed once more—to *Kruis.*

I had told Lakme this story when I talked with her about converting. For years, I had held the story close to my heart, my possible Jewish ancestry being a sort of justification for making the leap I was now contemplating. However, the week after reading Torah as a Jew, I felt an urgent need for distance. I wanted time to reflect on what was going on. I told Lakme I needed some space, and we stopped meeting.

That space grew into months, and finally I told Lakme I couldn't convert. The fact that I had wanted the story behind my name to legitimize me made me realize that being Jewish, at least for me, was not only about faith or spiritual community but also about ethnicity.

Wanting to be Jewish reminded me of wanting to be Navajo when I was younger, about reciting the Apostles' Creed in the

Diné language under my breath when I played with Bobby and Rudy Yellowhair, about how much I had needed to belong. Over time, it had been necessary for me to accept that I would never and could never be Diné. I decided that being Jewish was the same. To be myself, I had to give it up.

"Trying to convert has been really important," I told Lakme. "It made me realize more than ever that I need to make peace with my spiritual roots."

"Maybe you have to go deeper to do that," she said.

"You mean deeper than Christianity? Into Judaism?" I asked.

"Yes."

"I considered that." I felt serious regret when I said it. "But it doesn't feel right. It doesn't seem to fit for me."

When Lakme and I had shared that first dinner, she told me about an old Jewish concept that the late Rabbi Zalman Schacter-Shalomi was reviving. The Hebrew words for it are *ger toshav.* "It means *good stranger,"* she told me. "Someone who is ger toshav is not a convert, but they don't stand in the way of Judaism or harm it. They support Judaism. Ger toshav describes many non-Jews who marry Jews, don't convert, but participate in Jewish culture and support their children to be raised as Jews."

She had presented the concept as a possible alternative to conversion, if I would decide not to go through with it. "Yeah, okay," I said at the time, dismissing the idea as a poor second. It wasn't what I wanted.

The day I told her I couldn't convert, I asked, "Is there a ritual to make you ger toshav?"

"No, it's something you commit yourself to. A decision you make."

It was easy then to decide that I am ger toshav. A good stranger.

~22~

Longing for Home

Nelson Willy became a convert to Christianity while my father was the missionary at Teec Nos Pos. Before he could be baptized and take communion, he had to learn the catechism, which he studied with my father. "He learned the catechism faster than anyone we knew," my mother reminisced after driving two hundred sixty miles to attend his funeral. Mr. Willy had lived as a faithful Christian for more than fifty years.

A few months after the conversation with my mother, I was chatting with Nelson Willy's nephew. Robert told me, "Near the end of his life, Nelson started singing the old songs again." He meant traditional Diné songs.

This indicated something important to me. I didn't think that embracing Navajo traditions needed to be incompatible with being a Christian. But in this case, Mr. Willy had gone against more than fifty years of Protestant indoctrination to resume singing the sacred songs of his childhood. I specify *Protestant* because Catholics, as a rule, have been much more open to the integration of traditional practices with Christian ones—one more thing my father held against them.

My mother would be disappointed, possibly even appalled, if I revealed what she would think of as Mr. Willy's backsliding.

To the CRC missionaries, it would have meant that he was unworthy to partake of communion, that the church would have to discipline him. To me, it signified not necessarily an abandonment of the new faith but a deep need, felt by so many, to return to our spiritual roots, in much the way that Tirzah Firestone had returned to Judaism. Evidence of the power of longing for home.

Over the years, I found myself picking up the writings of Christians I respected. These were thoughtful, intelligent, inclusive, socially conscious people. I kept asking myself: How does Anne Lamott do it? Why is John Shelby Spong still a Christian? What enabled Marcus Borg to return to the Church? If they can be Christians, what can I learn from them? Could they be pointing a way that might allow me to return to the Church? Most of my family would contend that some of these folks are not Christians because they are not *their* kind of Christians. But they are people who have struggled with the beliefs that lie at the heart of Christianity. In the process, they found a way to claim Christianity for themselves.

I wondered too about all the Diné I know who have remained Christian. I understood Navajos who had left Christianity, but what about the ones who have stayed? What holds them there? I've asked myself this, but I've been reluctant to ask my friends. I felt that if they were content, I didn't want to sow doubt.

I also repeatedly asked myself an obvious question as I looked at the lives of the people who claim Christianity: Why would I want to be connected in any way with a church that had so roundly rejected me? Why would I want to belong to an institution whose basis for existence I no longer believed in? I was pretty sure my desire was the same as what got Nelson Willy singing the old songs as he approached death—the longing for one's deepest and oldest connections. As Jeanette Winterson, another lesbian raised to be a preacher, writes in *Why Be Happy When You Could Be Normal?* "If you are raised on the Bible, you don't just walk away, whatever anybody says."

Most of the time, I felt hopeless about the idea of returning to the Church. Part of me wanted to return, wanted to recreate what had become the greatest loss in my life. Yet I couldn't remake what I had lost and at the same time be myself. Besides, on the few occasions when I attended a CRC, I saw that it no longer looked much like what I'd left behind. It had changed too—in some ways for the better and in others that I didn't care for, ways that had done away with the marks of home. What I missed most often—the songs—had changed. An old hymn might be sandwiched in now and then, but mostly, new ones were being sung, projected on the walls without musical notes, which I need if the song is new and I'm going to harmonize.

The message in the CRC hadn't changed much, though. Oh, the minister sort of apologized when the catechism lesson on a particular Sunday required him to preach on hell and judgment, but everything else was essentially as it had been when I left forty years earlier. The Sufi poet Rumi, as translated by Coleman Barks, wrote in the thirteenth century, "It is right to love your home place, but first ask, 'Where is that, really?' "

I didn't know.

⋆ ⋆ ⋆

The prayers and intentions that people make in places of worship and other sacred spaces leave in their wake a special energy, a holy presence. One afternoon, a three-year-old friend and I were walking in San Francisco's Mission District. As we neared St. Paul's Cathedral, Ben asked, "Can you take me in the church?"

I was a little surprised, but I said, "Sure."

We made our way up a broad flight of steps and opened the heavy doors. A bank of votive candles flickered at the front of the dim sanctuary. People knelt between some of the pews in silent supplication.

After a few minutes, we stepped back out into the sunlight. Ben looked up at me and said, "There's something in there."

"Yes," I said. "There were people in there lighting candles and praying."

"No." He said it firmly. "There's something in there." He had felt that presence, that energy.

I felt that same Presence when I visited Salisbury Cathedral in England several years later. In the late '90s, I made a pilgrimage, taking in Westminster Abbey, a hermitage in Bradford on Avon, the ruined cathedral and abbey of Glastonbury, and the Chalice Well there. I climbed the Tor with its tower of the ruins of St Michael's Church and visited the great stone circle at Avebury. I ended the Avebury day with a trip to Salisbury Cathedral.

Just before evensong I walked through an opening in a tall, dark green hedge. As I entered the close, a palpable rush of soft energy surrounded me. The hedge cut off the sounds of the streets and marketplace, and I faced a broad grassy sward. To my left stood the immense limestone-and-marble Gothic cathedral, built in the thirteenth century and boasting the tallest spire in all of England. A feeling of peace enveloped me.

When I walked into the vaulted cathedral, the sacredness of the space was tangible. I was glad I could enter it not as a tourist walking about examining this statue or that stained glass window but as a participant in a sung worship service. I stepped into one of the carved wooden boxes and took my seat on a pew facing a long row of pews on the other side of the sanctuary. The singing began and echoed through the chamber.

Spoken word entered the service only once, when we all rose to recite the Apostles' Creed. I hadn't spoken those words for almost thirty years, but I doubt if I can ever forget them. I did not believe the words in the same way I once did, but I wanted to be part of that sacred communion at that moment in time, so I said them. I heard my own voice, and in that ancient place, I was joining others down through centuries of belief. It gave me chills just to be part of this, yet all the while I mentally translated each phrase into something I could agree with.

When vespers was over, I did not stay to read historical plaques or take a self-guided tour with headphones. I walked to the station to take the train back to Bradford.

Translating the Apostles' Creed in the cathedral that summer is a reflection of a major obstacle I ran into every time I considered ending my exile from Christianity. It was all about the two opening words of the creed: *I believe.* That is what a creed is—a statement of belief (directly from the Latin *credo, I believe*). I kept thinking that in order to satisfy my longing for home, I had to believe as I had been taught.

I started to see that the religious ventures I had attempted, from the Metropolitan Community Church on through Judaism, didn't work because I kept hoping I could recreate what I had lost. Yet I didn't want to *really* recreate it because I would end up with a replica of what had rejected me. Longing for intimacy, acceptance, and especially spiritual validation from family had played a significant role in my early attempts. I had been cast out of the Garden of Eden (not that the Church and all that went with it was Paradise—the flaws were abundantly clear to me, starting with a strong tradition for rejecting outcasts). But it had been my first spiritual home. At the gates of the garden stood the twelve-foot angels with one hand beckoning, teasing me back in, and the other holding a flaming sword to keep me out.

These guarding angels were my family. According to their God-given task, I couldn't be both in and out, which I suppose was what I actually wanted. I wanted to be able to be myself while enjoying the comforts of home. But those sword-toting angels couldn't be *themselves* if they allowed me to be myself. A dilemma, to say the least. Now I see that they, as representatives of the Church, did not keep me out by themselves. By failing to believe, I held myself back. The necessity for believing in order to belong was that deeply ingrained.

Not all traditions place so much emphasis on belief. Among Buddhists in America, a large number are Jewish. This doesn't surprise me for a couple of reasons. Like many Christians, many Jews, perhaps especially of my generation, have become disaffected with their own religion. Perhaps they had minimal to no religious upbringing to begin with. But more significant to me, both Judaism and Buddhism are religions that focus on practice more than belief. Following the commandments, including love of God and neighbor, service to others, and performance of rituals resulting in a conscious connection with God, is central to Judaism. With Zen, the form of Buddhism I'm most familiar with, it's sitting—meditation practice—as well as service—what we knew as karma yoga at the Scandinavian Yoga and Meditation School.

Christianity, and especially Protestant Christianity, is much more focused on belief. In the King James Version of the Old Testament, the Jewish Bible, the word *believe* and its variants are used a total of forty-five times. In the New Testament, which is less than a third the size of the Old Testament, some variety of *believe* is used 272 times. Over and over as a child, I heard the verses, "Believe on the Lord Jesus Christ, and thou shalt be saved" and "Whosover believeth on him shall not perish but have everlasting life." *Everything* depended on what we believed. Thus, there had been that division of the world into believers and unbelievers.

A story is told in the gospel of Mark of a father who begs Jesus to heal his son. Jesus tells him that if he believes, all things are possible. The man replies, "Lord, I believe. Help thou my unbelief." I get goose bumps when I read those words because of my inability to believe. I have uttered them often as a prayer. My prayer was answered through a different understanding of *faith, belief,* and *trust*.

Webster's offers two definitions of faith: belief and trust in God; and belief in the traditional doctrines of a religion. In the CRC, the second definition was the gold standard of faith. Everything came down to believing in the right doctrines. That feeling of free fall into God's safety net when I practiced the Third Step of my Twelve Step program transformed my understanding of faith, aligning it with the first definition: belief and trust in God. Faith was no longer an intellectual belief in certain doctrines or ideas *about* God. Faith had instead become utter abandonment to the goodness of God. This fits with the root of the word *faith,* the Latin *fidere,* which means *trust.*

I was again graced with a different understanding of *belief* when I attended a workshop on Celtic spirituality. The presenter, a stocky, ruddy Irishman, told us that the root of *believe* lies in the Old English *lēof* meaning *to hold dear or to love.* Thus, in a pure sense, to believe is less about intellectually holding to certain ideas about God and more about *loving* God.

I kept coming back to the story about Nelson Willy singing the old Diné songs on his deathbed—a story rich with meaning for me. It was about a return to Mr. Willy's spiritual home. It was about taking up a practice that held deep significance for him, even if that practice might conflict with Protestant *beliefs*—that is, Protestant ideas *about* God. Perhaps it was more about *loving* God, loving *Diyin,* the *Holy One*—about *trusting* God's inclusiveness, so different from the CRC's exclusiveness. In the end, it was about Mr. Willy being his core self.

~23~

Preparing the Lab

FOR YEARS, I HAD WAITED FOR RETIREMENT SO I COULD WRITE full-time. It was why I retired as early as I could, in 2010. But I'd no sooner retired than all the writing fuel in me seemed to have burned out. I had been writing for a long time, and the absence of kindling happens pretty often, as almost anyone who dedicates themselves to creative endeavors can attest. But I couldn't help asking myself, "Why now, when, for the first time in my life, I have that most precious creative commodity—time?"

It's often happened that the right book at the right time has crossed my path. Sometimes what I needed in a given moment has literally dropped off a shelf into my hands. That's how *The Best Year of Your Life: Dream It, Plan It, Live It* by Debbie Ford came to me when I was searching a bookstore for something completely unrelated. I found the title uninspiring, but I was willing to look inside, only because Ford had previously written a book with the much more captivating title, *The Dark Side of the Light Chasers.*

I took the book home, and because my life was definitely not at its best at that moment, when by all rights it should have been, and because I like structure that promises results, I began reading and doing the exercises. Debbie said that doing only one thing, the first exercise, would create powerful change in my life. That one thing was to meditate on the statement, "This is the best year of my life," for three minutes morning and evening. I was pretty discouraged, depressed really, which is something I hate admitting to myself. I thought, "This I can do. What have I got to lose?" So that's how I started.

The fourth chapter of the book, "A Clean Slate," started the preparation for what may have become the most significant experiment I've ever undertaken. It became a first step in preparing the lab for my experiment. The charge in this chapter was to list unfinished business and then do what was necessary to bring each item to closure—undone projects, tasks, relationships. I made my list of incompletions. Some things were simple but onerous—for example, turning the former bedroom that had become a large storage bin into an office.

High on the list, but not so simple, was an obstacle for which I had been blaming my family. For almost forty years, I had feared their narrow-mindedness and judgment, their further rejection where I felt most vulnerable—my spirituality. In the "completion" process, I decided that instead of continuing to hide my beliefs or lack of them, I would share my spirituality with them.

A short way into writing what I was calling my *Statement of Faith* (Appendix A), one of my nephews, a senior at his Christian high school, asked me to be part of an assignment. He had to ask questions of someone whose beliefs differed from his. I chuckled at how the Universe works and mildly chastised him for his assumption that our beliefs were different, since we'd never discussed my beliefs or his. Some of his questions helped me examine things I might not have thought of, speaking of my own assumptions.

When my statement was finished, I emailed my brothers, sisters-in-law, nephews and nieces over eighteen (not wanting to be taken to task for unduly influencing any minors), and a couple of my closest cousins. I gave them some guidelines on how to enter constructive interfaith dialogue, which I had adapted from Joel Beversluis's book, *Sourcebook of the World's Religions:*

An Interfaith Guide to Religion and Spirituality. The basic premise of the guidelines was that we would be sharing our faith for the purpose of knowing each other better, for enjoying deeper intimacy, not to convince each other of anything nor to label each other right or wrong. I said I would send my statement of faith to anyone who agreed to my guidelines. Most of the family, interestingly, chose to call the guidelines *rules*. Anna's Rules, to be precise. Sort of like *Robert's Rules,* I guess, and in a way, they were.

My family loves to argue, especially about passionately held beliefs. Several members have very strong convictions and, like my father, believe they are obligated to convince others to join them. Interestingly, the ones with the strongest views chose not to agree to the guidelines or read my statement. Almost everyone in the younger generation, though, wanted to know what I believed, despite the fact that most had accepted their parents' beliefs. No one offered much discussion, and all clearly tried to respect the guidelines. After the fact, my mother, who'd heard about what I'd written, asked for a copy, which I duly sent.

Most important to me was how freeing this process was. I had engaged in another, deeper, level of coming out, of being myself, so the people I cared most about could engage with me if they chose to.

★ ★ ★

My nephew Ryan is a tall, handsome fellow with curly blond hair, a strong jaw, and laughing blue eyes. He's smart and articulate and committed to social justice in an unjust world. In 2006, he began coming out to family and friends, and in 2007, became more public about his gay sexuality. His dad, Bob, was one of the most conservative of my brothers. Even before Ryan came out, though, Bob had shown a touching willingness to learn from his children, a humility that allowed him, in the aftermath of Ryan's news, to stretch himself for his son, as did his wife, Ard.

For a long time, Ryan and I didn't talk about our shared sexuality and church background, other than to minimally acknowledge that it existed. I felt that, like many LGBTQ people of his generation, he had little understanding, empathy, or interest in what someone of my generation—namely me—had gone through. I was mostly okay with that, glad that Ryan's experience was already so different from mine. I didn't want to burden him with my sad tale—to what purpose? I had no idea that the most significant healing of my life was going to happen through him.

Although Ryan didn't feel a need to share with me—he had his own friends for that—Bob and Ard had a lot they wanted to talk about, things they'd never wanted to talk about before. Ard said before anyone else, and more than once with genuine remorse, "We could've been so much more supportive of you. I'm so sorry." That heartfelt acknowledgement, while she was still struggling with her feelings and beliefs about her son's sexuality, was like the first layer of healing ointment applied to the family-church wound.

Ryan was still a student at Calvin College when he came out. He was highly thought of by professors and administrators. After he came out, he and my brother served on a panel at the college, addressing homosexuality and the Church. And things had changed enough that, even in the face of the Church's continued official stance on homosexuality, Ryan was asked to give the senior honors convocation address at Calvin.

I rejoiced for him that times had changed so markedly. At the same time, I couldn't help remembering the two boys who'd been discovered in bed together during my freshman year at Calvin. Fear had flooded me then, and I'd felt an overwhelming need to hide both my fear and my sexuality at all costs, lest I be associated with them.

Despite the acceptance and support Ryan got at home and at school—there are now a gender studies major, minor, and program at Calvin—the response he received from my mother and brothers (my father having passed away) was filled with condemnation and seemingly deliberate misinterpretation. The fact that Ryan, unlike me, remained in the Church, a professing Christian, didn't count at all with them; as far as they were concerned, *gay Christian* was an oxymoron.

Ryan wrote to all of us, a lovely letter, when he and his partner decided to marry in 2011. Because Devin was a grad student at Boston University, they would legally marry in Massachusetts. Having joined the Episcopal Church, they would have a commitment ceremony at the church in Grand Rapids with family and friends, and then marry later in Boston. Putting their money where their mouths were, Bob and Ard gave Ryan and Devin the same amount of money toward their wedding expenses that they planned to give their other children.

There was never any question but that Cheyenne and I would fly to Michigan for the occasion. One other brother, Rick, and his adult children and their spouses came. So did two sons of one of my other brothers. No one from Devin's CRC Iowa farm family was present.

A couple of days before the wedding, we all sat around the table in Bob and Ard's dining room, making decorations for the reception. The afternoon before the wedding, we survived a brownout while making salads for the rehearsal dinner picnic and had fun through the stress of it. All morning the day of the wedding, I had a blast snapping photos of the guys tying each other's ties, of Bob ironing one of their shirts, and posting the pictures on a social media site. I reveled in the joy of my nephew and my nephew-to-be. I was ebullient; although it wasn't my wedding, I had been looking forward with pleasure to a great symbolic moment.

* * *

St. Mark's Episcopal Church is the oldest public structure in Grand Rapids. Built in the Gothic Revival style of stones from the Grand River, it is a charming setting for a wedding, although, according to the Episcopal policy I would learn about later, this could not be called a wedding. It was still second-class.

Cheyenne and I sat in the front pew on the right of the sanctuary, a place of honor. The young people who acted as witnesses, besides three of Ryan's siblings, were friends from Calvin. He had adapted the liturgy from the ecumenical Christian community on the island of Iona, off the west coast of Scotland. It was beautiful, as was the sermon by the priest, whom I'd mentally castigated earlier because I thought he was the one responsible for the non-wedding wedding.

I was shaken and taken completely by surprise to feel tears rolling down my cheeks during most of the service. Not a few drops but copious flooding. Cheyenne put her arm across my shoulders. Even more surprising was how I sobbed in both Bob's and Ard's arms after the ceremony, when I only wanted to congratulate them. Surprised as I was, it wasn't a mystery. It wasn't as if I'd said to myself, "If only I'd had this." I didn't need to. The entire gestalt tapped into something far deeper than any words or analysis.

Afterward, I stood outside with everyone else, waving streamers as the guys ran our gauntlet and climbed onto their bicycle built for two with its "Just Married" sign and pedaled off, jaunty in their shirtsleeves and suspenders. Rick, two friends (one of them the Calvin College provost), and I went to a downtown pub for drinks in the hiatus between the wedding and the reception.

The reception was held upstairs in the St. Cecilia Music Hall, and sunlight flooded the room that was decorated in pale yellow, blues and grays. After the meal, the wedding party began toasting the couple. Rick's oldest son Noah and his wife Megan were master and mistress of ceremonies. Ryan and Devin's friends got up and told stories; glasses were raised. I was struck by how gay-savvy these Calvin students were, thanks in part to changes in the national media and also to their gender studies classes. I cried on and off and laughed too. Rick came over and hugged me, and we shed tears together. Bob and Ard stood with interlocked arms and toasted the couple. They were honest about the struggles they'd had when Ryan came out, and also spoke of their love for him and their joy that their son had found happiness. They cried and laughed. We all did.

Then Rick went up to the front, and I had a premonition of what he was about to do. I didn't want him to. I wanted this day to be about Ryan and Devin. He took care of that in his first words. He said, "I want to toast Ryan's Aunt Anna. I asked Megan if I could do that, and she said that I could if I connected it to Ryan and Devin. I want to toast her," he said through tears, "because she never had this. This recognition is coming much too late. Ryan and Devin wouldn't be having this celebration of their love today if it weren't for Anna and the groundwork she laid in our family." He raised his glass.

What happened next was like a great gust of wind. The entire crowd of a hundred sixty people gave me a standing ovation while I sat and breathed and allowed the love and support and recognition to flow over me. When the room quieted, my tears were gone. A great, gaping wound had closed. I spent the rest of the evening dancing, laughing, and being part of family pictures.

⋆ ⋆ ⋆

These two events—the earlier sharing of my statement of faith and the whole of Ryan and Devin's wedding and reception—had to occur before I could engage in the experiment that was to come. Only as I wrote this did I realize that a third essential event had happened three years earlier: my father's death.

My father had been the molder and shaper of my faith in so many ways. He had had such high hopes that I would follow in his footsteps and become a missionary at the level our church would allow for a woman. It is not too strong to say that he was devastated when he found out that I was a lesbian. All those times he tried to corner me when no one else was around, all the snide comments he made about me at family gatherings were signs of deep-seated anger, but I didn't recognize it until one of my brothers told me, "He's so angry about you."

I sensed his pain more than his anger, and I understood it. I was a huge disappointment. It was also painful for me to *be* a disappointment, and I was always on edge, knowing he might verbally attack me at any time. The rift between us widened without any sign of closing.

The last five years of his life, Dad suffered from increasing dementia and withdrew more and more into an inner world. I tried on one visit to talk with him about what had happened between us, but he changed the subject immediately. I had waited too long and had to accept that our timing did not match. I had finally confronted the subject when I was able to, and he was not able to hear me. His confrontational mode was a thing of the past.

The last time I saw my father alive, I had gone with family members for the hymn sing they held with him every Sunday at his nursing home. I was reveling in an old favorite when Dad looked directly at me. I can only describe the expression on his face as one of terror. I didn't know the cause of his fear, didn't know if he even recognized me, but I was intensely uncomfortable, and obviously he was too. I decided then that future visits would not benefit either of us.

On the morning of April 14, 2008, exactly a month before Dad's ninety-first birthday, Mom called. She said, "Your daddy has gone to glory." I immediately felt that I needed to see him, to spend time with him by myself. So I drove the 136 miles to Gallup and went directly to the funeral home. The body hadn't been embalmed and made up, so the funeral director told me I couldn't see him. I said I'd prefer to see him the way he was, and she assured me that I wouldn't.

I went out and sat on a bench in front of the mortuary and wept, as much for my defeat at the hands of the undertakers as for my loss. I didn't expect that anyone would take note, but I wasn't ready yet to drive over to Mom's house.

The director came out after a few minutes and said they'd changed their minds. If I gave them a few minutes, I could spend some time with my father's body. When they brought me to the small room, the embalmer tried once more to talk me out of seeing him. "He'll look so much better tomorrow. I promise you."

"It's all right," I said. "I need this. Thank you for changing your mind."

When I saw my dad, I understood their reservations, but from my hospital and hospice work earlier in life, I knew how people look soon after death. I just needed to have time alone with him after our time apart. I sat with him for fifteen or twenty minutes. I harked back to mealtimes from my childhood, how we decided together what Jesus might have meant when he said, "Don't put new wine into old wineskins." I remembered walks in nature with him on Sunday afternoons. I thanked him for teaching me to read Navajo at the same time I was learning to read English. I recollected the things he taught me about Navajo life, some of which were true and some of which were what a white man had learned from other white men. I chuckled over his corny sense of humor. I saw him walking from the car toward a store or a revival tent—anywhere—and pulling a small black comb from his back pocket to make sure his ever-thinning hair was still swept neatly back into less and less of a pompadour. I put my hand on one of his bony, liver-spotted ones and said, "Daddy. Oh, Daddy. I love you. Thank you for teaching me that there is a life of the spirit." Underneath his anger and disappointment in me, there had been love. I thanked him for loving me, and left the room, closing the door.

Two days later, we had family time in one of the funeral home chapels, and sure enough, Dad was all fixed up and wearing a suit instead of a body bag. Being with family was good. That night, we sat around Mom's living room telling stories about our dad. We laughed a lot together and had a few sobering moments. The next day, we held the funeral at the Rehoboth Church. Probably a third of the guests were Navajo people my dad had pastored. There was lots of hugging and joyful reunion. John Tsosie, the man who had comforted me at my sister Trudy's funeral, was there with his wife, Lila. People had driven from Teec Nos Pos, Tohlakai, and Toadlena to honor my father. They stood on the platform and sang his favorite hymn, "Victory in Jesus," in the Diné language.

It is evidence of my family's conflicted feelings about me—in some ways admiring me despite their condemnation—that they asked me to deliver the eulogy. We had known my father's death was approaching, and planned much of his funeral in advance. I wrote the words well before his death, crafting them with care so I could be true to the gospel-loving man my father was and also true to my own beliefs or lack of them.

At the cemetery, we gathered below the red rock outcropping where we used to sit for Easter sunrise services when I was in high school. A hole had been dug in the part of the cemetery known as *Missionary Row.* There, missionaries as far back as the legendary (to us) L.P. Brink, who died in 1936, are buried. One of my three minister brothers led the graveside service and had us recite in unison Psalm 1, which we'd memorized together at lunchtime all those years ago. We siblings lowered the homemade wooden casket into the hole on ropes.

Shovels were planted in the mound of dirt beside the grave, and everyone was invited to help bury my father. A Navajo woman who had driven her mother, one of Dad's early converts, down from Teec Nos Pos, was the first to grab a spade. She vigorously tossed dirt onto the coffin. She is a professional woman whom Rick and I know fairly well, and we both speculated later about her eagerness. I wondered if she were getting some kind of closure with my dad or with missionaries in general. Perhaps she felt something similar to what I experienced—a newfound freedom, a release that would allow me to take another step in my spiritual journey.

Part III
The Experiment

And I hope by thy good pleasure safely to arrive at home
—Robert Robinson, "Come Thou Fount of Every Blessing"

~24~
The Hypothesis

I MADE SO MANY FORAYS INTO VARIOUS SPIRITUAL TRADITIONS AND churches that I can't count them—starting with the Episcopal Church of the Holy Spirit in Gallup, then trying out the Metropolitan Community Church in Albuquerque. There was the yoga and meditation school in Scandinavia, Unity in Santa Cruz and Albuquerque, the Quakers in Salinas, California, the Unitarians in Albuquerque and Kalamazoo, a Jewish Renewal synagogue, the United Church of Christ. There was the Buddhist sangha, Lutherans in Copenhagen and Albuquerque. I walked into Queen of Heaven Catholic Church and right back out, and stayed only a few minutes longer than that at St. Michael and All Angels Episcopal Church; I had my brush with the Presbyterians in Cuba, New Mexico. Every now and then, for some family function or a friend's funeral, I entered a CRC and left with a sigh of relief when the event was over.

It made no sense whatsoever, the way I kept trying to find a Christian community that I could belong to for more than eight weeks. The fact was that the Church had long ago discarded me.

I once watched a street theater piece in San Francisco's Washington Square in which the players were clad as bag ladies and interacted with everyone in the park, including some women who actually were homeless. Again and again, the actors shouted, "We're the disposable people." Their words sliced into my heart. The Church had not excommunicated me, but its position was that I was not worthy of its sacred communion—the words of the hymn "Just as I Am" notwithstanding.

A friend who knew about my attempts (and not many did) told me more than once that I had to be a very gracious person to ever voluntarily enter a church again. My efforts probably didn't make much sense to anyone who witnessed them. It was not about graciousness but about need.

My kind and I weren't the only ones to whom the Church had done despicable deeds. I didn't have to look any further than the Diné friends with whom I'd gone to mission boarding school. They had been robbed of family, community, culture, and sometimes language. As if that were not enough, they had been emotionally, spiritually, and in some cases physically, abused.

I am not aware of any sexual abuse at Rehoboth. But a plethora of other examples stretch back through history: apartheid in South Africa, engineered by the Dutch Reformed Afrikaners, people religiously and ethnically related to my church; missionaries who had worked hand-in-glove with colonial governments to "pacify" indigenous peoples; John Calvin who burned Michael Servetus at the stake because he disagreed with him; witch hunts throughout history; the Inquisition, pogroms against the Jews, and church collaboration with the Nazis; the Crusades. So many grievous wrongs committed in the name of Christianity weighed heavily on my heart. The idea that I might ever tell anyone I was a Christian gave me great discomfort.

And then there was the issue of belief—or rather, my lack of belief. My Twelve Step program had given God back to me, and meditation had given me a way to connect with God more directly and deeply than ever before. But belief, the path to God that is the hallmark of evangelical Christianity? To be considered a believer in the CRC and other evangelical churches, there is a most basic, specific requirement—one must believe that Jesus died to save us from our sins and that this is the only way to God. I did not believe that I was evil from birth, and that Jesus had to die to save me from the fires of hell to which I would surely otherwise be consigned because of my evil nature and deeds. Again and again, my failure to embrace that specific belief seemed to me to form an obstacle to becoming part of any Christian community, even ones that were not evangelical. That is how deeply the teaching was engraved in my mind. It was why I'd walked out of the service at St. Michael and All Angels, which, as an Episcopal church, stood on the liberal end of the Christian spectrum. But the liturgy had contained too many references to the need for the blood of Jesus to wash away my sins.

And yet, I had persisted in one way or another for nearly forty years. My parents, the Church, and the mission school had all impressed upon me that the Church is where we receive spiritual nurture. Once Mom had asked, bewilderment in her voice, "Don't you miss church? I would miss it terribly if I didn't go."

I couldn't even begin to describe both how I missed it and how not going was such a relief, such freedom. I had learned in my exploration of other traditions that I could be spiritually nurtured in places and practices outside the Church. But the intense training I'd received did run deep.

Every religion has its mysteries. Intellectually, I continued, even through the driest of times, to be fascinated by the mysteries of many religions, and especially Christianity. Most religions seem to be an attempt to understand the mystery of what we call *God*. I had made peace a long time ago with that mystery as something ineffable, something I could grasp only in minuscule increments. To me, that mystery was part of God's essence. One of my favorite biblical stories is the one about Job. I like it because he struggles so with his God, questioning, wrestling, arguing. He comes away with such a sense of awe, such a sense of his own finiteness, expressed far better than I can say it, but how I feel it: "Lo, these are but the outskirts of his ways; and how small a whisper do we hear of him! But the thunder of his power who can understand?"

The mystery of Jesus, as opposed to God, still baffled me. It seemed that human minds had formed so much of the Jesus mystery. Over the years, I was intrigued whenever I came across new, often whimsical and humanizing, thumbnails of Jesus in popular culture. Leonard Cohen referred to him as a sailor when he walked on water; Dory Previn asked if he wasn't an androgyne; Simon and Garfunkel sang to Mrs. Robinson that Jesus loved her more than she could know; and Norman Greenbaum spoke on behalf of someone who wanted Jesus to recommend him to the Spirit in the Sky when he died. Clearly, others—four of the aforementioned being Jewish (although Greenbaum says referring to Jesus was just a marketing ploy)—were intrigued by Jesus too. I didn't believe Jesus died for me, but I loved getting new perspectives on the mystery of him. Maybe, just maybe, church could offer me some new understandings because the mystery of Jesus was something I kept being drawn to.

Only recently did I think about the matter of promises. I had made promises to God and to the Church when I was young, made them in all sincerity. But when all things spiritual, except for my connections with nature and people, ran out of me, I didn't feel that I had reneged on any of those promises. In my youth, I had often sung the words of a gospel hymn, "O Jesus, I have promised/to serve thee to the end." One day, this song came back to me with the insistence that songs sometimes do. As I hummed it throughout the day, I paused and wondered, "Is there something in the nature of making such a promise, any promise, that holds us accountable to the pledge?"

One of the books I'd read in my earlier attempts to reconcile with Christianity was *Living Buddha, Living Christ* by Vietnamese Buddhist monk Thich Nhat Hanh. He writes that if we do not make peace with our spiritual roots, we will always be at war with ourselves. I realized that my efforts at finding church had a lot to do with trying to make peace with my roots and thus peace with myself. I needed to be able to love my spiritual and religious roots as a way of loving a core part of myself. That didn't mean I had to be part of a church, but exploring church was a possible way to make peace with that part of me.

I took Thich's words to heart. I wanted to embrace my roots in some way. It wasn't because I believed that Christianity is the only path to God—or even that, as my brother Rick, who can acknowledge the existence of other paths, says, "It's the best, the most complete." It was because it was mine. Christianity was *my* tradition in a way that Judaism, Buddhism, and Native American traditions were not.

It turns out that, despite all obstacles, looking for home was the bedrock reason for the experiment I was about to undertake. If I could find it, I wanted the sense of belonging I'd once had with Grandma Havens in the chapel at Tohlakai; with those other missionary families who stopped and waited at an accident site in a snowstorm on Route 666; with the Bible Institute alumni who sang "Blest Be the Tie" beneath the red rocks; and with the two missionaries who took me out to dinner when I was hanging by a thread far thinner than they knew. I wanted to belong where belonging felt something like it once had. I wanted to find a way to create that without losing my soul. I wanted to belong to something bigger than myself.

* * *

When Holocaust survivor Viktor Frankl, author of *Man's Search for Meaning,* was liberated from one of Dachau's subcamps, he had the opportunity to emigrate to Australia. His sister and her husband, his only surviving family, had escaped there just before the war and wanted him to join them. Instead, he chose to return to Vienna and reestablish roots in the city that had been home from his birth until his deportation to Theresienstadt at the age of thirty-seven. Over the years, people often questioned his choice. "Didn't they do enough to you in this city?" they asked. "To you and to your family?" Frankl responded that he couldn't lump all the people of Vienna into the single category of those who had done him and his family evil. I think Frankl had another reason, a simpler, deeper one: Vienna was home.

In later years, when he had a visitor from the United States, Frankl took him into the city center. Pulling his friend into a coffee shop famous for its Viennese coffee, he ordered, "Smell!" Then he drew him into a bakery and said with delight, "Smell, freshly baked Viennese rolls." Vienna was not only home; it was the home that Frankl loved.

As a child and adolescent, even as a young adult, I had loved the church that was my home, the place that had offered me my first tastes of communion. But I was beginning to think that Thomas Wolfe was right: "You can't go home again." For one thing, home will never be the same as it was when you left, even if the house has only been painted a different color. The home I left, the church I left, is a memory, not a place.

For long periods of time, I would give up on the possibility of finding a spiritual home. Then I'd want to try again. I would read about someone else's amazing church experience. I would wish that their experience could fit me. Anne Lamott's St. Andrew Presbyterian sounded unlike any Presbyterian church I'd ever had contact with—a church that embraced her with all her irreverence. I mean, she can write, "I was fucked unto the Lord," and still be welcomed as a fellow Christian and even a Sunday school teacher in that church. But Annie's church is in Marin City, California. Even if I moved to the Bay Area, I wouldn't be living in Marin City. Nor would I want to cross the San Rafael Bridge every Sunday, driving past the oil tanks in Richmond and then San Quentin Prison, to get to church. But I was definitely jealous of Anne. Why couldn't I find what she had, in the place where I lived?

So I would set out again, less and less hopeful but compelled. One friend told me that I would always be a seeker, and I bristled. I didn't want to always be seeking. Or did I? My wandering life was not limited to floundering about in spiritual exile. By the time I was fifty-seven, I had moved sixty-four times, living in three countries on as many continents and in seventeen U.S. cities or communities. Research shows that people who spend a significant number of their developmental years in a culture other than their parents' exhibit a high level of restlessness as adults. I once had an office partner who observed, "You're always looking around the corner to see what's next." I asked myself if my spiritual seeking was just one more form of that general dissatisfaction, of trying, like the dog who turns and turns and turns, to find the exact spot and angle in which to settle.

I'd give up and lie down, then read something or have some conversation that shoved me back up again. I'd look around and start moving, sniffing in different corners, hopeful for a while. Then I'd give up again. Many times, I imagined starting my own spiritual community. "I'll call it the Church of the Storyteller," I thought. "We'll meet in my living room, start off with a potluck supper on Friday evenings. We'll follow the East African tradition known as 'Ladder to the Moon.'" In this practice, the gathering begins by sharing stories of the people's immediate lives, everyday occurrences from the week just passed. Then they are reminded of stories from their own past, and soon from the pasts of their ancestors—whether by blood or experience. From there, the stories become the stuff of legends whose truth lies in metaphor. At last, they tell their collective myths, the myths of humanity—creation, redemption, beginnings, and endings. What a wonderful church that would be!

I never put together what it would take to start such a church. Most of my friends who were interested in spirituality were already committed to paths they were satisfied with. Besides, I had founded, cofounded or been present at the inception of several communal endeavors: the Native American publishing house where I'd worked, the Lesbian and Gay Coop, three alternative schools, and more. I wanted something that was ready-made.

Despite my previous failed efforts, in January of 2012, I decided to try once more, although not with great optimism. This time, I framed my endeavor differently; I decided that if I were to have any chance of success, I needed to engage in a deliberate experiment. In science classes, we are taught that an experiment is based on a hypothesis, and the function of a hypothesis is to answer a heuristic question.

Three questions arose from the obstacles that always cropped up when I tried to become part of a spiritual community, specifically, a Christian one. There was no longer a place for me in the church of my youth when I decided to live my life as the person I was—a lesbian. So the first question was, "Can I be myself and be comfortable in a Christian community?" Second, "Can I find a Christian community that acknowledges the wrongs the Church has committed and tries to address them, in part through commitment to social justice and ecumenism?" Third, "Is it possible to be part of a Christian community as a follower of Jesus's teachings and way of life without believing that he had to die to save me from sin?" In the early days of the Church, people apparently didn't call themselves Christians. Instead, they said they were Followers of The Way, meaning The Way of Jesus. I could more comfortably call myself a Follower of the Way than a Christian.

My hypothesis, then, was this: "I can comfortably be part of a Christian community while being myself, including being a lesbian; being engaged in social justice; and being a follower of Jesus more than a believer." The rules of scientific experimentation also taught us to state the proposed answer to the heuristic question in the form of a null hypothesis. In this case, it would be, "It is impossible for me to be part of a Christian community while being myself, a lesbian; being engaged in social justice; and being a follower of Jesus more than a believer." Up to that point, I seemed to have proven the null hypothesis rather handily. Now I intended to deliberately engage in activities that I hoped could disprove it. That was my acknowledged bias.

Scientists keep a record of their research in a log, so I created one. I titled it, less than imaginatively, "Church Journal." On the front cover, I pasted a picture of what would become the third church I visited in my experiment. On the back cover, I pasted a portrait of Jesus that I especially liked. He appeared as I imagined a real first-century Mediterranean would look—with dark olive skin, dark hair, and beard. His brown eyes were kind and frank.

Well into my experiment, when I read back over my entries, I found that I asked myself over and over, "Why am I doing this? Why?" The simplest answer is not that I am especially gracious, as my friend suggested, but that I was compelled, although not for reasons most evangelical Christians would imagine or hope for.

⋆ ⋆ ⋆

In the early '90s, I served as the parent and youth program director of a Cambodian refugee agency in Oakland, California. One of my projects involved starting a community-based middle and high school in partnership with the Oakland Public Schools. Most students in our little school were involved with gangs, which has been a pattern for the youth of nearly every urban immigrant group in U.S. history. There are interesting reasons for this, but I won't go into them here. One boy, who was especially caught up in the gang life and often romanticized the battles between the infamous Bloods and Crips, said aloud to the whole school one morning, "We're Ms. Redsand's Bloods!"

My skin broke out in goose bumps. While I didn't want to encourage his identification with gangs, I knew he was paying a high compliment to me and to our school. This boy, who longed for the water buffalo he rode through the rice paddies when he was small, who drew idealized pictures of Angkor Wat, who now moved out into the night to steal car radios, this boy was shifting his loyalty in a way that was meaningful to him. He was *claiming* us as where he was *from*.

Gang-affiliated kids assess the lay of the land in a new situation with kids they don't know by asking, "Where you from?" They don't mean, "Where were you born?" or "What part of the city do you live in?" They mean, "What gang membership do you claim?" They are trying to find out if the situation is going to be safe for them. In my continued efforts to be part of a Christian faith community, I was trying to claim the place I was from, to be part of the gang again—Jesus's gang.

~25~

Same, Same, but Different

SOMETIME AFTER I WROTE AND SHARED MY STATEMENT OF faith with my family, after some of my deepest wounds were healed at my nephew Ryan's wedding, and after my father's death, I read Eboo Patel's *Acts of Faith: The Story of an American Muslim, in the Struggle for the Soul of a Generation.* I found myself talking about the book with very diverse people for many months after I'd read it. Patel begins by writing about how people with a commitment to pluralism have failed to reach out to the youth of our time. By contrast, Muslim, Jewish, and Christian extremists have avidly recruited young people to their numbers, all too often with horrifically violent results.

The author goes on to tell his own deeply moving and conflicted story of growing up Muslim in America. He tells how he rebelled, sought identity, explored other faiths, and eventually returned to the faith of his youth with a commitment to engaging young adults in interfaith interaction. Critical to his own progression had been his ongoing involvement in community service through the YMCA. Community service projects among youths from various religious and cultural backgrounds became the backbone of the organization he cofounded, Interfaith Youth Core (IFYC). In IFYC, young people are encouraged to remain true to their own faith while engaging in service projects and discussions on their shared and different traditions, and while working in harmony and increased understanding with one another.

Acts of Faith inspired me on many levels. Patel's own story was akin to Tirzah Firestone's, one that made me think that returning to the faith of my youth might be possible. It also helped me think more clearly about what I might want from a religious community and what I might hope to contribute.

Patel's book introduced me to the concept of Ubuntu. I wanted a church that would embrace that eastern African concept—that to be fully human, our souls need community. I had tired of what had become a lone spiritual journey. For many years, I had identified with a visual image of a solitary Navajo woman healer, sitting before a sandpainting and surrounded by discs bearing Native symbols. I saw my work as an educator of high-risk kids, a counselor, and a writer as the work of a healer. In some ways, the solitariness fit me; in other ways, I longed for change, for balance—for communion.

I believed that the work of the Church ought also to be a work of healing, as in the Jewish *tikkun olam*—healing the world. I wanted to journey with people who were working together to do just that. I believe that healing the world lies at the heart of Jesus's message and ministry. After all, he said that feeding the poor and visiting the sick and prisoners were akin to doing these things to him and for him. In the CRC, focusing on Jesus's command to feed the hungry and clothe the destitute had been referred to as the *social gospel* and reviled as *liberal*. It was much more important that we convert souls to Christianity.

However, as the minister of a church I would visit during my experiment put it, "Jesus came that the world might be saved. Therefore, if we are his followers, we should be engaged in saving the world." I took him to mean we should be saving the world not from sin but from hunger, war, and poverty. By extension, I thought I should be able to find a church that was fully engaged in communal acts of saving the world from hatred, fear, and greed—and the resultant disasters.

I knew I could perform acts of social justice with many organizations, but I wanted to be doing it from a spiritual motivation. A community that was committed to working for social justice was one variable that could prove or disprove my hypothesis.

Through reading *Acts of Faith,* I also understood that I wanted a group committed to an ecumenism that embraced more than various Christian denominations. I wanted something much broader, something that Patel's trajectory propelled me toward, something that could include Muslims, Jews, Buddhists, Native traditionalists and more. At the very least, I needed a church that was open to working toward such comprehensive unity.

People often use the words *spirit* and *soul* interchangeably, but to me, *spirit* is about my relationship with God, Higher Power, the Source, the Holy One—call that Presence what you will. With the tools I learned in yoga and meditation and the practices I learned from the Twelve Steps, I had regained a life of the spirit, a life in which I made my best effort at conscious daily contact with God.

The word *soul,* on the other hand, connotes something earthier. It speaks to what we're about here on this planet. It is about relationships with people, animals, plants, home, and food—the sacred in daily life. It can be about how spiritual principles are lived out in the everyday world, heaven on earth perhaps. Not that I believe in heaven as a physical place. My desire to be part of a faith community was about soul. My soul wanted spiritual contact on the earthly, horizontal plane, spiritual contact with others.

* * *

When Cheyenne and I visited a friend who runs an orphanage in Cambodia in 2008, if we looked interested in a vendor's wares but then turned away, the vendor would quickly bring forth something similar, perhaps in a different print or a slightly modified style. Always the eager words, "Same, same but different," accompanied the new product.

That was what I was seeking. I wanted something that was "same, same but different" to satisfy the needs of my soul. I wanted the traditions, the practices that I had so dearly loved—the old hymns that I still sang around the house, in the yard, or when I was driving. I wanted a certain meditative solemnity before worship—no jazz combos playing what masqueraded as a prelude. Swelling organ music for me, preferably from a pipe organ. I wanted a recognizable liturgy, a form to worship services that was similar week after week. And I wanted the bread and wine of communion. These would form "same, same" for me, if I could find them.

Some of the things I wanted had not actually been supplied in the reservation chapels or the more formal church at Rehoboth. The drama queen in me liked a level of pageantry that was consciously absent in the CRC. No surplice-wearing ministers with colorful stoles for us, no Christ candle lit at the beginning of the service. Definitely no incense. We did have an organ—pump on the reservation, electric at Rehoboth—but not a pipe organ. I loved the swell of organ music we did have, especially when Miss Hartgerink played Bach, but I fell in love with the majesty of a pipe organ when I went to Calvin, and I have been in love ever since.

Some pageantry could be supplied by nature, and even the CRC couldn't stop that. On a summer evening, the setting sun suffused the sanctuary at Rehoboth with golden light that lifted my heart to a rarefied plane. During monsoon season, incense would have been pallid compared with rain on parched earth and the pungency of newly washed sagebrush. My imagination provided the rest of the ceremony I craved. When the minister intoned at the end of the service, "Now unto him that is able to keep you from falling, to present you faultless before the presence of his glory with exceeding joy, to the only wise God our Savior, be glory and majesty, dominion and power, both now and ever. Amen," I imagined the hand of Jesus holding me up, taking me to the great golden throne of God, and my heart swelled with "exceeding joy."

As for "different," I looked for intellectual and spiritual stimulation, new ideas, new interpretations, new perspectives, new understanding. I craved openness, affirmation of diversity that included me and many others. I wanted to ask questions and hear the questions of others, questions that weren't limited by the accepted evangelical paradigm. I wanted mission to be about showing God's love through compassionate action, not about converting people to Christianity. Though I wouldn't have expressed it that way in the beginning, I was looking for warmth and acceptance.

In the end, I summarized "same, same but different" like this: I wanted a form that was traditional but a spirituality that was open. I happened, one Saturday, to switch on the radio, just as Garrison Keillor quipped on *A Prairie Home Companion,* "She was looking for a church where the lambs were sort of free-range." The audience and I laughed. I had no idea what had come before this line, but I recognized myself as someone in search of a fold that was more free-range than what I'd grown up with—certainly freer than what I'd been subjected to on that Sunday when I was sixteen.

★ ★ ★

My deliberate experiment began on Martin Luther King Sunday in 2012. King was not only a civil rights leader but also one of the greatest liberation theologians we have known. This was a poignant concurrence, since my departure from the Church began as a liberation issue; I had been theologically disenfranchised.

I entertained some special guests that MLK weekend. Paolo was a former missionary's kid, what we in the know call an *MK.* The Baptists had sent his parents to Italy (not a country I immediately think of as fertile ground for Protestant proselytizers). Kristen was a self-described *ambivalent* Catholic. Others might call her *lapsed,* a term neither of us has ever heard applied to anyone but Catholics. She had last attended a Lutheran church because she wanted to sing in its outstanding choir. Kristen and Paolo were both doctoral students in second language acquisition and teaching at the University of Arizona.

We'd been having deep conversations all weekend around my kitchen table and during a long walk in one of Albuquerque's oldest neighborhoods. We covered language and language learning, multiculturalism and life in other countries, gender roles, popular culture, religion, and spirituality. Several times, I mentioned ideas from *Acts of Faith*.

I was in the seriously thinking stage, about to launch my experiment, but after my many previous attempts, I couldn't bear the thought of trying once more on my own. I asked Paolo and Kristen if they would go to church with me on Sunday. By then, I had discussed my heuristic questions with them, and the third had become the most important to me: Can I be part of a Christian community simply as a follower of Jesus? Is there a faith community where it is possible for me to do that with integrity?

Wonderful friends that they are, Paolo and Kristen were enthusiastic about helping me take the first step. In fact, when I tried to back out on Sunday morning, ostensibly for their sakes, they wouldn't let me.

I had picked First Presbyterian Church for two reasons—the beauty of its spacious nave and its pipe organ, which vies with the one at St. John's Episcopal Cathedral. Both claim theirs is the largest pipe organ in New Mexico. I'd been in First Presbyterian once before, though not for a service. The cream brick edifice had been a stop on a pipe organ crawl I had joined a few years earlier. That day, when our group entered the space with its vaulted, polished wood ceiling and royal blue and red glints from intricate stained glass windows, one of the crawl members, not a churchgoer, said in hushed tones, *"This is a sanctuary."* I had to agree. When the opening run of Bach's *Toccata and Fugue in D Minor* resounded through the expanse, I was electrified.

The sanctuary and the organ did not disappoint on MLK Sunday. The rest of the service did. The sermon was uninspired and uninspiring, and the singing of both the congregation and the choir was anemic. People were moderately welcoming, though it felt like a matter of form. This church would not satisfy my soul needs. But the visit would provide a modicum of momentum for the next Sunday when Kristen and Paolo would not be there to bolster my weak resolve.

As it turned out, the momentum was pretty puny, and I nearly dropped my experiment. I had chosen St. Andrew Presbyterian Church for the following Sunday morning as the next step in my research. Five years earlier, Fonda, a woman I'd met at a school counselors' workshop, had talked about the church in a way that appealed to me. I'd thought I might, maybe, give it a try sometime. The building stands directly across a flood-control arroyo from my branch library. For five years, I had glanced at the modern-looking structure at least once a week when I checked out books. But I didn't follow up on my chat with Fonda.

The sanctuary at St. Andrew was an irregular hexagon with warm peach-colored walls and two stained glass windows, one abstract and the other with a southwestern theme. Its rust, fabric-covered chairs were arranged so it was possible to see nearly everyone in the small congregation from any of them. I sat in the last row, close to the door, in case I had to leave in midstream, as I'd done during other test trials.

Almost right after I sat down, a small white-haired woman came over and sat next to me. "Everyone's telling me, 'Go over and ask her who she is.'"

She said it with such straightforward mirth that I had to laugh with her, and I felt at ease. I told her my name.

"I'm Shirley," she said. "Are you new in town?"

"No. I'm looking for a faith community where I can be comfortable."

"Well, you're welcome here," she said. "I'm the court jester. Right?" she asked for confirmation from the gray-haired woman in front of us.

"Court?" said the woman, who seemed to be made of sterner, more-precise stuff.

"Well, then, the church jester," Shirley amended, unperturbed. She stayed seated in my row and appeared quite satisfied with herself. I liked her.

A few minutes later, a tall rail of a man about my age sat in the chair to my right, held out his hand, and said, "I'm Joe. I'm the outreach elder."

I introduced myself again and got the question I would be asked many more times over the next few weeks: "Are you new in town?"

I gave the same answer, and Joe said, "We welcome you wherever you are in your faith journey."

Tears welled in my eyes and throat. Those were words I had needed to hear from the voice of the Church for a very long time. As the question became predictable at St. Andrew, I would hear variations on Joe's words in response to my answer—"You have to follow your path." "Many of us have been wounded by the Church." "People who come here are looking for a compromise." Here I was in a mainstream church, a church of the Reformed tradition (the Presbyterian Church belongs to the family of churches in the Reformed tradition), being seen and welcomed seemingly without condition.

Except for playing the piano for the Christmas Eve service at the Cuba Presbyterian Church and visiting it one other time, I hadn't attended any Presbyterian churches during my time in exile. Of the mainstream Protestant churches, the Presbyterian is closest to the CRC, also being in the lineage of John Calvin. That is probably why I had almost totally avoided it and why I now sought it out. Perhaps it would supply me with "same, same but different."

After that first venture into St. Andrew, I tried one more Presbyterian church. This one had a well-employed pipe organ, and the congregation had long since decided to remain where it was when the neighborhood changed and became widely known in Albuquerque as the *War Zone*. Both the pipe organ and the church's commitment to stay and serve in a needy area of the city were pluses to my way of thinking. At first, I planned to alternate between this church and St. Andrew during my experiment. But I felt a certain coolness here, perhaps in part because of the traditional rows of pews where you look at the backs of people's heads, whereas St. Andrew was warmth itself. In all the ventures I'd made into churches over the years, only at St. Andrew did individual after individual come up to welcome me and engage me in real conversation. I didn't go back to the church with the pipe organ. Sigh.

~26~

Saturday Nights and Sunday Mornings

For several months I attended St. Andrew most Sundays. Nearly every Saturday evening, I went through a pre-church ritual, but it was not the ritual of the Saturday nights of my childhood. On those nights, my father brought one of the little boys' high wooden stools into the kitchen. One by one, my brothers climbed up, and Dad pinned a soft old sheet around their shoulders. He got out his electric clippers and proceeded to give them all buzz cuts while he told stories about his boyhood on the farm in southwest Michigan.

The rest of us huddled around to listen, while my mother peeled potatoes for Sunday dinner. Each of us in turn took one of our twice-weekly baths. My mother, having submerged the potatoes in cold water to prevent discoloration, supervised the baths and brought children to bed. When the haircuts were done, Dad polished shoes and lined them up on newspapers. His last chore was to mix up the coffee cake and dot the batter with margarine and brown sugar and sprinkle it with cinnamon. This ritual of preparation went on every Saturday night, so we would appear clean and beautiful before God and his people, and to avoid doing unessential work on the Sabbath.

During my experiment at St. Andrew, my Saturday nights involved preparation too, though of a very different sort. It began with a feeling of anxiety in my solar plexus, and it soon became apparent that the anxiety was about going to church the next day. Hardly a Saturday passed without a struggle over whether or not I would go. These were some of the many times I asked myself, "Why am I doing this?" Often I decided I wasn't going. Then Sunday morning came, and I went anyway.

One Sunday, I had caulked the bathtub and shower with a material that required seventy-two hours to cure, so I hadn't had a shower for two days. "The perfect reason not to go," I thought. Yet, inexplicably, I took a birdbath and went.

From the beginning, I did some things to insert myself into the community. If I were to truly disprove my null hypothesis, I needed to fully explore whether I could be part of this gathering. I engaged from a spirit of curiosity, the spirit of a scientist. I started right away to attend Adult Christian Education, the Presbyterian name for adult Sunday school class. The topics were wide-ranging: feeding the hungry, immigration reform, health and mental health in spiritual life, sermon postmortems, preparation for communion, and proposed single-payer health insurance in New Mexico.

One of the first Sundays, Joe, the outreach elder, who liked to call himself the Minister of Propaganda, led a discussion on how to draw more people to the church. I was interested first of all in the motivation for wanting more people. Was it to save souls? If so, my interest in St. Andrew would be nipped in the bud. The congregation, as with many mainstream churches, is aging, and it became apparent that drawing more members was needed to keep the community vital, as attrition would take its course. Somewhat to my surprise, I wanted to share my thoughts. I felt I might have a unique perspective as someone who had only been attending for a few weeks. I talked about the fact that, even though I knew pretty well how to "do" church, when I read the St. Andrew bulletin, so much of the church's culture was taken for granted by the members that I was often puzzled as to what certain phrases meant.

"Like, what are Two-Cent Meals? What is Small Change? What does Historical Jesus do besides meet on Thursdays? What is Spiritual Formation? Who or what are Famous Friends? To me these are codes that members assume everyone understands, but I don't. How will I know if I might want to participate if I have no idea what something is? Visitors who are potential members might appreciate a brochure that explains these exotic terms." That might sound a bit crotchety, and I'm pretty sure I didn't say it quite that way, but I did want information. I also made a point of sharing the fact that St. Andrew was doing something right—that I had felt truly welcomed there from the beginning.

This was when I first met Jan, who would make an important contribution to my experiment as time went on. She was taking notes during class, and when I spoke up, she said, "I would like to talk to you." I could tell she meant it, so I stayed after class and added things that I would like to see at St. Andrew while Jan took more notes on how to draw people into the church. I also shared a thumbnail sketch of my story.

Since doing social justice from spiritual motivation was one reason I wanted a faith community, I decided I needed to come through with some action. St. Andrew offered a variety of opportunities for this. The Mission Focus during the service often brought in speakers to tell about community projects such as Habitat for Humanity; Project Share, which feeds meals to homeless people; and Barrett House, a shelter for women and children who have been victims of domestic abuse. Service possibilities are also mentioned in the bulletin and the monthly newsletter. The easiest was addressing hunger by bringing food offerings for local projects and later helping to serve hot meals at one of them.

One opportunity listed in the bulletin especially interested me: tutoring sponsored by the church in one of Albuquerque's barrios. I joined two St. Andrew members, Jack and Lori, to tutor struggling first and second graders who were attending summer school. As a former reading teacher, I had fun using my skills with beginning readers, and I enjoyed seeing that I was making a difference in young lives. When the project ended, I counted Lori and Jack among my special friends at St. Andrew.

I also looked carefully at what I could commit to in the way of advocacy when the next legislative session began. Many church members were actively lobbying for fair treatment of New Mexico's considerable immigrant population, for job creation, and for educational funding and policy initiatives.

Despite my active involvement and my curiosity, I sometimes felt anxious, almost panicky, about church, and I didn't know why. Maybe I was afraid of becoming trapped in something that had once been like an abusive romance—something I had once loved and later despised. Even more than that, I feared that I was not behaving with integrity. Sometimes I felt like a phony, standing there singing my heart out when I didn't believe many of the words of the hymns. Always reading the Bible passages while most everyone around me just listened to the minister read them. I didn't do that to impress anyone. I just wanted to better grasp the words from the pulpit. I worried too that when I took notes in my Church Journal, the way I used to take sermon notes, it might look to others as if I were sanctimonious.

I asked myself, "Am I really the person I look like to the rest of the people in the sanctuary?" I worried that maybe I only kept coming back because it would make a good story—the possible return of a Christian from years in exile. Mostly, I couldn't explain either the anxiety or what compelled me to continue my experiment, but both were at the root of my Saturday night questioning of whether I would attend church the next day.

Sometimes I was afraid that Christianity had died within me, that not a single heartbeat was left to revive me. Tears came during nearly every service, and, except for a little water brimming in my eyes, they seemed trapped in my throat. At times, I felt as if I were an animal trying to give birth, filled with unutterable groaning, fearing that what was being birthed was something dead, macerated, shriveled. I first heard that word *macerated* when one of my aunts gave birth to a baby that had been dead inside her for ten days—at least I remember it as ten, which seems much too long now. I wondered if this was it—if I feared trying to belong to a church because Christianity as I'd been taught it had died in me a long time ago.

But no, my tears were signs of life. They were salt water, the essence of life in the lip of my eyes. They were the amniotic fluid of this new existence, this being in Christian community that was trying to be born. Tears were a sign to me that I might be in the right place.

You'd think it would be fear of rejection or oppression once more, of harsh judgment of my sexuality that kept me asking why I was doing this. But oddly enough, that never seemed to be an issue. I say oddly in part because five years earlier, when Fonda, the counselor at the workshop, told me about St. Andrew, I asked her how LGBTQ people were received there. She said, almost too quickly, "It's not an issue."

I wanted to say, "Not an issue for whom? It's an issue for me." But I didn't, because I felt that her intent was pure.

When I started attending St. Andrew and came out to people (usually when they asked me the standard question, "Are you new in town?"), I explained that I had been "unchurched" for about forty years. I often casually slipped in that I had left the church of my youth because there was no place for me there as a lesbian. No one ever batted an eye. It wasn't an issue for them, and I discovered that it wasn't for me either. Evidence of that was the fact that it took several weeks for me to either check or notice St. Andrew's specific inclusion in its welcome statement: "We are striving to overcome all divisions that separate the peoples of God from God and from one another, whether race, ethnicity, gender, sexual orientation, marital status, age, physical or mental ability, education, socio-economic status, or cultural background."

Welcoming gays and lesbians as members has been the policy of the Presbyterian Church USA (called the PCUSA, distinguishing it from other less progressive Presbyterian denominations) since 1978; however, as with the lesbian interim pastor at the Cuba Presbyterian Church, gays in relationship were not allowed to be ordained or to serve as pastors. My friend Elaine was ordained, but until her stint in Cuba, she had not been open about her committed relationship with her partner. In 2011, all of that changed when the church's General Assembly decided to allow gays and lesbians in committed relationships to be ordained ministers. Though the decision is still cause for division in the church at large, it was a big moment.

Interestingly, however, something had changed in me. I did not even notice the 2011 milestone go by, as I was still not particularly interested in the Presbyterian Church then. Only later, as I pursued my experiment more deeply, did I discover this change in policy. The policy of the church at large did matter to me. I was happy about it, of course—rejoicing, even. But what mattered more was that there was a place for me at St. Andrew as an out lesbian—just as I am.

It is a measure of my development as a spiritual being that I was more concerned about whether there could be a place for me as a person who didn't hold to the belief that had been instilled in me as the all-important one. Joe's moving response to me on that first Sunday, "We welcome you wherever you are in your faith journey," and subsequent responses from others suggested that there could be. I would face more of a question as to whether I had been able to shed my deepest attitudes about spiritual belief.

I could embrace the Jewish and Buddhist emphases on spiritual practice. But my intense training had been that belief was what mattered. How you live your life after you believe is in some ways secondary. Except maybe when it came to sex. This was the legacy of the Reformers, who wanted to leave behind the Roman Catholic emphasis of their time on penance and indulgences. Some evangelicals don't like the message in the biblical book of James, emphasizing that faith without works is dead.

To me, it seems as though the belief pathway may be easier than the practice one. All you have to do is believe or say you believe, and you are in. Practice involves a conscious daily commitment. But what might it mean practically to be a follower of Jesus's teachings? St. Augustine addressed this question by taking it to the ridiculous. He asked if it meant that we should attempt to walk on water. Acknowledging the unlikeliness of doing this successfully, he concluded that Jesus's followers should pursue his path of righteousness and charity. And I would add inclusiveness, which I think was Jesus's most radical teaching in word and deed. He welcomed and associated with the outcasts of Jewish society in his day—Samaritans, adulterers, tax collectors, lepers, women, the poor.

As my experiment progressed, I would come back many times to the question of being a follower rather than a believer. The people of St. Andrew seemed to think it was up to me whether I said I was a Christian or a Follower of The Way as the ancient pre-Christians did. Therein lay the rub, and also the gift. It was up to me to decide if I could be a genuine participant in the church, possibly even a member, without believing that Jesus died to save me from my sins—the evangelical gold standard.

~ 27 ~

Old Questions and New Answers

AS I TRIED TO RECONCILE WHO I WAS WITH THE TENETS OF Christianity as I'd known them, I quickly progressed from reading about Christian views of homosexuality to issues that truly made it hard for me to consider myself a *believer* according to the definition I'd been taught. Looking at the Bible as the authoritative Word of God—the way I'd learned the meaning of *authoritative*—no longer presented an option for me.

This was something I kept grappling with, and as I read scriptures from other traditions, I knew that the Judeo-Christian words were the ones I still loved best. They offered wisdom that I resonated with. Often, it wasn't different from Buddhist or Hindu wisdom, but it came to me in the language of home. I had never stopped loving the Bible, whether or not I believed in it the way I'd been taught.

I especially love the Bible's central teaching that love is everything. That teaching is embodied in the most essential Jewish prayer, the Shema Yisrael—"Hear, oh Israel, the Lord our God, the Lord is one. And thou shalt love the Lord thy God with all thy heart, and with all thy soul, and with all thy might." And in another place, "Thou shalt love thy neighbor as thyself." The first has been called the Great Commandment, the addition the Second Great Commandment.

Early on during my experiment I read *The Bible: A Biography.* In it Karen Armstrong, a former Catholic nun who became a religious and biblical scholar, tells the fascinating story of how the Bible was written. One thing that stood out for me was how portions of it were composed, rescripted, and revised, often many times. Why? Because the writers were redesigning their work to fit the needs of the readers of their times.

I went on to learn that only since the nineteenth century has the Bible been thought of as exclusively literal. Until then, few people had read Genesis as a historical account of how the world began. It was freeing to find out that the scholars who put together the Jewish and Christian canons placed competing versions side by side without comment. It was especially liberating to read that early biblical authorities insisted that any interpretation that fostered hatred or disdain was illegitimate.

At other times, as I read Armstrong's book, I reacted against it. Even though I'd given up the belief that the Bible was the authoritative Word of God, a part of me *felt* that if it wasn't, what was the point? It seemed that something I'd given up intellectually still lived in my reptile brain. Emotionally, I was still attached in some way to the old paradigm. I felt rather than thought, "If I give that up, what's really left?"

Depression overtook me for a time as I read. First, I grieved what I'd lost—the assurance that comes from black-and-white thinking; afterward, I was comforted. There could be another way to approach this spiritual book that had meant so much to me. I was reminded of a phrase from a book of sermons and prayers by Episcopal priest William L. Dols, "Just because it didn't happen doesn't mean it isn't true." To me this meant that there is a greater Truth than what is found in words that were obviously written by humans. Some of the stories in the Bible may not have happened in history; they are a metaphor that informs us of a deeper Truth. This different way of looking at the Bible removed, among other beliefs, the necessity for believing in Jesus's sacrifice for my sins.

During my time of exile, I only picked up the Bible if I wanted to find a specific verse. But from all those years at my mother and father's table, the Bible was woven into the fabric of my being. Every so often, a verse would come to mind offering a fresh perspective. One day, a passage from Psalm 118 popped into my head. Jesus had quoted this verse when the religious and political leaders were opposing him: "The stone that the builders rejected has become the chief cornerstone." I had been taught that Jesus used those words to claim himself as the foundation of our faith.

That day I thought, "Wait a minute. A cornerstone is not foundational, at least not in the twenty-first century. A cornerstone functions as the message bearer of the building, telling when it was built and sometimes who built it." I realized that Jesus was probably not talking about himself as the underpinning of a new religion. He was once again bringing his message of inclusion. He was saying, "The outcasts of this world have a story to tell, a message to bring. The rest of the world, the establishment especially, needs to hear it."

I went so far as to think, "Maybe Jesus was even talking here about me."

Probably, he was thinking of the same people that inspirational speaker Jacob Nordby referred to when he wrote, "Blessed are the weird people—poets, misfits, writers, mystics, painters, troubadours—for they teach us to see the world through different eyes."

* * *

I hoped that St. Andrew would open me to something new within the faith tradition that I wanted to reembrace. I especially yearned for a new understanding of the mystery that is Jesus, which was still troublesome to me. I did not think that the young rabbi intended to start a new religion, and yet here I was, trying to find out if I could rejoin that religion by following his teachings. As I've said, I believe that God is by nature a mystery; Jesus, on the other hand, seemed to be more of a human-made mystery. Now I was looking to this community to help me unravel the enigma.

I was not to be disappointed. At St. Andrew, I had found a group of people who were exploring the mystery of Jesus. They were seeking ways to follow his teachings and his way of living as best they could in the twenty-first century. Almost from the beginning, I realized that many of them, like me, were refugees from fundamentalist or evangelical Christianity.

At one point, I attended a group that was studying the historical Jesus. As we talked, Max said, "I find it bizarre that people think of the Bible as a historical document."

I thought, "What was utterly common in my upbringing is bizarre to you. How refreshing to hear such a different reality."

Then Dick, a retired minister asked, "How many of you were raised to believe that the Bible was literally, historically accurate?" A forest of hands went up, and chuckles went around the table.

I would discover that Max had not been raised in a church as most of us had. The contrast between his thinking and what most of us had been taught brought home just how difficult it can be to get over Old Think.

One of the loveliest moments of meeting the New Jesus was actually a case of meeting him in ancient times. Bill, a white-haired, white-bearded orator who was also a retired minister, was preaching that day. He told us about visiting the Roman catacombs, where early Christians had hidden from the Roman authorities.

"They also made art there," he said. "Painting murals on the walls. I've seen many of those paintings. But I've only seen the one I'm telling you about in photographs. It's one of Jesus tending sheep. He's dancing on the hillside and playing a panpipe."

"Oh," I thought, "how very lovely—a dancing, joyous Jesus, making music. So different from a suffering, hanging Jesus." I thrilled to this new vision and couldn't help laughing. I felt as if I had just met an artist who'd known a side of Jesus that I wanted to know too.

Someone else had said from the St. Andrew pulpit that Jesus, by his life and teaching, shows us what God is like—loving, forgiving, powerful, and healing. Another preacher put it in even more metaphorical terms, saying that Jesus was the face of God. These perspectives helped me gain a new appreciation for the mystery of Jesus.

I recalled that my deepest, most intimate impressions of Jesus had come through fictional interpretations by authors like Lloyd C. Douglas, Sholem Asch, and Lew Wallace. In their respective novels, *The Robe, The Nazarene,* and *Ben Hur,* I had sensed what people surrounding Jesus must have felt when they encountered him. Those writers seemed to be seeking the answer to questions I was asking myself: "What was it that made people drop everything they were doing to follow Jesus? What was it about the stories Jesus's followers told after he was gone that made people even then want to follow him? What is it about him that makes people want to follow him today?"

Each of those writers portrayed Jesus as a man who embodied pure, unsurpassed Love—without condition, without limit. In their books, Jesus *was* Love. As a teen-ager and young adult, I had stepped into the shoes of the characters in those books. When I did, I felt that immeasurable Love. It had not been sermons from my early life, or the catechism, or even Bible stories that helped me truly encounter Jesus as the Love that was his essence.

It was that Love in him, I'm quite sure—because, as John says, "God is Love"—that made the three disciples fall down before Jesus and say, "My Lord and my God." This I know, not from any sermon or book but from the direct experience I'd had years earlier with my therapist and spiritual teacher.

My first summer at St. Andrew, we had many guest preachers, as our regular preacher was on sabbatical. One of them, speaking about the Gospel of John, said, "John keeps circling back to the idea of God in this human being, Jesus. He keeps coming back to the Divine in all of us, to greater and lesser degrees."

As she said it, I thought, "God in Jesus, God in my therapist, God shining through all of us. So we cannot help seeing God, feeling the Presence, the Love."

Catherine, another guest preacher, spoke one Sunday about my greatest stumbling block in the institutional Church. She said, "Thank God for his love that saves us."

I felt her words wash over me and thought, "Not Jesus's blood. God's love." That I believed.

I heard one sermon about the story of David and Goliath. It was Bill again who reminded us, "King Saul wanted the stripling David to wear his armor for protection as he went to meet the giant. David didn't want to, but he dutifully tried it on. It's hard to refuse a king.

"Then David said, 'I can't wear it. It's too heavy for me. I can't move with it.' So he took it off."

What Bill said made me realize that I couldn't move forward with someone else's armor, their faith—not my family's, not the CRC's peculiar brand, not Islam's or Judaism's, not even St. Andrew's. It has to be my own faith that propels me.

On another Sunday, I heard Catherine, guest preaching again, say, "Thanks be to God for the variety of perspectives in the Bible." These were not words I would have heard in the church of my youth. Thus at St. Andrew, I began to gather unto myself a new theology, one I could draw upon for my spiritual practice and growth.

~28~

Men in Straw Hats

THIS CHAPTER IS ABOUT WHAT I LIKED AT ST. ANDREW. BUT lest anyone think I saw only through rose-colored glasses, know that the chapter that follows is devoted to things I did not especially care for.

★ ★ ★

A Navajo friend once told me that his grandmother had taught him, "If you find a place where you feel the presence of God, go to that place often."

I have two places like that. One is the place I think of as the spiritual heart of the Navajo Nation—the Spider Rock overlook at Canyon de Chelly. The canyon, composed of flowing red sandstone, figures large in Navajo history and teachings. Chinle Wash runs through it, giving it fertile, watered ground for peach orchards, corn, beans, squash, and melons, and for grazing sheep. De Chelly was home to many Diné who made it their last refuge when Colonel Kit Carson and his troops rampaged through, burning orchards, crops, and hogans and raping women, finally forcing the tribe onto the Long Walk to Fort Sumner in central New Mexico in 1864.

The top of the 800-foot-high column known as Spider Rock is considered to be the home of Spider Woman, who gave aid to the Monster Slayer Twins so they could rescue the Diné from giants that roamed the land. Spider Woman is honored as a chief deity and is also sometimes used to encourage children's obedience, in a role not unlike the bogeyman's in Euro-American culture. It is Spider Woman who taught Diné women how to weave their gorgeous and holy rugs.

For me, the rock shelf that stands 200 feet above the top of Spider Rock and a thousand feet above the canyon floor is a place of profound silence and powerful energy. Here I have heard the whirring wings of wheeling ravens and swallows. I have stood in awe as a veil of swirling snowflakes made the Rock appear close enough that I could touch it. I have heard the crackle of cornstalks being harvested on the canyon floor and the bleating of sheep along the wash, reminding me of the human connection that is one with the canyon. Here my solar plexus and my limbs go completely soft, and my heart space opens wide. I have come here again and again to feel the Presence of God, to meditate and to pray.

The other spot on Earth where I have often gone to meet the Holy One is quite different from Canyon de Chelly: Muir Woods, the great redwood forest just north of San Francisco. Here I enter the place known as Cathedral Grove, and the silence, the solemn joy I feel in the presence of the giant majesties overwhelms me. I am in the Presence. Often, tourists from huge buses are there too, but even German and Japanese chatter cannot dispel the quiet power. Beyond the Grove, the tourists turn back, and there is no denying the Source of Life in the green of the ferns, the bubbling water, and the trees. The trees—what a gift!

I have also felt the Holy One's presence in churches, as I did in the great cathedral of Salisbury, as my young friend Ben did in St. Paul's Cathedral in San Francisco. I did not especially feel the Presence in the St. Andrew sanctuary. I did feel genuine warmth from the people who welcomed me. Once in a Twelve Step meeting, when the topic was Higher Power,

Jacob, a prematurely balding young man stood up and said, "I find my Higher Power in other people." I thought he meant that in the sense of the Hindu *Namaste,* sometimes interpreted as, "I greet the Divine in you." In that sense, I did feel the Presence at St. Andrew, but I didn't have the feeling of awe that I find at Spider Rock or in Muir Woods; I felt more a sense of comfort, of being embraced.

In many churches and also in some synagogues, there is a time in the service when people reach over their pews or get up and walk around to greet each other. In the Presbyterian Church, it is called "Passing of the Peace." Everyone who can gets up and walks around, shakes hands, or embraces others. They say, "Peace" or "Peace of Christ" or "Peace be with you." And sometimes, they start chatting about other things.

In the past, I've found this a bit artificial, hence uncomfortable, but at St. Andrew, people seemed so real, so truly glad to see me and greet me and each other, that these encounters were filled with warmth and meaning. Nor did this happen only during the formal meeting and greeting time. Members made a point of extending themselves. People sat next to me and introduced themselves and chatted a bit. I began to tentatively consider that I might be finding the Presence of God in this place, that maybe I should, as the Navajo grandmother suggested, come here often. I had the sense that being at St. Andrew could represent a homecoming.

Shortly after the Sunday school class where I suggested information that someone new at St. Andrew might need, Jan, the note-taker, called and asked if we could get together for lunch or tea. I'm always a bit reluctant to meet socially with someone I don't know well. But I reminded myself that if I wanted community, I had to at least reciprocate when people extended themselves. At that meeting, we shared our stories of leaving Church, and I asked Jan about how she had returned. I craved other people's stories about walking away and coming back. Over time, I would ask more and more people for the tales of their journeys.

★ ★ ★

One Sunday after the service, I noticed four white-haired men in white, short-sleeved shirts standing in a row near the entryway. They sported narrow dark ties or bolo ties, and three of them wore cream-colored straw fedoras with dark hatbands. For a moment in my mind's eye, I saw the old-style missionaries of my father's generation and older, men he is buried beside now. These men could have been talking about the sermon, about missions, about baseball, or the weather. But I saw in that little conclave such a tableau of familiarity, giving me one more sense of homecoming.

After I had gone to St. Andrew for a few weeks, I noticed that when I drove to church, I saw other vehicles that also might be headed for a church service somewhere. The streets were Sunday-morning quiet, and I smiled to myself, feeling as if I had joined a flock of people who shared the habit of rising early and dressing nicely, even if twenty-first-century casual, and going to similar places for similar activities. This felt like something larger than St. Andrew, something also communal.

More than almost anything at St. Andrew, I loved singing the old, familiar hymns of my childhood. My heart opened with joy when we sang those songs. I rarely cared for the new or unfamiliar hymns, the ones where I had to carefully read the music in order to sing my part. I kept wishing for the glory of a pipe organ, even though Jean, the St. Andrew organist, was gifted on both piano and electric organ, and often the music director joined in with excellent guitar accompaniment. Sometimes, a trumpeter, flutist, or violinist participated.

Certain songs took me back to specific times and places. "Blessed Assurance" was the song we sang every morning in the tabernacle at the Southwest Bible and Missionary Conference. When we sang, "Blessed assurance/Jesus is mine/Oh, what a foretaste of glory divine" at St. Andrew, memories of running around with friends, of my crush on Marilyn, of giving my heart to Jesus in the dining hall all came flooding back.

Sometimes, when the accompanist played the introduction to a hymn, the words that came to mind were Navajo. Instead of hearing "Holy, holy, holy, Lord God almighty," I heard, *"Diyin, diyin, ei God, Ayoogo nidziilii,"* and I had to make an effort to recollect the English words before we started singing.

One Sunday, we sang the old, familiar hymn, "What a Friend We Have in Jesus." I didn't have to think at all about getting the harmony right. For the first time, I listened as I sang. I heard voices lifted in joy all around me. I *heard* communion, and I sang purely from my heart. My eyes were wet with tears of joy.

After that, I started noticing that many in the congregation at St. Andrew sang the old songs with an exuberance that pulsated throughout the sanctuary. I saw the elation on their faces, saw them rocking and swaying to the music, as I did. I was not alone. I was not the only expatriate trying to come home.

★ ★ ★

Before I would give any money to the church, knowing that some of it went to missions, I wanted to know just what was meant by *mission* at St. Andrew. In the CRC, it had meant converting people to Christianity. If the CRC had a medical mission or a program to feed the hungry, the ultimate goal of that program was to turn the recipients into grateful Christians. At least that's the way it was when I was growing up. I did not want to be part of anything like that.

When I first considered putting money in the offering basket, I called Jan to ask her what *mission* meant. She referred me to Joe. He told me the Presbyterian Church had given up converting people through its missions fifty years ago. "What it means," he said, "is that we are doing our best to show Christ's love by feeding, healing, bringing clean water, advocating for people's rights, and educating." This was something I was willing to participate in; in fact, this kind of mission precisely represented one of my reasons for wanting to be part of a spiritual community.

I saw that the people of St. Andrew took to heart Jesus's words: "I was hungry and you gave me food; I was thirsty and you gave me something to drink; I was a stranger and you welcomed me; I was naked and you gave me clothing; I was sick and you took care of me; I was in prison and you visited me. . . . Just as you did it to one of the least of these who are members of my family, you did it to me."

And the words of the Jewish prophet Micah: "And what does the Lord require of you but to do justice, and to love kindness, and to walk humbly with your God?" Nothing in either passage said God required me to believe that Jesus had died to save me from my sins.

The people of St. Andrew had so many concrete ways of reaching out to the poor and needy of the community that it took months for me to be aware of most of them. Many homeless people spend their days and often their nights in a large city park across from St. Andrew. During the week, the church provided them with sack lunches. On Sundays, many of them joined in worship. When communion was celebrated, they came forward with everyone else, assured of their welcome. After the service, church members served people from the neighborhood a hot meal, whether or not they had come to the service. At any time during the week, people could come in for toiletries, socks, warm clothing, blankets, and bag lunches. The church bought bus passes from the city for them. These park dwellers were part of the St. Andrew community, although they seemed to remain mostly on the fringe.

On communion Sundays, congregants brought bags full of groceries and left them at the communion table, to be taken later to the barrio community center where I had tutored. Every other month, on a Saturday, members prepared food and served it at a city project that feeds dinner to close to two hundred homeless people every day. Church members appeared to do it all with cheerfulness and enthusiasm. I never saw any one-upmanship either. The people they served seemed to feel comfortable and truly but not ingratiatingly thankful.

The church also joined with other Presbyterians, Catholics, and Methodists to raise the money and construct one Habitat for Humanity house per year. Presbyterian women raised money to fund social and educational grants around the world. These people were teaching me about what it meant to be one of Jesus's followers.

Periodically, my atheist friends get indignant about the fact that churches are exempt from paying taxes. I think these friends don't realize how much of the money many churches take in goes to alleviate suffering locally and around the world. Perhaps there should be a distinction between funds that go to pay the minister, the choir director, and the mortgage and funds that go into serving the community. On the other hand, it is the existence of the building and the paid and unpaid people in it that inspires and makes these outreach programs possible. A short time ago, I might have agreed with my friends protesting the tax status of churches, but I've come to see it a bit differently after observing business as usual at St. Andrew.

* * *

In many traditional indigenous societies, where survival was at a premium, every member was considered essential to the group's continued existence. What other societies might consider liabilities are turned into assets. At one time, in an old Diné legend, men and women were in such conflict that they decided to live separately—men on one side of a river, women on the other. They soon discovered that they were ill equipped to live apart because they had only learned the survival tasks assigned to their gender. Men who lived as women and women who lived as men saved the day on the two sides of the river because these people knew how to perform the tasks of the opposite gender. They were essential to the whole.

I witnessed something akin to this at St. Andrew. Different church members took in a man who had been rendered homeless by medical expenses. As he recovered, he began to volunteer by helping to serve the hot meals after church on

Sundays. A woman who had been pushed out of her previous church because of mental health issues that impinged on others' sense of decorum sang beautiful solos at St. Andrew and was applauded for them. One Sunday each month, after the service, a group called Comfort My People met. It was a peer support group for individuals and families living with mental illness. In so many ways, the church community showed that it valued each individual.

Whenever I told friends that I was attending church, I described St. Andrew as progressive. However, I know from some members that there has been strident political conflict at times between Republicans and Democrats, conservatives and liberals. Though what I continued to feel was unity of purpose and respect for differences, I knew that if I stuck around, I would eventually come face to face with some of those conflicts. Conflict in itself is not bad, and I credit both the pastor and the congregation's own overriding desire for harmony and communion that a sense of unity remains. The lively spirit of inclusiveness was also reflected in the liturgy—no more "Our Father," for example. Rather, "Creator God."

~29~

Ebb and Flow

In every significant relationship of any duration, there exists an ebb and flow. There are times of closeness and harmony, times of conflict and distance. This was true in my relationship with the community at St. Andrew, much as in any relationship. My experiment involved much more process than result, and soon, without realizing it, I had surpassed the eight weeks that had been my lengthiest church attendance since exile began. Inevitably, I was sometimes disappointed with the community. Did I mention that there was no pipe organ?

When I was a child and a teen, faith community happened without any effort on my part. It was just a fact of life. But as I observed life around me at St. Andrew, it became clear that if I wanted true community and communion, I would have to get more deeply involved than simply doing what would prove or disprove my hypothesis. This is what community is—a group of people who are *involved* with each other in common goals, activities, and even, yes, beliefs. It is far more than eating bread and drinking juice or wine together, no matter how frequently or infrequently it happens. I had seen that, despite differences and conflicts, the people of St. Andrew were a community because they *did* things together, things they considered important.

The first way I got involved in St. Andrew's activities had been by bringing food to the table on communion days. On the one hand, I liked the way this food reflected the nourishment we received when we took communion. On the other, I have to say that I am not so enamored of giving out food. I would rather see a more long-term approach, teaching people to fish rather than handing them a fish. I would like to see the development of a microfinance project along the lines of the model begun by Nobel Peace Prize recipient Muhammad Yunus, author of *Banker to the Poor: Micro-Lending and the Battle Against World Poverty.* This approach to alleviating poverty and hunger lets people provide for themselves with dignity and pride. It changes whole communities and even countries.

On the other hand, I also recognize that stopgap measures to address hunger in emergency situations through food pantries and soup kitchens are necessary. I also know that some people may never be able to use a micro-loan because of mental illness, entrenched addiction, or long-lived homelessness. While I admired the open-hearted generosity of the St. Andrew community, I was somewhat critical of a handout rather than a hand-up approach.

I do need to add, though, that St. Andrew participated in Bread for the World, a letter-writing campaign intended to influence legislators to enact policies for combating hunger. Members worked to influence such short-term policies as SNAP, better known as food stamps, and ones that address the deeper causes of hunger. They have successfully impacted such initiatives as Tax Relief, Unemployment Insurance Reauthorization, the Job Creation Act of 2010, the Earned Income Tax Credit, the Child Tax Credit, rural economic development programs, and programs addressing the HIV/AIDS pandemic.

⋆ ⋆ ⋆

Many St. Andrew parishioners were active in a citywide organization called Albuquerque Interfaith (A.I.), which works for change through the democratic process, focusing especially on workforce development, improving public education, and ensuring fairness for immigrants. During a legislative session, for example, members lobbied successfully against a bill the governor had proposed to deny drivers' licenses to undocumented immigrants, a policy that would not be good for immigrants or the safety of the general populace.

A.I. members draw spiritual support for their work for immigrants from a command in Leviticus to welcome the strangers in our midst. During the Mission Focus at a service shortly before the legislative session, a young immigrant mother spoke movingly about her gratitude for the opportunities she and her children enjoy in the U.S. and about their needs and hopes for the church's support.

I was excited about getting involved with A.I., not only because I felt aligned with the projects it supports but also because it is an ecumenical group consisting of Catholics, Protestants of many stripes, Unitarians, and Quakers, as well as educational and social work organizations. The members set aside whatever differences exist among them and work together for the common good. Despite my eagerness, I was disappointed to learn that *interfaith* only referred to a diverse group of Christians (except for the Unitarians and Quakers). Where were the Jews, the Muslims, the Buddhists, the traditional Native Americans? Being part of a group that created unity from diversity was as important to me as, perhaps even more important than, the work we set out to accomplish. I decided that if I joined A.I., I would want to commit to working on expanding the membership to embrace more diversity. I told that to a couple of the most active St. Andrew members of A.I., and they were supportive, but it wasn't their mission.

⋆ ⋆ ⋆

One of the things that impressed me deeply at St. Andrew was its warmth and service to the homeless in the neighborhood. One Sunday, though, I had to acknowledge that the church's hospitality was not always unconditional. As the service was winding to a close, a homeless woman began to speak loudly about how difficult and painful her life was, how many tragedies had befallen her. She wept noisily and wetly. Her face had the puffy red tinge of an alcoholic, and her speech was slurred and dramatic. It took me back to the exaggerated, self-pitying behavior of alcoholics I had known in childhood on the Navajo Reservation.

The guest minister seemed to be at a loss, somewhat embarrassed. I saw that he wanted to be compassionate but also that he wanted to end the service by cutting her off gracefully. A pall of unease fell over the community. The woman continued, despite the pastor's response. Then one of the congregants, a woman about my age, got up and sat beside the blubbering, sweaty woman, put her arms around her and gently rocked her. In that embrace, the woman quieted while the service proceeded to its close.

The sermon that morning had been about God in the form of Jesus coming as a blood sacrifice because blood sacrifice was the paradigm for redemption in his day. The preacher speculated that today, perhaps God would come as a computer geek. To me that seemed unlikely. After the woman of the congregation went over to the suffering woman and unhesitatingly held her, I was certain that God had just come to us in the form of a drunken homeless woman, and only one of us had had the courage and grace to meet the Holy One. The irony of our failure to respond, in conjunction with the sermon topic, was not lost on me.

In those moments, I loved St. Andrew for that one brave and loving woman. And I couldn't help questioning myself. Why hadn't I been the one to reach out? My excuse was that I was too new, not really part of the community. In the midst of my judgments about both the church and myself, I tried to be compassionate.

I reminded myself of the humanness of communities I'd been part of in the past. There was Rehoboth Mission with its backbiting and meanness among the missionaries themselves, and mistreatment of Native students in the supposed interest of saving their souls. There was its rejection of Jennie and Alice for loving each other and, by extension, of me. There was also the connection, whether I liked it or not, between me and the Reformed Bible Institute alumni who sang "Blest Be the Tie" at the foot of the red rocks.

Shortly after Cheyenne's birth, we lived in a women's community in New Zealand. Sometimes, relationships there got messy. But it was also a community that knew how to work together and accomplish farming and building projects. We knew how to play together as well, swinging into the rushing creek after steaming in the sauna, building solstice bonfires, and playing a feminist version of Dungeons and Dragons.

From time to time, after my yoga courses in Sweden, I lived in the ashram in Copenhagen. People there complained about the woman who shirked her karma yoga assignments or never made it to morning meditation. And still, delicious, vegetarian meals made it to the table where we sat and joked and ate together. And still, the yoga classrooms were kept spotless, and once in a while, we all walked down the street together for falafel at Shawarma Huset. And still, morning meditation happened.

If I were truly to be part of a community, it would have to be for better and for worse. Like any community, spiritual ones are gatherings of people sometimes sharing a common purpose and sometimes at cross purposes that must be worked out.

* * *

The ebb and flow of my relationship with St. Andrew went on for an unprecedented seven months. I continued to ask myself nearly every Saturday night and Sunday morning, and also sometimes during the week, "Why am I doing this?" I continued, most Sundays, to show up, to enjoy myself, to have tears wet my eyes, and to deliberately involve myself in church projects, mostly to find out if I wanted to be part of them on an extended basis. I felt discomfort and satisfaction in close to equal measure.

The ebb tide had to flow around one very large obstacle. It had to do with my own process, not with anything intrinsic to St. Andrew. I was repeatedly disturbed by the issue of coming out, not as a lesbian but as a churchgoer. My feelings were similar to ones I had when I first started coming out sexually, except that they were not as intense. On one side of the issue stood my family. It might seem as though I should be eager to tell them I was attending church pretty regularly—a church of the Reformed faith, no less. Of course, it wasn't one of the approved Reformed denominations, so there was that little hiccup. I didn't want to hear their assumptions or judgments about the suitability of the church that I might or might not end up choosing.

Most of them would see little virtue in St. Andrew because it was too liberal. I imagined a conversation like this with one of my three preacher brothers:

Him: The Presbyterian Church will take anybody.
Me: As far as I know, so did Jesus.
Him: (Pause). Yes, but he had requirements.
Me: Yes, to love God and your neighbor as yourself.
Him: To believe that he died to save you from your sins.
Me: He never said that.
Him: The Bible says it.
Me: You're a preacher. What do you know about how the Bible was written? Oh, this is pointless.

There was more to it than my family's approval or lack thereof. What if my null hypothesis were to be proven in the end? As often as I struggled of a Saturday night with whether I would attend on Sunday morning, as often as I asked myself why I was doing this, even though my attendance at St. Andrew had lasted longer than attendance anywhere else, I wasn't at all sure that I wouldn't permanently stop going from one Sunday to the next.

Sure, there were things about St. Andrew that I liked and admired, and I found a certain level of comfort and familiarity there, but what if this place and these people couldn't become home to me? What if I couldn't commit to this or any other spiritual community? What if St. Andrew couldn't commit to me? I had been open with people about the things I didn't believe. My fear that I might not be acceptable came from the old assumptions of what it meant to be a believer.

And then there was rebelliousness. A part of me just didn't want to give my family the satisfaction of my concession that perhaps there could be something of value in attending church. I had to admit that I received a certain amount of gratification from being a free agent, a renegade Christian (if I could even call myself a Christian), a maverick. Moreover, I didn't have any real hope that my belonging to a church would increase our ability to share our spiritual lives with one another. Did I say *belonging?* To a church? I certainly wasn't there yet.

I mentioned to only two of my brothers that I had been attending church for a time. Rick, who was able to acknowledge more spiritual realities than his own, seemed baffled. Despite that open space, he was more entrenched than I was in the necessity for belief. He knew I did not believe, except in God. "Why would you want to?" was his only response when I told him about St. Andrew. Bob, Ryan's father, was simply, quietly supportive, as is his way.

As difficult as it was to open up and share with my family that I had been attending a Presbyterian church, I worried even more about telling my friends—agnostics, atheists, Buddhists, practitioners of Native spirituality, Jews both observant and secular, and so-called New Agers. These were the people who had supported me all these years, stood by me through the hard times. We had been spiritually in alignment to greater or lesser degrees. Christianity carries so much baggage for so many of them, as it has for me, that I dreaded coming out to them. I was living in hiding once again from people who were my own.

I am part of a monthly book group, and the members are all lesbian. I love this group. The thriving LGBTQ community we enjoyed in the days when we clung together because we were all we had has shrunk. My book group has become some of the community that slipped away. We have a common understanding that makes our gathering the most relaxed of any social group I'm part of. I laugh more with them than with any other set of people, and we always seem reluctant to part at the end of our evenings together.

One day after I had engaged in my experiment for a few months, the book group was sharing a snack before beginning our discussion. We sat on a flagstone patio under a handcrafted *portal,* sipping cold limeade and eating chips and salsa. We looked out over the llano, the high plains that figure prominently in Rudolfo Anaya's classic, *Bless Me Ultima.* I sat at a round table with four of our eight, and one woman asked if any of us could ever imagine embracing Christianity again. Three of us had been raised as Christians to one degree or another. My stomach went weak, and I swallowed hard. Another of the three had had a pretty similar upbringing to mine within the Presbyterian Church. She'd even been born in a mission hospital in the Navajo Nation, and a few months earlier I had told her about my experiment. She had told me she didn't think she would ever go back, but I couldn't wiggle out of telling the women at the table what I was doing because of what I'd told her.

Carefully, in as few words as possible, I talked about the experiment. I hastened to explain the distinction I drew between being a believer and a follower. "Oh," one woman said, "you mean to follow the teachings of Jesus?"

I was relieved by her quick grasp of it. I was further surprised by how little energy my confession generated among my friends and how matter-of-factly they seemed to accept what I was doing. Gradually, I took the leap to mention St. Andrew with other friends, always saying that it was in a progressive branch of the Presbyterian Church, always distinguishing between believing and following or practicing.

Caryl, the last school principal I'd worked with, was raised Catholic and might now be described as a student of New Age thought. Our approach to education and to life was in clear alignment, and ours had been my most satisfying work relationship with a supervisor, a great note on which to end my career. This was in part because we were also in agreement about basic spiritual principles. One evening over margaritas and green chile enchiladas, I told her, with some trepidation and all my disclaimers, that I'd been attending church. At first, she laughed; I couldn't tell if it was with skepticism or nervousness. But as we talked, she acknowledged the general breakdown of community in our society and said she understood why I would want to pursue this avenue.

Another friend, Jean, was an agnostic and in a relationship with a vocal atheist. She had an initial caveat when I told her about my experiment, "As long as you don't tell me you believe in all that stuff." I didn't bother saying that I didn't need her permission, one way or the other. Soon after she said it, she spoke of her own need for spiritual community and said I'd inspired her to look into a nearby Buddhist center where she thought she might be comfortable. I began to realize that I needn't have worried about my friends; the desire for meaningful sharing in community seems to be nearly universal, and for that, I was grateful.

~30~

The Test Again

FRANK YATES, THE PASTOR AT ST. ANDREW, SOUNDED AT FIRST fearful like a good ol' boy from Texas. The barest piece of that characterization is true—he grew up in Texas in a fundamentalist home where the belief system was in many ways similar to the one I grew up with. Frank was solidly built, cheerful, funny from the pulpit, warm, and down-to-earth. The children of the church loved him; this was evident on more than one occasion during Time for Young Disciples, when they answered questions like, "Who is the most beautiful or most important person in the church?" with a resounding, "Frank!" The answer, of course, should have been something like, "Everyone." The adults, including Frank, laughed.

After I had attended St. Andrew for a few Sundays, Frank asked if I would like to visit with him. We met in his book-lined study where the titles are evidence of the fact that this guy with a down-home Texas drawl is a scholar with a Ph.D. and teaches religion at the University of New Mexico. He was far from being a good ol' boy, his conscientious objector status during the Vietnam War being just one indication of that. I told Frank a brief version of my growing up years, my exile from the Church, and the home I was hoping to find somewhere, someday, maybe at St. Andrew. I came out to him as a lesbian and a doubter who thought she might want to be a follower, as someone who embraces the great mystery that is God but is still trying to grasp the human-made mystery of Jesus. I told him I did a lot of reframing during services in order to understand the liturgy and sermons in a way that I could accept with some integrity.

"A lot of people at St. Andrew do the same thing every Sunday—that reframing," Frank replied.

When I told him about my missionary-kid status, he said, "My wife grew up at Laguna Pueblo. Her parents were Presbyterian missionaries there."

A little later, I told him about Fonda having been my first contact with St. Andrew, then added, "That was five years ago. I've been considering checking it out ever since."

"Well, you wouldn't want to do anything precipitous," he said. We both laughed. "By the way," he added, "Fonda went to Hope College."

"Really?" I felt a frisson of excitement. Hope was Neale's old school and Calvin's archrival. That information about Fonda's and my connection would later become important to me. I knew right then that in all probability, she and I had lots of points of commonality. Perhaps the most significant would be our common Dutch heritage and upbringing in sister churches. Frank in those moments granted me one of his great gifts—offering tie-ins, links to the church and its people.

He also shared some of his own faith journey out of fundamentalism. When I told him I had conducted groups and workshops on healing from fundamentalism, he gave me another gift. "I could have used one of those groups at one time," he said. To me it was a sign of Frank's generosity and humility, which I'd noticed in the way he spread both the work and the honor at St. Andrew.

Frank placed himself in relationship to my belief or lack of it by saying, "I'm pretty orthodox theologically, but I support others where they are in their varied beliefs." This, to me, characterized perhaps Frank's greatest talent, aside from his knowledge and skills as a teacher. He was a unifier. Once more,

I heard about how the people of St. Andrew's congregation ran the gamut from very conservative to very liberal.

He told me about some of the wrenching political conflicts, particularly after what many liberals viewed as the stolen presidential election of 2004. At that point, I still hadn't experienced any clashes. I believe that the genuine warmth pervading the St. Andrew sanctuary, the feeling of communion there, had something to do with Frank's belief that people of widely divergent theological and political stances can come together in love and truly care for one another, and the way that he, as the pastor, put that belief into practice.

A few weeks after we met, Frank left on sabbatical. In the three months that he was gone, the people of the church came together and filled in in many ways. I learned that several retired and inactive ministers were part of the congregation, and some of them preached. Others took care of pastoral needs, and things went along smoothly, at least from my uninitiated vantage point. I did not absent myself any more than I'd been doing already. That told me that I was not at St. Andrew because of some central figure, which had been the case when I attended Unity of Santa Cruz. Rather, I was there for the community. In fact, I became more involved while Frank was gone, as this was when I started tutoring, bringing food offerings for hunger projects, and learning more about Albuquerque Interfaith. I also joined a pair of teachers from the congregation in a protest against excessive educational testing at the state capitol in Santa Fe. And this was when I asked Jan to tell me more of her story. Cautiously, I was contemplating the possibility of becoming a member of St. Andrew.

When Frank returned from his sabbatical, the joy in the sanctuary was palpable. His sermon that first Sunday was part travelogue because he had visited holy sites in Turkey and Greece and part joyous thanksgiving. He spoke from a text that made me want, for the first time in forty years, to memorize a Bible verse again. The verse proffered a prayer of thanksgiving, which Frank said was his favorite biblical prayer after the Lord's Prayer. I loved the opening lines for their inclusiveness: "I bow my knees before the Father [okay, "Father" is not so inclusive, but I valued highly what came next] from whom every family in heaven and on earth takes its name."

To me, that phrase said that God is the God of all, regardless of religion or unbelief, of race or nationality, sexual or gender orientation, regardless of any difference. It reminded me of a conversation I'd had with my father years earlier. He was talking about Tibetan prayer wheels. His face bore that peculiar, nervous smile that told me the topic embarrassed him. "They think when they spin the wheel," he said, "however many turns it takes, that's how many times their prayer goes up to their gods."

"Dad, there are lots of ways of praying," I said. "When I pray, I pray silently. I don't ask for specific outcomes. If I'm praying for someone in particular, I just lift them up. I think God reads that, and God knows what they need better than I do."

"What God are you praying to?" His question was an accusation, and I heard his scorn.

I did my best to keep my voice light. "There's only one God, isn't there? Isn't that what you taught me?"

He didn't say anything.

But yes, I loved Frank's text—the God "from whom every family in heaven and on earth takes its name." Including the Tibetans who use wheels and flags to pray.

⋆ ⋆ ⋆

While Frank was gone, I had continued to keep the log in my Church Journal. I had also continued to ask myself why I was doing this. Somewhere in there, I came close to the decision that I wanted to formally become part of the community at St. Andrew. To become a member. I couldn't have said exactly why. In fact, becoming a member seemed to be the next step in the experiment, as odd as that may sound. On some level, I knew that unless I took this step, I wouldn't know whether my hypothesis had been proven or disproven.

After the service on Frank's first Sunday back, he came up to me and asked if I'd like to visit again. I had planned to ask him. We got together that same week.

I had made a prayer request on Sunday, and Frank started our session by bringing that up.

"Oh." I smiled. "That's not what I want to talk about. Thank you, though. Actually, I've been wondering how I could become a member."

"Well, you came to the right person. There are a few ways," he said. "You could be baptized."

I shook my head. I had been baptized as a baby at the First CRC in Grand Rapids, wrapped in the soft, silver-threaded white shawl my grandmother had knitted just for me. I knew my baptism would count with the Presbyterians. "I've been baptized," I said.

Frank nodded. "You can transfer your membership from a previous church."

I laughed, thinking back to when Neale and I had attended Fort Wingate CRC, next to the big BIA school where I'd once taught Sunday school. "I doubt if the last place I was a member—forty years ago—would still have any records to pass on."

Frank chuckled with me. "Well, you can also come before the Session and reaffirm your faith."

I nodded. That was not only fitting; all along, as I considered joining, I had felt a need to do just that. I wanted a meaningful rite of passage, something to mark the significance of this next step in my spiritual journey. It also felt like an action that would bring to full circle my meeting with the thirteen men who had sat around the table when I was thirteen in that church basement in D.C. Here I would declare what I believed and perhaps also what I did not believe, keeping in mind that so much of Protestant Christianity is about belief. Frank told me the Session would meet in three weeks, which happened to be my parents' wedding anniversary, and we agreed that I would meet with them then.

A day or two after I arranged with Frank to take this leap, I sat down and wrote out what I wanted to say at the meeting. Talking about myself in front of a group makes me more nervous now than when I was that bold thirteen-year-old. I end up forgetting most of what I want to say. I wrote a little about my journey, my time in the wilderness, and what St. Andrew had come to mean to me as I had continued my search.

The Apostle's Creed may be the most well known of several Christian creeds. I once knew it as well in Navajo as I did in English. Growing up, I had said it in each language at least once every Sunday. At that vespers service in Salisbury Cathedral, I'd found my way clear to repeat it as I mentally translated parts of it that were hard for me to say. As part of my reaffirmation of faith before the St. Andrew Session, I decided to write each step of the creed in my own words (Appendix B). I wanted my rewrite to say what I meant about my beliefs within the Christian faith. When it was done, I felt that the words reflected my ever-evolving understanding of God, Jesus, the Holy Spirit, and the Church at that moment in time. I felt that my words also reflected the spirit of the original. I set my confession aside to await what felt like the night of reckoning, as if I were setting forth once more to pass the test.

~31~

Panic Saturday

I HAVE MY SHARE OF NEUROSES—RUMINATING ON THINGS I have no control over, especially things past, nervous anticipation, occasional depression, a little healthy paranoia—but I'm seldom, if ever, given to panic. Two Saturdays before I was to meet with the Session, I slid into that mode. I had taken a leap just by setting up this meeting, and now I wanted a balloon to come along and lift me up and out of the chasm.

I have spent a good bit of my adult life working with immigrants—mostly Cambodian war refugees and Mexican economic refugees. No matter how much they need the refuge they hope the U.S. will offer, in the beginning, and sometimes for many years afterward, they find the act of coming to live here frightening. One friend told me he had been terrified by the noise of the flush toilet on the plane from the transition camp in the Philippines. "I thought it was going to suck me out of the plane," he said, now able to laugh about it. After immigrants have been here for a time, they have other occasional causes for panic. It comes with the awareness that this is not a vacation or a refugee camp; this is for real; there is no turning back.

As I got closer to joining myself formally to this faith community, I considered that it might be permanent. All the times I'd asked myself, "Why am I doing this?" now came crashing in on me, suffocating me, ambushing me with the feeling that I couldn't possibly belong at St. Andrew, that I was an illegal immigrant, about to be exposed as a fake. The issue of belief reared up in front of me like a hooded cobra.

Some people become frenetic, hysterical when they panic. Not me. As if I'd already been shot through with venom, I felt paralyzed. By ten that Saturday morning, I had crawled back into bed and fallen asleep. Periodically, I woke and asked the questions I'd plagued myself with throughout my experiment—evidence of one of my neuroses. And I asked some new questions too.

Question number one, of course and yet again: "Why am I doing this?" Also a repeat question: "Why on earth do I want to join a group whose most basic tenets I don't believe in?" And: "Am I a fake for even trying?" Between sleeping and ruminating over these questions, I started to think I would email Frank to say I needed to postpone my reaffirmation of faith until the next month. Then I thought I needed to cancel it indefinitely. Or possibly permanently. I knew for sure that I wouldn't go to church the next day. Maybe I would be taking a break for several weeks. Maybe permanently.

As I cowered, immobilized, I thought of an art show I had visited a few years earlier. All thirty pieces in it—from an original etching by Rembrandt to ceramic pots, from a fabric collage to a series of four black and white linoleum prints—had as their subject the Prodigal Son. The well-known story is of a son who takes his inheritance early, leads a debauched life, ends up on the skids, and finally returns home to a lavish welcome from his father, to the dismay of his older brother who had stayed home and done the daily grind.

I was most deeply moved by the contemporary depiction of the story in a series of prints Steve Prince had made in 2004. The second, titled "Prodigal Appetite: Halloo," reminded me of my years in addiction. "Prodigal Journey: Exit Wounds" called forth the pain resulting from addiction. "Prodigal Return: Your Past May Be Stained but Your Future Is Untouched" left me with a feeling of hopelessness. I felt at the time that, unlike the prodigal, I would never be able to find my way back home.

As rich as the exhibit was on many levels, I was almost angry with the friend who had suggested I see it because it brought up such feelings of despair. I had long identified with the prodigal as the one who left home. I had thought, "If he could return, maybe I can too." On Panic Saturday, I was afraid my only choice might be to give that up.

* * *

It is my practice to take one day a week off from writing, except for journaling, which I do almost every day. Saturday is not my day off, but I couldn't move out of my quivering huddle to touch a pen or a keyboard. Four times a year, I am invited to write for the Religious Perspectives column of my hometown newspaper, the *Gallup Independent.* My deadline was fast approaching, and I hadn't settled yet on a topic. I was thinking of a story in Rachel Naomi Remen's *Kitchen Table Wisdom* that I might connect with my upcoming piece. By mid-afternoon, I had hauled myself far enough out from under my covers to reread some of the book, hoping it would move me toward writing.

Soon I was caught up in stories other than the one I'd been thinking of. My reading became less about the column I should have been writing and more about my state of panic. One wise gift from Auntie Rachel was the suggestion that it is necessary to grieve what we have lost to be able to love again. I thought about the years that had followed my leave-taking from the Church, the mission, and our table at home—the altar around which my family still gathers from time to time. I recalled how my beliefs had poured from me effortlessly when I walked away from the Church and how I'd felt little more than relief.

One year, not too long ago, I went on a tour of Christmas lights with two friends from my book group. Both are Buddhists now, but one had been a devout Catholic while the other had had little religious upbringing. The former Catholic and I talked about leaving our respective faith traditions, and for the first time, I acknowledged to someone else and to myself, "Losing my faith and my community has been the greatest loss of my life." Yet as I read Auntie Rachel's words, I realized that I had done little grieving for that loss.

The times when I had cried were mostly connected with my family. I had lain on the bed in my apartment in Copenhagen and sobbed when my brother Ed felt compelled to write that he believed the Bible commanded him to shun me because of my sexuality but that he couldn't do it because of his love for me; nevertheless, he added that I should turn from my wicked ways. By the time my brother Ron wrote that God had turned me over to the devil, I had no tears left; I felt only sorrow that he understood so little.

Now, on Panic Saturday, as I read Rachel Remen's words, I wondered if it had become impossible for me to open my heart to love and commit to St. Andrew and its people because I had not fully grieved what I'd lost in the first place. I realized that my loss was perhaps not so much about a tradition or an organization called *church* or *mission.* I had lost safety and certainty. I had lost what was comforting in its familiarity. Most of all, I had lost people. Community, after all, is made up of people, of individuals.

A good many of those in the mission community had meant something to me but were now part of my life only tangentially or not at all. There were nurses I'd worked with at the hospital when I was in high school and college—women who had taught me the skills I needed to be an operating room technician and nursing assistant, enabling me to work my way through school. Those women had, in their own way, loved and nurtured me, and I had loved them. There were the two missionaries who took me for dinner to Furr's Cafeteria when I was struggling, unbeknownst to them, with faith and sexuality. There was the fifth-grade teacher who terrified me so that I missed fifty-three days of school that year, the woman for whom I later felt great compassion because I saw that her intense anger quite possibly came from frustration about her own unlived sexuality. There were the single women who could have been bitter about their fourth-class status in the missionary world but instead showed kindness to me and to other students they ministered to.

Those people I lost were all white. The story was different with Navajo Christians. Although I saw them just as infrequently, when I did see them, great delight passed between us—no holding back. There was Ella Descheeny who gave me my Diné name. There was John Tsosie who comforted me at the funerals of my sister and my father. There were people from the chapels at Teec Nos Pos and Tohlakai. There were people with whom I had attended the mission school. There were colleagues I had worked with in the Navajo bilingual education movement. They always welcome me without reservation, regardless of whatever stories they might have heard about me. My Diné friends were not part of the loss I needed to grieve.

On that Saturday, still under the covers, I laid aside Rachel's book and wept for the people and the church and the mission—the life that was gone from me.

Maybe the tears will never be completely spent, and certainly no love can be quite so deep, so innocent, so much a part of me as those first loves. But when I was done with crying on Panic Saturday, I thought of people at St. Andrew for whom I felt great tenderness. They were the ones I especially looked for when we walked around the sanctuary for the Passing of the Peace. They were the ones I talked with after services.

I realized too that I was different at St. Andrew from how I am in most settings—friendlier, more outgoing, less hesitant to show myself, reaching out to others who seemed to need a moment of kindness. I acted there as if I already belonged. I liked myself this way, and I felt that the warmth that infuses St. Andrew had produced a transformation in me.

I stayed under the covers reading, and I came to a story that was about Rachel herself, not one of her patients (she is a physician). Interestingly, the story was titled "Going Home." She told about being part of a research program for medical professionals at Esalen in Big Sur, California. There she was exposed to ideas calling into question so much of the status quo in medicine, so much of what she had been taught, that she wanted to run away. The program director asked her first to do an exercise in which she closed her eyes and opened to an image of what she was feeling. When she interpreted what she saw, she was able to stay with the program and eventually become the healer that she is today.

I decided to try the exercise. The image that came to me immediately, not too surprisingly, was a cross. On the heels of that image came the understanding that the cross represented a crossroads for me. And with that knowledge came a shift. It did not mean I was back on track to reaffirm my faith. But it did release me from the panic-induced paralysis to know that I would continue to examine the place where the crosspieces met. I still felt I needed a break from church.

The next morning, early, as I often do on Sunday mornings, I met for breakfast with my friend Paula, who happens to be a former nun. Then, without anxiety, without planning to, I went to church. Afterward, I couldn't help feeling that it was meant to be. On that Sunday, a guest preacher helped return me to a love for the gospel according to John, helped me understand John's version of Jesus better.

After the service, I hung out for an unprecedented hour talking with Fonda, my Dutch American friend and fellow school counselor. We exchanged stories about our common heritage, which we had done often. A white-haired woman pushing a walker stopped to chat with us and mentioned that she had taught at the Presbyterian boarding school, Wasatch Academy, in Utah. That was another connection for me because I knew CRC missionaries who had sent their teen-agers there before Rehoboth had a high school. Nancy now volunteered in the New Mexico Presbyterian historical archives, and I promised to visit her there some Wednesday because I find local history so fascinating. Another woman stopped by to say she hoped the other two were trying to get me to come to women's Bible study, which I politely declined.

Fonda and I stayed talking when the others moved on. She mentioned a nephew who she's sure is gay, a young man who lives in an extremely conservative, homophobic home. Then I made my second unplanned move of the day and told her about Panic Saturday. She listened with compassion and reminded me that I could be part of the St. Andrew fellowship without becoming a member. She said too that she would pray for me in the week and a half leading up to my meeting with the Session.

I still couldn't articulate why I had thought I wanted to become a member at St. Andrew, but Fonda's words clarified one thing: I didn't want halfway measures. I was at the point of all or nothing. The fact that she would be praying for me was a comfort.

⋆ ⋆ ⋆

In fiction writing, a device known as *deus ex machina* is much disparaged. The stratagem is a hallmark of lazy writing in which a problem is solved not by the agency of a character but through fate or divine intervention. A favorite maneuver is the killing off of characters not to further the story or explore issues of life and death but because the author could not come up with a more challenging and satisfying ending or solution to a problem.

A week after Panic Saturday, an event occurred that, if this were a work of fiction, would definitely be limned as *deus ex machina.* My heavy, metal security door slammed hard on my left Achilles tendon, which I had ruptured and then reruptured twenty years earlier. My skin turned purple and black within seconds. I iced it right away, but the pain was intense and the area around the tendon swelled. After a visit to urgent care and a specialist, I was consigned to crutches and one of those obnoxious black boots, and told to get an MRI to determine the extent of the damage. I felt physically and emotionally vulnerable. The injury became my perfect excuse to postpone the reaffirmation of my faith. In the back of my mind, I held open the option of sliding out of the sights of St. Andrew permanently. I knew I could screen calls and not answer emails from church members. But I couldn't do it without feeling shame.

I didn't do that. I answered calls and emails. I let Frank include me in Sunday prayers. Three weeks later, when the MRI results showed that my Achilles had not even partially ruptured, I was freed from crutches and the boot. I rescheduled my meeting with the Session and returned to church, having survived Panic Saturday.

~32~

Passage

THE CRC WAS THIN ON DRAMA. I THINK ONE REASON OUR church eschewed ritual was because it smacked too much of the dramatic—communion only four times a year, for instance, instead of what we thought of as the Catholic pomp and circumstance of daily mass. Ironically, by making it such an infrequent event, our church had increased the intensity of communion, at least for me. In the same way, there also was none of the splashiness of baptism by immersion that the Baptists were so fond of. We made do with lukewarm water sprinkled onto the forehead from a little silver sherbet dish.

When I was about seven or eight and my family still lived at Teec Nos Pos, the trader from Beclabito moved up to Durango, Colorado. He had become a Christian, in part through my parents' efforts, and when he was going to be baptized in a Baptist church, we drove up to witness it. Not only would we be attending a Baptist service but we also would be traveling a good distance on a Sunday, forbidden in those days lest we should participate in the work of a gas station attendant who would instantly become our manservant. That was how we interpreted the commandment to "Remember the Sabbath day, to keep it holy . . . the seventh day is the Sabbath of the Lord thy God: in it, thou shalt not do any work, thou, nor thy son, nor thy daughter, thy manservant, nor thy maidservant."

At the service, I watched with barely contained breath as the maroon velvet curtains to the rear of the pulpit opened. Behind a half-wall stood the pastor, still in his suit and tie, and George, wearing a white gown gathered at the neck like the ones Christmas choirboys wear. The pastor plunged George out of sight below the top of the wall to the sound of great sloshing and the familiar words, "I baptize thee in the name of the Father, the Son, and the Holy Ghost. Amen."

After the service, I begged to see the font, which turned out to be a disappointing cement trough with descending steps on one end. The minister's trousers had remained mysteriously dry, and he laughed when I asked about it. "I wear hip waders," he said. After the service, we went for a late night snack to George and Jean's house to fortify ourselves for the long drive home.

Captivated by the ceremony of it all, the next morning, I dressed my brothers and sister in bathrobes and proceeded to dunk them down to the living room floor, pronouncing the sacred words. My mother overheard me, and, using that Dutch word for mocking what is holy, admonished, "That's *spotten.*" To my surprise, though, she didn't forbid the baptisms. "You need to find different words," she said.

I began again. "I baptize thee in the name of Iggly Wiggly Piggly. Atah." I continued to baptize the other kids until they tired of their much less interesting roles.

⋆ ⋆ ⋆

Despite the CRC's view of it, I did like drama in a church service if it was to be had. In the late spring, when I hadn't yet talked with Frank but was considering membership at St. Andrew, I fell into my desire for a to-do. Around that time, I happened to drive up to Jemez Springs to meet a friend and soak in the hot springs. The drive there is always meditative, with its wide tapestry of blond mesas, blue-black mountains in the distance, and endless sky before you get to the village of San Ysidro. Afterward comes the fertile valley of Jemez Pueblo and then the great red canyon. The cottonwood leaves had burst forth in the shiny light green of new.

The possibility of joining St. Andrew was on my mind. All the way up to the springs, I listened to a CD of sacred songs recorded by my friend Paolo in both Italian and English, one of them about a return from wandering. Paolo has a sweet, clear voice, and he also sang his own version of "Jesus Loves Me" in both languages. I felt Paolo's love as he sang, and I imagined him singing at the service in which I would become a member. Soon I was choosing all the music for the service. One song I especially wanted to hear in what I was now thinking of as *my* service was this:

Softly and tenderly, Jesus is calling,
Calling for you and for me.
See o'er the portal, he's watching and waiting,
Waiting for you and for me.

Come home, come home.
Ye who are weary, come home.
Earnestly, tenderly, Jesus is calling,
Calling, Oh sinner, come home.

And then I had to laugh at my inner drama queen. I mean, I say that I'm not one, but she's there inside me—for sure. I knew, in fact, that the service wouldn't be anything like what I was imagining. I had seen new members join at the third Presbyterian church I'd visited during my experiment. The ceremony, if you could call it that, amounted to just an announcement, with the pastor warmly telling a bit about the new members. They happened to be refugees from Sudan, and obviously had a much more dramatic story than mine. This was one more way in which the Presbyterian Church was not too different from the Christian Reformed—not a whole lot of drama, although more. When it comes down to it, becoming part of a community is not all about me; it's about the community. The drama queen thing would have been about me.

⋆ ⋆ ⋆

We were approaching fall on a balmy evening when I parked in front of St. Andrew to meet with the Session at last. After Panic Saturday and the *deus ex machina* of my tendon injury, I'd made a decision to move forward and set my doubts aside, moving into just-say-yes mode. Sometimes taking action when I am in doubt removes uncertainty.

Before I read the statement I'd prepared, I mentioned to the Session how I'd come before the elders in another church in the Reformed tradition when I was thirteen, to profess my faith. "I feel like I'm coming full circle tonight," I said. "Only then, the elders were all men. It's affirming that there are women present here."

There were other differences. My age made me feel more equal than the time before. I was also pretty certain that this process was not a test I had to pass, that I had already been accepted by this fellowship. It was more of a self-imposed test, one of the final proofs of my hypothesis.

More than fifty years earlier, I had walked into a room where the thirteen men were already seated around that massive table. In my mind's eye, they are all wearing black suits, white shirts and black ties, though I doubt that was the reality. On this evening, I saw plaid shirts, print blouses, jeans, and capris.

I didn't think I was nervous; my hands were warm until it came time to speak. I explained that I'd written something because I find it hard to talk about myself in a group. Then my voice went all raspy and wouldn't clear, so I read it as if through a scraper. I saw people nodding, being attentive, and I heard some affirming vocalizations now and then. The group did not have any questions for me. Frank asked me, "Do you want to be a member of St. Andrew Presbyterian Church?"

"Yes."

Everyone around the table clapped. Then he talked about what he hoped I would contribute to the community.

"I wanted to join in part to serve," I said.

And that was that. Frank hugged me, and so did Joe, the outreach elder, who then walked me to the front door. I went out to my pickup in the falling dusk. If I'd been expecting anything different, the meeting would have been anticlimactic.

That was Tuesday. Before Sunday, when Frank would announce to the congregation that I had become a member, I needed to do something for myself to ritualize the step I was taking. I know for a fact that other members of St. Andrew have been on similar journeys and returned from exile. But without knowing me well, people couldn't possibly know the magnitude of the step I was taking; I needed to acknowledge its importance to myself.

I wanted a baptism of sorts—a washing, a cleansing and closing of the past. I wanted to demarcate the end of my years of wandering from this new beginning. If I had converted to Judaism, part of the ceremony would have been a ritual bath in a *mikvah.* I considered the privacy of the bathhouse in Jemez rather than one of the outdoor springs where others might be partaking of the waters and talking. But my schedule that week didn't allow time for the drive.

My nephew Joshua had served as a missionary in Tibet for five years. He returned to the States so altered by the experience that he left his mission organization and church. He had continued on a path of learning from spiritual traditions other than Christian, much as I had. It has been my privilege to walk this part of the journey with him, sharing ideas, books, and love. The same Tuesday I went before the elders, Josh sent me a surprise gift: an album called *Beyond: Buddhist and Christian Prayers,* performed by Josh's favorite Tibetan singer, Dechen Shak-Dagsay, with Regula Curti and Tina Turner, who has long been a practicing Buddhist.

All those years ago, I had baptized my brothers and sister. Now I decided that I would baptize myself. I set up speakers and ran a bath with olive and lavender oils, lay back and listened to the nurturing meditative prayers and chants blending the two traditions. The timing of Josh's present was perfect, unbeknownst to him. It helped me honor how I've learned and will continue to learn from many traditions as I committed myself once more to following the faith tradition in which I'd grown up.

After the bath, I did one more thing to commemorate the meaning of this step for myself and also to share it with others from my new community. I singled out six individuals or couples who had been especially helpful in welcoming me to St. Andrew, assisting me with learning the ropes and coming to this decision. I hand-made note cards and wrote thank-yous to each, telling them how they had been part of my journey.

I found out that St. Andrew does a little more than that other Presbyterian church did during the new-member announcement. First of all, instead of saving it until the end of the service, Frank made the announcement just before the Passing of the Peace, so lots of welcomes could be offered, and they were. I also received a basket stocked with symbolic gifts—among them a loaf of bread to remind me of the Bread of Life and a candle that stood for the admonishment to be a light to the world.

I had to go up to the front of the church to be welcomed and receive my basket. Being on display, so to speak, made me nervous enough that I couldn't feel much else. However, right at the beginning, when Frank spoke his words of welcome, my eyes filled with tears, affirming for me once again that this was a step I needed to take. That I was coming home—home not to the CRC in Teec Nos Pos or Tohlakai or Rehoboth but to my new, "same, same but different" home: St. Andrew Presbyterian.

A small, unremarkable action that I took just before the service on the day I joined finally answered the question I'd been asking myself for the previous nine months: "Why am I doing this?" The answer could not have been simpler.

On one of the chairs in every row in the sanctuary lies a brown vinyl folder. Inside it is a pad in which each person in attendance can write her or his name, address, and phone number. Next to the name are three columns labeled *visitor, friend,* and *member.* In the beginning, I checked the visitor column. At some point, maybe after the first time I met with Frank, I started marking *friend*—not a significant enough shift for me to have noted when it happened.

On this Sunday, I checked the *member* column. I had crossed the threshold of my new home. That was when I received the answer to my perpetual question. I was doing this for a very plain reason: I wanted to belong.

The Latin root of the word *religion* is *religare* meaning *to bind together.* Binding can be restrictive, and that was how I bore it as a young person needing to come out, just as foot binding in Chinese culture was tragically, painfully constrictive. On the other hand, mothers in many traditional cultures, including the Diné, swaddle their babies to provide a sense of security and offer muscle strengthening through isometric movement against the binding.

As I joined St. Andrew Presbyterian Church, I was not binding myself only to this group of Christians. I was still bound as well to that group of missionaries, Diné and Dutch, with whom I'd known my first taste of the Love that is God. I will always be bound to them, sometimes liking it, sometimes not. At St. Andrew, I was rebinding myself to people around the world who claim Christianity as their religion.

Being bound reminds me of Chaucer's Canterbury pilgrims, a flawed group if ever there was one. As they traveled along, they could find their close association irritating, but they also enjoyed safety in numbers and the gift of entertainment as their fellow pilgrims unfolded their tales.

In my forty years of exile, I was mostly a lone wanderer. As I progressed on my solitary journey, my path often crossed the paths of other pilgrims, some solitary like me, some attached to faith communities. Our crossings offered rich sharing and learning. Some of those pilgrims remain an ongoing part of my spiritual network—women and men from around the world and many different faiths, people with whom I hope to always be able to share succor. These relationships continue to be important to me, maybe especially because they represent points of contact so essential to a lone traveler. During one service at St. Andrew, the verse, "My grace is sufficient for you" turned up in the liturgy. I realized that these spiritual points of contact along my journey all represented grace that had been enough for me, that I had been watched over all along my way.

When I checked off *member* on my membership Sunday, I had no doubt that I had cast my lot with the St. Andrew group of pilgrims. I was committing myself for better and for worse. In some areas of my life, I haven't been that good at commitment—intimate relationships, longevity in jobs, and places I've lived. I have stuck to my work as a writer, and I've no doubt been best at commitment in the role of a mother. I have learned in my relationship with my daughter that staying through the rough times brings the deepest rewards. Childhood illnesses and problems and situations calling for consequences are the times of strong bonding.

I suspect if I show up for the tough times that are bound to occur at St. Andrew, I will grow as a person and also feel more a part of this faith community. I have already been entertained by some of my fellow pilgrims, not with the bawdy tales of those folks en route to Canterbury but with stories of their own faith journeys.

Belonging at St. Andrew is not only about being part of this local gathering but also about claiming kinship with something bigger, something with a history that reaches back through the ages. In *Kitchen Table Wisdom,* Auntie Rachel tells the story of a young woman who had not been brought up as an observant Jew. She was to prepare the Seder meal for her Orthodox boyfriend and forty of their friends. She found herself with four sets of dishes, completely overwhelmed by what she should do with them, where to put things. Suddenly, she was struck by a vision of the women before her who had shared in this dilemma—her friend's mother, her own grandmothers, women in Eastern Europe, in Israel, in Babylon, women in mansions, women in tents and caves. From that vision of preparation and celebration far bigger and older than herself, she drew a tremendous sense of belonging and also the strength she needed to continue her preparations.

The something bigger than me is the Presbyterian Church, the Reformed faith, the Church Universal, the Jewish faith, the people I see driving to church on Sundays, to temple on Friday evenings, people I know who sit in the tepees of the Native American Church. We are all part of that great cloud of witnesses with whom I cast my lot when I joined St. Andrew. We all bear witness to the law that says that the Whole is greater than the sum of its parts. Every Sunday at St. Andrew, after a confession of sin and assurance of pardon, we sing a short *"Kyrie Eleison,"* Greek for *Lord, have mercy.* It is a very old part of the Christian liturgy—Eastern, Catholic, and Protestant—and this too reminds me that I have rejoined something much larger than the small congregation that worships across from my library.

I am glad to be part of something bigger, but it's still hard for me to say that I'm a Christian, with all the baggage that that entails. In fact, I rarely say it. But I do try to keep Dorothy Day—who was a passionate Roman Catholic, a Christian anarchist, and a servant of the poor—in mind. She is my model for sojourning with an all-too-human group of pilgrims, a woman who saw the many flaws of her church, especially the wealth of its princes, yet remained committed to being part of it. I can also take Jesus as my model. The people closest to him were just as human as the Christian Church today—squabbling about who was the greatest, failing to understand Jesus's ministry, unable to be true friends when the chips were down. But Jesus didn't give up on them, as the story goes.

~ 33 ~

The Silver Cup

When I lived in Copenhagen, Hermy, a Dutch friend from the Netherlands, had an expression I'd never heard from my Dutch kinfolk in the U.S. She often talked about making a thing round. She was referring to finishing something in a harmonious way, bringing things full circle.

Joining St. Andrew made several things round for me. The most dramatic, one of those events that would strain credibility in a work of fiction, was a second-hand reconnection with Jennie—Jennie of Jennie and Alice, Jennie of that watershed day in my sixteen-year-old life.

It happened the Sunday before I became a member. Fonda wanted to introduce me to her sister, who was visiting from Michigan. We started right away to play Dutch bingo—who do you know that I know? We got to talking about Rehoboth, and Fonda's sister said they had a cousin who'd been a nurse at Rehoboth. "But it was a long time ago."

"What was her name?" I asked.

"Jennie De Vries."

It's a wonder my heart didn't leap out of my chest. I didn't even blink when I said, "I knew her. She was only a few years older than I was. I was a junior and senior in high school when she was at Rehoboth."

The sisters didn't seem to think it was odd that I could place her so specifically within my own timeline, and I could tell from their expressions that it was highly unlikely they knew much about Jennie's time at Rehoboth, including the fact that she'd been asked to leave—certainly not the reason for her being sent away. I've always wondered what happened to her after the last time I saw her and Alice in the supermarket. Indirectly, she had played such a pivotal role in my life.

Alice's family had homes in a ponderosa pine forest off the road between Gallup and Zuni. On and off over the years, I wondered if the two women lived in a hogan or a cabin out there in the security of isolation. It's what I imagined for them. Once, in a Native arts and crafts magazine, I saw a photo of Alice working as a silversmith, so I knew a little about her life after that night. I speculated as to whether the two were still together.

Now Fonda's sister supplied a piece of the answer. Jennie had come back to Michigan at some point, married, and lived for the past many years with her husband in Texas. I didn't get the impression that Fonda and her sister had ever been close with Jennie, nor that her comings and goings were in any way unusual or significant to them.

I was so taken aback by this incidental encounter, that I emailed some friends who knew my story. One of them thought I should contact Jennie, tell her about her role in my young life, and give her the opportunity to tell her story. "I never question synchronicity," Monica wrote.

I don't question synchronicity myself. I do ask what I'm meant to take from it or do with it. I haven't ruled out the possibility of one day contacting Jennie. But I think back to how closed she and Alice were when they came through my check stand that night. I think about how unaware her cousins seemed to be about that slice of her life. I felt I needed to respect Jennie's apparent choices. For now, the purpose of this indirect meeting with her is simply about closing that circle, making Jennie's and my connection round, as Hermy would say. I take meaning too from the fact that this rounding took place at St. Andrew through Fonda, who first told me about the church. And that is enough.

* * *

In another circling around, I am reminded that my father groomed me to become a Bible woman, someone who passed on the Church's standards of living in God's presence. He encouraged me to ask questions, to probe for understanding, though always within that received framework. He wanted me to fulfill the Calvinistic role of priest within acceptable guidelines for a woman—teaching Sunday school, leading ladies aid societies, witnessing door-to-door. This is what it means to be a priest—to perpetuate the status quo within a religion.

I did not become a Bible woman. I did become a spiritual seeker, questioning and questing, though most of the time outside my father's and the church's framework. I think that even though St. Andrew is not the Presbyterian brand my dad favored—he would call it by that anathema *liberal,* while I would say *progressive*—he would have been glad I joined a church of the Reformed faith.

I sent my mother a note the Monday after what I've lightly thought of as my swearing in. I told her I'd been attending St. Andrew for about nine months and had become a member. I also said I knew St. Andrew wasn't within the Presbyterian branch she would prefer. She sent me a gracious reply. Perhaps her words even spoke for my deceased father, but more peaceably than he might have put things. She wrote, "I know you'll be a blessing there and that you'll be blessed and also find some good friends." My mother and I have come a long way together since that Sunday when I was sixteen.

* * *

When I was in college, I worked summers at the mission hospital. I stayed in the nurses' lodge with several other women on the hospital staff. I often worked nights and got to know some of the RNs well because in that small hospital, only two of us at a time worked the night shift. One of them was Hattie Veurink. Hattie destroyed many of the stereotypes of a Dutch Christian Reformed village girl of her era from small-town Minnesota. She drove a VW camper van and took herself on mini-retreats on her days off. She was an upcycler long before recycling and upcycling became popular. She liked to listen to and absorb ideas from younger people. Miss Hartgerink, who had introduced me to mysticism, also introduced Hattie to it, and Hattie had embraced it. Other nurses sometimes poked fun at her for her eccentricity and the spiritual preoccupations that sometimes caused her to make mistakes at the hospital.

I liked Hattie and found her openness to be a sort of refuge, though I held some things close to my chest when I was with her, particularly my sexuality. The summer before I left for Boston, I read a fictionalized life of the prophet Jeremiah. One evening, the two of us stood in the living room of the nurses' lodge watching the sky turn from blue to orange to mauve to gold and coral. I told Hattie about Jeremiah's encounter with the flowering almond branch. Then I confided, "Hattie, I want to be a prophet."

Caught up in the idea, she responded, "Maybe you will. Maybe you will."

A prophet is not a purveyor of received wisdom, of orthodox thinking in the way that a priest is. A prophet's voice resounds from the wilderness, from lessons learned while wandering. Hattie, is one of those people, recently passed on, that I wish I could sit down and talk with, to say, "Maybe, just maybe, I can say I've come full circle with this too."

Who can claim to be a prophet without immediately engendering scorn, especially from her own people, the ones who know her? But if a prophet is a voice from the outback, if a prophet does point out a different way, another way back home, then maybe I can say that this is another completed circle.

I can't help thinking of my dreams in connection with the idea of being a prophet—the dream of tossing a ball of light with like-minded people in orange robes. Perhaps the members of St. Andrew are some of those robed light catchers. Or the dream of leading a service in the old Rehoboth church.

* * *

For many years, I lived with depression as a fact of daily life, at times receiving treatment from mental health professionals. Now when it strikes me, which is seldom, it usually takes several days, occasionally weeks, for me to admit to myself that I might possibly be depressed. By the Friday after I became a St. Andrew member, I was feeling heavy inside, as if I were drowning in unshed tears. Saturday night brought a gorgeous, full harvest moon, and whether that had anything to do with it or not, I got only two hours of poor sleep. Sunday morning, I admitted I was depressed. I used the depression, lack of sleep, and feeling overwhelmed to decide that I wasn't going to church. Then I tried to figure out what was causing my emotional state.

Naturally, I wondered if the commitment I'd made to St. Andrew the week before could be the main cause. Even though Joe, the outreach elder, had told me the previous Sunday that 90 percent of St. Andrew members probably agreed with my reframing of the Apostles Creed, my early training—that to be a Christian and a church member, I must *believe*—clearly went deep. I had been upfront about what I did and did not believe, but I still couldn't shake the unsettling feeling that because of my lack of belief in that one thing—Jesus's blood atoning for my sins—I was a fake.

On top of thinking I had joined disingenuously, I felt guilty for skipping out on church that morning. Here I was, a freshly minted member, absent. People would be looking for me, expecting me, and I wouldn't be there. I started wishing I hadn't joined. After all, a certain amount of obligation goes with commitment to a community. At the very least, one should show up.

I moved through that Sunday without getting rid of the heavy, waterlogged feeling. Monday evening I cried all the way through bingeing on seven episodes of *M★A★S★H,* the '70s TV show. Yes, there are many moving scenes, often delivered with dark comedy and profound commentary on the human condition, especially about love and war. I often shed a few tears when I watch the show, but this was a deluge, and it didn't depend on anyone's lines. These tears were about washing out my depression and the grief that lay beneath it.

When the tears were spent, I realized that I still grieved the old—the faith community I'd lost, while I was glad to be free of its narrowness. I missed the individuals I'd loved and who had loved me. I grieved not only the lack of compassion for me and anyone else who didn't meet the right criteria for belonging but also for community members' inability to be gentle with themselves.

I grieved simpler things—those long wilderness Sundays in which I was free to do whatever nurtured me—or didn't—no questions asked by me or anyone else. Somewhat to my surprise, I also missed the romance of questing that had been the hallmark of the past forty years. I do not mean to say that I won't go on questioning, but the quest for a faith community seemed to be done. I recognized too that for me, there would always be tension between my need for solitude and my need for community. It would probably always be necessary for my spiritual and emotional wellbeing for me to take the occasional Sunday for myself.

I couldn't help wondering if I was giving too much place to grief. And then I found comfort in these words by Anne Lamott:

> All those years, I fell for the great palace lie that grief should be gotten over as quickly as possible and as privately. But what I've discovered since is that the lifelong fear of grief keeps us in a barren, isolated place, and that only grieving can heal grief; the passage of time will lessen the acuteness, but time alone, without the direct experience of grief, will not heal it.

When I'd gone through this surge of mourning and making meaning of it, I began to look forward to the next Sunday, the first Sunday of the month, which is communion Sunday. It would be my first communion as a member of St. Andrew. It turned out to be World Communion Sunday, when Christians around the world note that through communion, we are in relationship with one another. It affirmed my belonging to something much bigger and older than St. Andrew—belonging to a group with diverse beliefs, practices, nationalities, races, and continents, sharing communion through the young rabbi who was one of God's great messengers of compassion and inclusion.

I felt different on this Sunday at St. Andrew—that I was settling in with this group of people. I had lost some of the self-consciousness that comes with having lived a solitary life. My contemplation during the silences was deeper, more present, less focused on ego. As I watched people wend their way up to the altar, I had the sense of a long line of people practicing an ancient ritual, a love feast. When I stood to receive my chunk of bread and dip it in the juice, I was as conscious of the presence of my fellow communicants as I was of myself. I didn't think it then, but now I see: This *is* communion—more awareness of the connection with others than of oneself. It is the communion I longed for all those years as a girl, waiting to be allowed to pass the test. When I pinched off my piece of bread from the loaf, the server, not someone I knew but who knew me from seeing me at the front two Sundays earlier, used my name. She said "The life of Christ for you, Anna." One more moment of coming in from the cold.

I returned to my seat and watched others as they walked back from the communion table—elders bent over their walkers, children with sparkling eyes, friends looking serious and friends with slight smiles, people from the neighborhood who live in the margins during the week and partake of community at St. Andrew on Sundays. I watched people chewing their bread, deep in thought, solemn. I noticed how one chewed with large jaw motions, another so delicately that she must nearly be chewing on nothing. And I wondered if this wasn't part of why I love communion so much; it is so very basic, so very human, this remembrance of Jesus in one of his most human moments, and we the participants communing at our most basic—eating, nurturing ourselves, and sharing that fact with one another.

The communion cups at St. Andrew are ceramic, big and thick. We don't drink from them. We dip our bite-sized chunks of bread into them. But as I dipped my bread, I couldn't help thinking of "Lonely People," the '70s song by Dan and Catherine Peek. Dan's group, America, sang for us, the ones who had been shut out. They sang for us who feared that communion with others had passed us by. They urged, "Don't give up until you drink from the silver cup."

Throughout my experiment, I had probed for complex answers about why I was doing this. It turned out that all I really wanted was to belong. It was about being a part of something bigger than me, something with a history—my history but also a history that reaches far, far back beyond me. It was about being related to that artist who painted a picture of the pan-pipe-playing Jesus on the catacomb walls. It was about belonging to a gathering of humans and sticking with them for better and for worse because we are learning together how to be the face of God in the world. It was about standing at the foot of those great, splendorous red rock waves, breaking bread with others and singing "Blest Be the Tie That Binds." I had endured until I could drink from the silver cup.

Epilogue

NEARLY FOUR YEARS AFTER I FIRST WALKED THROUGH THE doors of St. Andrew, I still attended there most Sundays. I joined the Social Justice Committee—still called then by its old name, the Mission Committee. I found it ironic that this would be the first committee on which I would serve at St. Andrew. A few short months after I became a member, I was asked to be a deacon. In the Presbyterian Church, deacons are like shepherds, caring for the flock in times of sickness and other needs, organizing greeters and people to serve meals at Project Share, that sort of thing. I probably had the heart and skills to be a deacon, but I was planning to move away from Albuquerque quite soon. When I decided to stay, I was asked to be on the committee that nominates people for deacon and elder positions. Then I was asked to be on the committee to select an interim pastor in anticipation of Frank's approaching retirement. New blood is highly appreciated and put into service at St. Andrew.

On and off, I still went through those Saturday night bouts of asking myself why I was doing this. Sometimes I felt hypocritical and hollow because I didn't believe Jesus had died to save me from my sins. And I didn't believe *that* because I didn't believe the Bible was authoritative; instead, I thought of it as inspirational and instructive. I knew too many people who would say, "What's left to believe if the Bible isn't God's word?" And I would come back to only being able to say along with those ancient folks, "I am a follower of the Way. I don't pretend to be anything else."

Then along the way, I became friends with a retired minister who attends St. Andrew. Catherine willingly and with a sense of humor engaged in discussions with me as I continued to grapple with my deeper questions. She offered fresh perspectives from a long personal history with the Presbyterian Church. I began to see even more clearly than before how different it was from the CRC.

When Catherine understood how I felt about the Bible, aside from the issue of authority—how much I loved it, had continued even during my wanderings to learn from it, that it touched me in a way no other scriptures did—she wrote me, "Because of all that, because you opened your heart to the Bible and to the people in it, because it won't let you go ... buckle your seatbelt, because I am about to say something that you may not like . . . the Bible has some authority in your life. That doesn't mean that it is inerrant or that it is the authority for your Islamic neighbor or that we beat people over the head with it. It just means that it has deep lasting power for us and that we turn to it over and over and over again for sustenance and strength. That's a lot of what the authority of scripture means to many of us . . . at least, what it means to me."

Those words settled into me like a smooth, oval stone sliding into still water, water that was ready and waiting to receive it, to let it ride to the lakebed. Oh yes, I return to it over and over and over again for sustenance. Yes, it has deep and lasting power for me. Of course that means that it has some authority in my life. This put a whole different light on the concept of *authority,* a much more nurturing meaning, one that placed the Bible before me as something alive, waiting to be searched and fathomed for my growth.

* * *

I've heard people call those who attend church only on Christmas and Easter *Cheaster churchgoers.* I have always loved Christmas and happily attended those ecclesiastical celebrations, but on my first two opportunities at St. Andrew, I skipped church on Easter. I wasn't at all sure I would go on my third chance. I don't have trouble believing in the possibility of resurrection. There are yogis reported to have risen from the dead. There is D.H. Lawrence's explanation of Jesus's resurrection in *The Man Who Died*. There is the idea that the resurrection is symbolic of new life, especially as its celebration comes with spring.

But part and parcel of Easter in the evangelical world is the belief that Jesus died to save us from our sins. Although St. Andrew was not an evangelical church, the teaching that I must embrace that fundamental belief was so deeply ingrained that I found it difficult to celebrate Jesus's resurrection. On my third St. Andrew Easter, I got all caught up in needing something new and springy to wear, which had never been a concern before, even growing up. In the end, I went, wearing something not at all springy and definitely not new.

It had rained the night before, and drops of water on the grass and long-needled pines in the park across from the church sparkled in the bright sun. I took a short walk around the park, breathing deeply the scent of the fresh-washed ponderosas. Thus fortified, I walked into church and was assailed by the heady smell of Easter lilies bringing with it memories of Easters past. The sanctuary was filled with infectious joy.

The sermon that day was a choir cantata that began with an invitation to see in Jesus's mercy a portrait of his grace. Moved, I thought, "This is what following Jesus means—being merciful and gracious, sacrificing for others, especially for the ungracious and unmerciful because they are the most in need of grace."

After the cantata, Frank read from the gospel of Matthew, "Now the eleven disciples went to Galilee, to the mountain to which Jesus had directed them. When they saw him, they worshipped him; but some doubted."

We *thought* the cantata was the sermon, but Frank could not resist giving a teeny one himself, and we chuckled as he launched into it. In that short discourse, he gave me the takeaway of the day, perhaps the takeaway of the year. "Some of us standing here today" Frank said, "are believers. Some of us are doubters. But we don't stand here and throw the doubters under the bus."

Involuntarily, I did a fist pump and whispered, "Yes!"

* * *

Shortly after Easter, Frank would be retiring. Then it would be up to the two elders in charge of worship to make sure the pulpit was filled from week to week. One Sunday a couple of weeks before Frank's departure, Bill, one of the worship elders, casually asked me, "Have you ever gone to seminary?"

I chuckled and said, "I might as well have." Then I explained, "Growing up, we read the Bible and discussed it after every meal and before going to bed. In high school, I took Reformed Doctrine and Church History. In college, I studied Old and New Testament Theology, Reformed Doctrine, and Calvin's *Institutes.*" Then I said, "You know how 'Red or green?' [referring to chile] is the New Mexico question?"

The elder nodded.

"Our family question was, 'When are you going to seminary?' Except they never asked me because I was a woman and a lesbian." I found that humorous at this point in my life, but Bill seemed to take it rather seriously.

His next question was a shocker. "Would you like to preach some Sunday?"

Completely taken aback, heart pounding, I could only emit a squeaky, "No."

"Not even about Viktor Frankl?" Bill asked.

Most people in the church knew I'd written a biography of Frankl because Frank had mentioned it when I stood in front of the congregation to have my membership announced. I had also done a Q&A on the book with the Women's Book

Group. But who would preach on a subject like Viktor Frankl? Sermons are supposed to be based on the Bible. Aren't they? They were in my CRC world. They are in the Presbyterian Church too, for that matter.

"Maybe," I said. I dropped my head, full of reticence. My stomach clenched. Feeling that mere politeness required it, I said, "Thank you for asking. I'll think about it." I didn't see this as an honor or even as a call to service. I found it weird that I would be asked, and I expected that to be the end of it. I didn't know that St. Andrew had a long tradition of asking its lay members to preach.

The next Sunday, I stopped by the church office before the service to put a couple of books that Frank had loaned me in his box. The act was symbolic of a farewell to someone who had helped me find my way into St. Andrew, who always greeted me as though seeing me brought him real joy, a friend and a scholar with whom I could carry on precious discussions about the Bible.

As I turned to leave the office, the other worship elder and I nearly collided. I should have known, as collaborative as things are at St. Andrew, that she would have been part of the decision to ask me to preach. Janet is undeniably the most genuinely enthusiastic person I know. "I really hope you decide to preach for us," she said.

My eyes widened. I had been giving the possibility some thought during the week. "I have reservations," I told her. "I was thinking I might ask Bill if I could talk with him face-to-face, but maybe I could meet with you."

"Absolutely. Let's email about a time."

A few days later, we met for tea. I talked about my main reservations: "I'm not really very good at public speaking. Plus, I am a doubter."

Janet chuckled. "I wouldn't want to hear a sermon from anyone who didn't have some doubts," she said.

"Okay," I said, "so what parts of the service would I be expected to perform? I mean, I don't pray aloud—just as an example."

"You can do as much or as little of the rest of the service as you want to," she said. "One of the pastors can take care of anything you don't want to do."

I reluctantly agreed to speak. "But I can't call it *preaching,"* I said, "and I'll only offer the message, not the other parts of the service." Everything I laid out was fine with Janet, and we went on to talk about other aspects of our lives.

I did bring the message a few weeks later, though I still hadn't gotten to the place of saying I was preaching. My talk brought together the stories of Esther from the Old Testament and Viktor Frankl from the Holocaust with a little Rumi and Joseph in Egypt thrown in (Appendix C). I couldn't help reflecting that in a sense, I had fulfilled my father's wishes for me. I didn't become a Bible woman, and he probably would not have been pleased that as a woman, I was "preaching" in church. But things had, in some sense, come full circle.

★ ★ ★

I have accepted that I will probably always move between doubt and belief when it comes to the Church's creeds. Sometimes the waves of doubt will be so large as to create crisis—but this offers an opportunity to deepen my faith, to plunge beneath the waves. I have also come to see that, regardless of how the Protestant Church emphasizes belief, I have taken on Christianity—following the life and teachings of Jesus—as my spiritual practice. It's rather simple when I keep my eyes on that.

In fact, I have gone through a few crises since joining St. Andrew. The biggest one occurred when I withdrew from taking a leadership position as an elder. During training for the position, I realized that there were two essential questions I could not answer in the affirmative before the congregation. Deeply discouraged, I began to doubt that there was any reason for me to stay connected with this communion of Christ in any way. Several members met with me to share their own experiences of doubt and how they had resolved them. One of the retired ministers and I had some enlightening conversations about my theological sticking points. Nevertheless, a few months after the crisis had flattened into mere uneasiness, I planned a trip of about five months' duration. Secretly I thought, "During this time I can quietly slip away without anyone noticing. If that's what I choose."

However, by the third Sunday of my trip, I actively missed people from the church. Beyond that—and this surprised me—I missed the church service, missed being there. Once more, I accepted, "For better and worse, these are the people I am journeying with."

The elder training session made me realize that the Presbyterian Church is strongly centered on creeds—belief—and not so much on the mystical path. Recognizing the relative absence of the mystical at St. Andrew, I also identified for myself, possibly for the first time, that I am a mystic. There is a hymn that goes, "There is a place of quiet rest/Near to the heart of God." Meditation, the mystical path, takes me to that place of quiet rest. It is about my direct relationship with God, a heart-to-heart relationship. I wanted St. Andrew to be a place where I could slip into that quiet rest that took me to the heart of God, and that did happen occasionally—when I made a conscious effort in that direction. However, I began to accept that church is about relationship with God through people and through a more-active approach, not a receptive one.

In my counseling practice, I often saw couples in which one or both members expected all their emotional needs to be met by their partner. This unrealistic hope put tremendous pressure on the relationship, which then threatened to implode. I had acknowledged early on that there was an ebb and flow to my relationship with St. Andrew. As I worked my way through this crisis, I began to understand that the St. Andrew community could not meet all of my spiritual needs. My personal practice would always be essential. One of my friends at St. Andrew, an ordained but not active Methodist minister, participates in a Buddhist community besides attending church. Like him, I might want to add a meditative community to my participation at St. Andrew. I may be taking up another search, acknowledging that the friend who suggested I would always be a seeker might be right.

* * *

It happened around my one-year anniversary at St. Andrew that Jan, the woman who had so generously shared with me the story of her faith journey and answered my questions about the church's quirks, died quite suddenly. I knew that she was gifted in many areas, but at her memorial, I learned of multiple talents I hadn't been aware of. I knew too that I wasn't the only one she had touched so deeply, but I got a glimpse that day of her profound and far-reaching influence in the lives of the St. Andrew community and the world at large.

The entire service was a celebration of Jan's life, including recordings of her singing in her operatically trained voice. The last song our packed sanctuary sang was "I'll Fly Away." The piano introduction was full of energy and spilling notes. We started singing, and suddenly several members lofted tambourines, rattles, and clappers. One woman, a close friend of Jan's, danced down the aisle and up to the front. I started to cry—hard. Some tears were for how I would miss Jan and how I wished I'd had a chance to say goodbye face-to-face, to tell her how much she'd meant to me. All over the church, people began hugging each other. Mostly, I cried for the privilege of being part of this group of Christians that could so fully, so meaningfully celebrate life—people who could mourn together and rejoice together. I wept in gratitude for communion.

* * *

A momentous event took place during my second year of membership at St. Andrew. Once a year, churches in the PCUSA send delegates to a national decision-making body, the General Assembly. After the Supreme Court ruling in 2013 that the Defense of Marriage Act was unconstitutional, eighteen states had made same-sex marriage legal. In 2014, St. Andrew and some other churches brought an overture to the General Assembly requesting that pastors be allowed, according to their consciences, to marry same-sex couples in states where it was legal. The overture passed with a large majority, making the PCUSA the nation's largest mainstream denomination to allow same-sex marriages. With pride and joy, I posted on a social media site, "That's my church."

~Appendix A~
My Statement of Faith
(Sent to my family in June 2011)

ALTHOUGH I DIDN'T KNOW I WAS PREPARING FOR THE MOST important experiment of my life when I wrote what I called my *Statement of Faith,* it was an important step in resolving some of the conflict I'd had with my family. It did not necessarily resolve things for them, but it did for me. Before I would send anyone my Statement, I asked them to agree to the following guidelines.

Dear Family,

I've been aware for a long time that in our extended family, people avoid asking me about my spirituality. While that has been a relief in some ways because asking brings with it the potential for conflict rather than open sharing, avoidance brings with it tension and lack of intimacy. It's been sad for me not to feel comfortable sharing my spirituality in our family because it's such an important part of my life and yours. I would like to share my faith statement with you, but only if you can make the agreements outlined below.

1. If you agree, and I send you my statement, we may enter

into dialogue about it. The purpose of our dialogue will be to know and understand each other better and especially to understand one another's spirituality.

2. We will be open to each other in order to learn from each other.

3. We will really listen to each other and respond to what the other person says rather than what we assume they are saying and rather than waiting to make our own favorite speeches (probably writing in this case).

4. We will be honest and sincere and treat each other as equals as we speak and listen, not having a spirit of I-am-right-and-you-are-wrong, which is not an attitude of equality.

5. We will not make assumptions about where we agree or disagree.

6. We will work to find as many areas of agreement as possible.

7. We will be willing to examine our own beliefs critically as part of the process.

8. We will not make statements that denigrate what the other person believes.

9. You will not share my statement of faith with anyone who has not made these agreements with me. In other words, I will be the only one to send out my statement of faith.

If you can make these agreements, I'll be happy to send you my statement of faith as an attachment. It's five and a half pages, single-spaced and covers these topics: "Faith or What I Don't Know," "Belief," "God," "Names," "Me in Relationship with God," "The Bible," "Prayer," "Jesus," "Christ," "The Holy Spirit," "Religion," "Christianity," "Other Religions," "Proselytizing," "Life Mission," "Music and Ritual," "Sin," "Death," "Heaven and Hell." Please note that I have not sent this email to anyone who is under 18, and I may have missed some who are over 18. If you choose not to participate, I have no hard feelings. I'd like to engage with you spiritually, but I want it to be for creating intimacy and harmony, not to tear us further asunder.

The Statement

Faith or What I Don't Know

Faith is dynamic. As I grow in faith, some of my beliefs change. What I am about to set forth is what I believe now [2011]. Most of it I have believed for some time, so I don't expect it to change any time very soon, but as something dynamic, of course, it could change tomorrow.

What I don't know is as unquantifiable as the grains of sand in all Earth's deserts. But that, I think, is what faith is all about. If I knew everything there is to know about God and spirituality, I wouldn't need faith. If I had an answer to every question, the way catechisms seem to propose to do, I wouldn't need faith. If I had no doubts, faith would be meaningless—without doubt, no faith. It's like the way darkness is necessary for a candle to make light beyond just the sight of the flame when I'm looking right at it. I believe others can best know my faith less by what I say than what I do.

Belief

Christianity, quite possibly more than any other religion, emphasizes the necessity of belief. Redemption in Christianity is dependent upon belief. Judaism and Buddhism, on the other hand, are based on practice more than on belief. There's some talk about practice in Christianity—for example, "Faith without works is dead." But the core of the gospel message is that you believe. Islam may be that way too; I don't know enough about it to say.

The problem that can arise from belief is that people hold so tightly to a belief that 1) when contrary evidence is given, they can't be transformed and 2) even more serious for our world is the corollary—that people feel they must defend their beliefs. This can lead to conflict, violence, and oppression. Really, I think that faith must be more about trust than belief.

For a long time, I tried to only live a life of Spirit and not hold beliefs. I didn't want my beliefs to lead me to intolerance. Then I had to realize that, no matter how much I tried not to, I had beliefs. And I decided that I needed to know what they are, not so I could defend them but so I can share, exchange, know and be known.

God

I believe in God. A God far beyond my comprehension. A God I get to know in the tiniest of increments, and I haven't even begun to scratch the surface. The 26th chapter of Job says it so incredibly well, ending with the 14th verse: "Lo, these are but the outskirts of his ways; and how small a whisper do we hear of him! But the thunder of his power who can understand?" (RSV)

I do not think God is a person. I think God is a Presence, a powerful, active Presence of Love. I don't understand Love very well at all. If it's something to be understood. Even though I don't believe God is a person, I do most often personalize God because it's how I'm able to best connect with that Presence. Connect consciously, I mean, for I do believe I am connected all the time, just not very aware of the connection most of the time. I want to love God, but most of the time I don't really know how. I'm often surprised when people say they love God, because I think, "Boy, how do you do that?" Maybe wanting to love God is part of why I personalize God. As a Presence, I believe God is without gender, race, or ethnicity. I don't think God "minds" if we assign gender or other personal characteristics to God in the service of making contact as best we can, given our human frailties.

Names

The Danes have a saying that a loved child has many names. So maybe I love God more than I know, since I delight in many names for God, though I probably use *God* and *Goddess* the most. Some of the ones I love are: *The Holy One, Yod-HayVovHay* (Hebrew), Presence, *Source, Creator, El Elohim* (Hebrew), *Diyin* (Navajo), *Yahweh, El Shadai* (Hebrew), *Spirit, Love, Hashem* (Hebrew), *Adonai* (Hebrew).

Me in Relationship with God

I am always in relationship with God but not always aware of being in relationship. I believe this is true of all people and all sentient beings. I believe that since God is Love, and I am God's image-bearer, Love is also who I am and that my task on Earth is to actualize being Love. I'm not very good at it yet. God, of course, is communicating, reaching out, all the time. I just miss noticing, probably most of the time. But I think, really, that that communication comes from every part of life, if only we see it, hear it—through people, serendipitous events, books, nature, animals, music, scriptures, meditation. Meditation, maybe more than anything, has the potential, not only during meditation, but at other times too, of making me more aware, awake to the communication. I think this is because, as Jesus said, "The Kingdom of Heaven is within you." He made it as a general statement that didn't hinge at all on people believing in him for salvation, as I read it. And I experience meditation as a very strong way to make conscious contact with the Kingdom within.

The Bible

I love the Bible, though I usually only read it any more to look for something specific. I don't read it, in part, because I memorized so much of it that when I need some words or a story from the Bible, they come to me.

I believe that the people who wrote the Bible wanted or needed to share their experience of God in their lives and in their communities. They were also sharing their beliefs about God. Often the people who wrote about events were not the ones who were there when the events happened. We know this pretty surely about the writers of the gospels, who probably wrote forty to seventy-plus years after Jesus's death. They were writing from stories they'd heard and how those stories affected them. I think the Bible is also stories that people told each other to explain big questions—like how good and evil came to be, why there are sea animal fossils in places where there are no seas, what God is like, what God wants of us, etc.

I also believe that there is plenty of evidence that much of the Bible has, over the millennia, been tampered with, altered, sometimes by mistake, sometimes on purpose to serve the power desires of church leaders. And to satisfy their greed. I know some things were put in or taken out because people in power liked or didn't like something. Also, the original writers apparently rewrote and revised many times to serve the needs of the people of their times.

I guess it's obvious from what I've said so far that I don't believe that the Bible is the inerrant Word of God. Oh, and the canon is another thing, how books were picked and chosen to go along with pre-held beliefs of certain powerful men who wanted, naturally, to retain their power. I believe God speaks to us all, inspires us all for our growth and guidance and service, when we're in conscious contact with God. This doesn't mean that I think we should all be going out and writing Bibles. But I do think sometimes we're guided to write our experiences for the purpose of sharing them with others. That's why there are so many inspiring books out there to bless us. The Bible often inspires me in the organic way I mentioned—when a passage comes to me.

I learn from the Bible all the time. I've read scriptures of other religions, and none has quite the power to deeply touch me that the Bible has. I think that's because of the long and deep history I have with the Bible. I opened my heart to it as a very young person, and once you open your heart to someone or something, that's a lasting thing. So through the Bible, I first opened my heart to God and to the people who had met God in days gone by. This, I think, aside from much of the beauty intrinsic to the Bible, is why it remains my favorite scripture.

Prayer

I don't really pray out loud any more, definitely not publicly. Recently, when I was asked to, I did, and it didn't feel right for me afterwards. I think for me, it becomes performance when it's aloud with others, no longer prayer.

When I pray, I make conscious contact with God. I feel God in my heart, my mind, sometimes in my chakras. I pray for peace in the world. My prayers for individuals are a silent holding them up, like offering them and their needs to God. Even when they've asked me to ask God for specific things in specific ways, I don't do that, because I believe that God knows far better than any of us what we all need. So it's like turning that person and their needs all over to God.

I do set intentions in my own life, things I would like to have accomplished; in my process of setting an intention, I give my intention to God, too.

Jesus

People, when they've read some of what I've written about my spiritual journey and Jesus, have said that it comes through very strongly that I have really loved Jesus. A lot. That surprised me, because I wasn't really aware of it. I believe that as God's image-bearers, since God is Love, Love is what we are, in our essence, too. But we as Love are mostly not shining realizations of it. The love is in us; it is us, but we haven't brought it to fruition (mostly). I think the stories of Jesus's amazing, healing powers and the words he spoke are testament to his being one of the most highly realized bearers of God as Love. I think people who walked with him on Earth were bowled over by that love. I think it's exactly why they fell down before him and said, "My Lord and my God." In part, I think I know how they felt because I've experienced wanting to do what they did before one person with whom I felt God's love pouring over me and through me. If anyone ever feels that love pouring through me, even in small measure, I'll be so happy.

I don't really understand the mystery of Jesus's death, any more than I understand the mystery of anyone's death—

maybe less, since so much has been made of it. I don't think Jesus had to die for anyone's sins. I think that idea came from early Christians applying to Christianity the Jewish idea of animal sacrifices for atonement. And I think the Church leaders used it to have power over people, to say, "You need the Church in order to be saved." It was like job security for them. And they used fear of hell and separation from God to maintain their power. It also brought them money. Lots of it. I think most people today who promote the idea that we need to believe in Jesus's sacrifice for our sins are sincere about it. But I think the idea got started for the wrong reasons.

I think we are in relationship with God regardless of what we believe or do, but it's not always a good relationship on our end. I think Jesus, embodying, incarnating Love as he did, can redeem us if we follow him, as disciples. I don't have any trouble believing in the possibility of the virgin birth, miracles, resurrection. I've seen and heard of too much of this kind of thing happening throughout history and experienced some miracles myself, so I believe they're possible. In Jesus's case, I don't know for sure they happened, but they're not critical to what I can learn from him and his great power—Love.

Christ

Christ is from the Greek *Christos* and means the same as *Messiah* or *Meshiach* from Hebrew—*The Anointed One,* the one anointed to redeem, repair, restore the Earth and all that is in it, its people included. *Christ* has become a part of Jesus's name, but really, it's a role, a task, not an identity. I think we are all anointed to redeem, repair, restore the broken world, that this is our purpose. I don't see it as unique to Jesus, but he may have, in his life, fulfilled that purpose more fully than most. He is one of the exemplars we can follow in our attempts to fulfill the redemptive purpose. I think just how each of us is meant to fulfill the purpose of redemption is unique to each of us and that a big part of our task is to learn how we are meant to do that. It's why I love this poem by Rumi, the 13th century Sufi poet, so much:

There is one thing in this world that you must never forget to do.
If you forget everything else and not this, there is nothing to worry
about, but if you remember everything else and forget this, then you
will have done nothing in your life.

It is as if a king has sent you to some country to do a task, and you
perform a hundred other services, but not the one he sent you to do.
So human beings come to this world to do particular work. That
work is the purpose, and each is specific to the person. If you don't
do it, it's as though a knife of the finest tempering were nailed into a
wall to hang things on. For a penny an iron nail could be bought to
serve for that.

Remember the deep root of your being, the presence of your Lord.
Give your life to the one who already owns your breath and your
moments. If you don't, you will be like the one who takes a precious
dagger and hammers it into his kitchen wall for a peg to hold his dipper
gourd. You will be wasting valuable keenness and foolishly ignoring
your dignity and your purpose.

The Holy Spirit

For me, another name for *God* is *Spirit*. I don't think (and this goes with my not thinking God is a person) that there are three persons, a Trinity. I really don't have any idea where that came from—the Trinity idea. But I think the Holy Spirit comes closest to being the essence of God—Spirit, indwelling us (another name for the Kingdom of Heaven), the source of all life, the Breath of Life (what *Spirit* comes from—inspiration, inspire [as in breathe in]). If I could say I love God, it is Spirit I love. And it is Spirit I love in you and in me.

Religion

I think religion is a mistake because it tries to organize God into things like catechisms, into human-made rules, regulations, institutions. It's an attempt to control behavior. It's a vehicle for power-over. I think one reason people want religion is because it's a way to have community. It's a way to feel safe. It can be a way not to have to think too much. It's a way to have all the answers to life's most persistent problems and questions. It can be a way not to have to take responsibility. It's not the same as spirituality, although, despite all its inherent weaknesses, it can be a path to spirituality; that's its good bit. But it's not the only way to spirituality. Maybe a good way to really make use of it is teaching children about many religions, introducing them to the practices, too, so they can choose what fits best for them. Or just teaching a neutral meditation practice, like observing the breath; that facilitates an opening to Spirit.

One of the big problems with religion is that members become so invested, so identified with their religion, that they think theirs is best for everyone and they often become intolerant of others' religions or even the ways their coreligionists practice their common religion. And the intolerance often leads to horrific violence.

Christianity

I believe that Paul invented Christianity, not Jesus. I don't think Jesus intended to start a new religion. I don't think he saw his death as payment for our sins. I think that was invented afterwards by someone who believed there had to be sacrifice. I think Paul was sincere but probably, incidentally, on a power trip.

Christianity has, however, been a good pathway to God for many, just as other religions have. Like any religion, I believe it is human-made, not God-made, and as prone to flawed thinking and action on its behalf as any religion. In fact, it is one of the religions most bent on imposing its beliefs on others.

Other Religions

Like Christianity, other religions are human-made and prone to flaws. Many people continue to practice the religion they grew up with, whether or not it is suited to them. Ideally, I believe, people would be given information to allow them to choose, if any, one that fits them best.

I learn from many religions. I am probably most drawn to Judaism, also as the root of Christianity, which ought to have remained Judaism, transformed by Jesus as one rabbi and by other rabbis over time, as all religions do to differing degrees transform over time to fit the times. I will probably never choose one religion but continue to learn from many in order to grow spiritually.

Proselytizing

I believe in sharing one's faith in an exchange where the goal is to know another person better, promote understanding between two people, and learn from one another for our spiritual growth. I believe in living my faith so that others might say, "She has something I don't have, and I want that something. How can I get it?" I believe in overtly sharing a non-fear-based faith with people who are living in a fear-based one, to give them another option. I don't believe in overt proselytizing to people whose faith is working for them pretty well and not fostering fear. Because faith is a human experience, I don't think any one faith is best for everyone. I don't support Christian proselytizing through fear of damnation any more than any other fear-based proselytizing by any other religion.

Life Mission

I believe my mission in life is to embody Love. I take the Shema (Hear, O Israel, the Lord our God, the Lord is One. Thou shalt love the Lord thy God with all thy heart, with all thy soul and with all thy mind, and thy neighbor as thyself.) and Micah 6:8 (. . . And what does the Lord require of you but to do justice, and to love kindness, and to walk humbly with your God?) as commands for my life mission. After that, I believe the individual task is to learn what my unique way of fulfilling that task is meant to be.

Music and Ritual

Belief tends to rely so much on the intellect. And I think other pathways than intellect take us nearer to God. I believe that music and ritual are such pathways, as well as meditation and prayer.

Sin

I believe it's pretty clear that no human being is perfect. I include Jesus in that, by the way, believing he was just as human as we and no more a son of God than we are children of God. I believe it is part of the human condition that we are broken, in need of healing. I have seen that healing happen in many ways—through spirituality as it exists inside and outside religion, through connection with nature and music, through psychotherapy, through body therapies, through medicine (in every sense of *medicine*), through Love (especially and ultimately) and many other modalities. In general, I don't see Christians as more whole than others. I don't believe that healing or redemption from our brokenness is a one-time deal as in being "saved." Rather, I believe it is a lifelong (perhaps many lifetimes) process.

Death, Heaven, and Hell

The great mystery. As I grow older and thus closer to death, I try more and more to comprehend it, to imagine what it is really like to die. What I think happens after death is based on stories told by people who have been pronounced dead, then resuscitated. Regardless of their beliefs, what religion they professed or whether they were atheists, their stories have the same elements—going down a long tunnel and emerging into brilliant white light and a profound sense of being loved, being met by a person from their religious belief who was important to them or by a family member or friend who had died. What happens after that must be the great adventure. I do believe there is evidence for reincarnation. I think the people of Jesus's time, including he and his disciples, believed in it. I have read that Constantine had references to reincarnation removed from the Bible. But the story of the Mount of Transfiguration suggests it as a common, acceptable concept. I think the attachment we have to this body being permanently attached to this soul is a materialistic one and that we are spirits having a physical experience in this lifetime with all the tasks and learning that entails.

When I left the church, for a period of time I denied that I was a spiritual being, and I had nothing to do with spirituality (I thought, not realizing I am always connected with God, regardless of my awareness or lack thereof). Not believing in Heaven or Hell was part of that. And yet, somewhere in the rooms of my mind, there was a heaven because, when I thought of Trudy and Grandma Kruis, they were both there. It was just a little oddity I had. Now I don't know about heaven, probably not really a "place" in the way we think about place. I don't believe in hell, based on peoples' after-death experiences.

~ Appendix B ~
What I Read to the Session
Including my version of the Apostles' Creed (September 2012)

I have to begin by giving thanks for St. Andrew. I don't think I could ever have given up hope that I could find a Christian faith community that I could be part of, because, in some sense, I have continued searching for nearly forty years for a spiritual home. The Hebrew word for Egypt is *mitzrayim,* meaning the narrows. In a reversal of what I was taught to expect, the Reformed church in which I was baptized and made profession of faith, became my Egypt when I couldn't be accepted as a lesbian. The church became my narrow place, so when I left, the old hymn, "Out of My Bondage," became a song about my release from it. A rabbi friend of mine told us at Seder that when the Israelites left Egypt, they entered the wide, open wilderness. He said that the wilderness belongs to no one and is a symbol for spiritual teachings. Spiritual teachings belong to no one, he said; hence, they belong to everyone. My nearly forty years outside the church were my wilderness years, and I learned from the spiritual teachings of many traditions during that time.

A few weeks ago, in the bulletin's call to confession these words spoke to me and affirmed me and my journey to St. Andrew: "Our Loving God has called us, not to a set of beliefs but to a relationship of trust." In St. Andrew, I have found a faith community where I can share that relationship of trust. During the past forty years, I was always trying, through reading, through sharing with others, through writing, to find a way to reconcile who I am with the Christian faith in which I was so immersed as a young person. It is not because I believe Christianity is the only way to God or even the best way; it is because Christianity is *my* way, *my* tradition. Thich Nhat Hanh wrote that if we do not make peace with our spiritual ancestry, we will always be at war with ourselves, and for me that peace-making has been essential.

To me, faith community is less about my relationship with God than it is about my relationship with others who are trying to follow Jesus and his teachings in practical, everyday life. It is about learning to follow Jesus in all our human imperfection. It is about practicing social justice with people who are acting from shared spiritual motivation.

My faith in God has not been in question for a long time, and over the years, it has only grown, though, of course, with ups and downs. However, to have faith in Jesus has required quite a lot of work on my part. The mystery of God is inherent in God's being, but the mystery of Jesus seems to me in large part to be man-made, so it requires much more work to understand.

In preparation for my reaffirmation of faith, because the Apostles' Creed is one of the creeds embraced by the Presbyterian Church, I have written a version of the creed that I can say with integrity and which I'd like to share with you. I hope it won't in anyway be an obstacle to my becoming a member of this fellowship.

> *I believe in God, and I do my best to love God*
> *with all my heart.*
>
> *I believe in God's son, our brother and my Master*
> *Teacher, Jesus,*

Who is for me the human face of God,

Who lived, taught, healed and reached out to outcasts and inspires me to do the same, who was crucified for putting the rulers to shame, whose last supper, death and resurrection convey to me that redemption is a journey from death to life and that love is greater than death; who, when I follow him, daily redeems my life from destruction. In this sense, he is my savior.

His soul, as is mine, is eternally with God.

He teaches me to discern right from wrong, to distinguish loving actions from fearful ones that can lead to hate and hurt.

I believe in and love the Holy Spirit, the manifestation of God in whom I live and move and have my being.

I believe in the church as the hands and feet, the ears and tongue of God. I believe without reservation in the communion of the saints.

I believe in the great gift of the forgiveness of sins.

I believe that my body is mortal and that my soul is immortal and has always been and always will be in and with God.

The Presbyterian Church is not exactly the home I left, but it has enough of the same traditions, the same beliefs, and similar practices, that I know pretty much how to do it. I feel comfortable most of the time and definitely welcome. I am near tears, good tears, nearly every Sunday service, and they are tears of recognition, of grief for what I lost, and of return from exile. This journey has been very much about how God's grace has always been sufficient for me and guided me through every life lesson, including taking me to St. Andrew.

Below is the original Apostles' Creed:

I believe in God, the Father almighty,
creator of heaven and earth.
I believe in Jesus Christ, God's only Son, our Lord,
who was conceived by the Holy Spirit,
born of the Virgin Mary,
suffered under Pontius Pilate,
was crucified, died, and was buried;
he descended to the dead.
On the third day he rose again;
he ascended into heaven,
he is seated at the right hand of the Father,
and he will come to judge the living and the dead.
I believe in the Holy Spirit,
the holy catholic Church,
the communion of saints,
the forgiveness of sins,
the resurrection of the body,
and the life everlasting. Amen.

~ Appendix C ~

For Just Such a Time as This Esther 4:9–14 (The Message I Gave At St. Andrew on June 29, 2014)

No doubt you're familiar with the story of Esther, so I'll only summarize it briefly. There are four main characters in the story: Esther herself; her Uncle Mordecai, who raised her because she was an orphan; Ahasuerus, king of Persia and ruler over 127 provinces from Ethiopia to India; and Haman, the king's racist, self-important, right-hand man. A fifth character, God, is notably missing—never mentioned once directly. We'll come back to this.

The Esther story is so full of coincidences that an editor today would insist the writer get rid of most of them. I counted thirteen in all. There isn't time to mention all thirteen, but watch for them. I'll point out some as we go. The first apparent coincidence is the fact that Esther even became queen—through the unseating of the former queen who refused to be objectified before the king's guests when all of them, including the king, were in their cups.

After Esther became queen, when Mordecai, an observant Jew, refused to bow before Haman, Haman decided to get rid of all the Jews in the 127 provinces. He paid the king a hefty bribe to set a date for the annihilation. In profound mourning, Mordecai sat at the king's gate wearing sackcloth and ashes. When Esther sent down some decent clothes, he rejected them. Instead, he asked the servant who brought them, "Go! Charge Esther to go to Ahasuerus and beg for her life and the lives of her people."

Esther said, "I'm afraid to go to the king. He hasn't asked for me for a month. I could be executed for going to him without being requested—unless he holds out his scepter when I appear."

Mordecai sent Esther a second message: "Don't think you're going to escape this pogrom just because you live in the palace." Then he uttered these words of both faith and kindness, prodding the young queen to action. "Perhaps, Esther, you have come to royal dignity for just such a time as this." Mordecai thus suggested that Esther's ascension to the throne may not just be a coincidence.

Brave Esther went. The king was happy to see her. He asked what she wanted. She invited him and Haman to dinner. The king asked again what she wanted. Still fearful, she invited the two to a second dinner. Incidentally, one reason for her fear was probably the fact that she hadn't told anyone she was a Jew.

Haman decided he couldn't wait for the scheduled pogrom to get rid of Mordecai, so between the first and second dinners, he had a seventy-five-foot gallows built to hang his nemesis. Now comes another of the thirteen coincidences: Ahasuerus couldn't sleep after the first dinner. What did he think would put him to sleep? A reading of the annals of the kingdom. Yet another coincidence: He discovered that a while back, none other than Mordecai had saved him from an assassination plot and had never been rewarded.

The next morning, he asked Haman, "What shall I do for someone I want to honor?" Of course, Haman thought, "Who else would the king want to honor besides me?" He suggested that the man be dressed in the king's own robes and crown and be led about the city on the king's own horse by one of the king's highest nobles. Oh, the humiliation, when Haman had to lead that horrible Mordecai through the city. Yes, another coincidence.

At the second banquet, Esther gathered her courage and asked the king, "Please, spare my life and the lives of my people." She pointed to Haman as the man who was planning to destroy her and the rest of the Jews. Enraged, the king left the room to walk in the garden. Haman threw himself on Esther's couch to beg for his life. Ahasuerus returned to find Haman in that very compromising position. He ordered Haman hanged on the gallows prepared for Mordecai. Mordecai became his right-hand man. You see what I mean about coincidences. The Jews were saved because Esther accepted the idea that she had come to the throne for just such a time as this.

★ ★ ★

Fast-forward now to a possibly less familiar story—1941 in Vienna, Austria. Another pogrom has begun, this one of such unbelievable proportions that we call it the Holocaust. In 1938, Hitler had annexed Austria in his grab for land and power. Viktor Frankl, a thirty-four-year-old Jewish neurologist and psychiatrist, had already developed the theory and practice of logotherapy. His concept was that the most basic human drive is a search for meaning and the fulfillment of that meaning. Viktor believed passionately that he could help people heal from depression and anxiety by helping them find purpose in their lives. He felt compelled to spread his ideas among mental health practitioners worldwide.

As the deportation of Austrian Jews began, Viktor applied for a visa to the United States. When it was granted in 1941, he was deeply troubled. He knew that if he went to the U.S., he would survive possible death and be able to promote logotherapy. But his parents were elderly. Not yet knowing the true nature of the death camps, Viktor thought he might be able to help them survive.

In his dilemma, Viktor went into St. Stephan's Cathedral in central Vienna. Surrounded by immense granite pillars, brilliant stained-glass windows, and rows of flickering candles, he listened to someone practice the magnificent pipe organ. He searched his heart, asking whether his responsibility lay in caring for his parents or in escaping to safety in order to disseminate his work. As he left the cathedral without an answer, he thought, "Isn't this the kind of situation that requires some hint from heaven?"

When Frankl arrived at home, where he still lived with his parents, he saw a piece of marble lying on the table. His father had salvaged it from the rubble of a razed synagogue. A single Hebrew letter was engraved on the marble. Viktor's father told him that the letter came from one of the Ten Commandments, the only commandment to use that letter. "Which one?" Viktor asked.

His father replied, "Honor thy father and thy mother, that thy days may be long upon the land which the Lord thy God giveth thee." Viktor knew that this was the guidance he had asked for. He stayed with his parents in Vienna and later accompanied them to the Tereisienstadt Concentration Camp.

If Frankl had escaped the camps by emigrating, he would have been spared great suffering. The practice of logotherapy might have been widely distributed among psychotherapists. But it is the story of how Viktor was able to find meaning in the darkest places on Earth that ended up touching the lives of so many ordinary people.

When he was released at the end of the war after surviving four concentration camps, Frankl learned that of his family, only his sister in Australia had survived. He was deeply depressed and suicidal. It was his belief in life's purpose that kept him from acting on his feelings at that point. He couldn't help thinking that there was a reason his life had been spared. In a space of nine days, he dictated *Man's Search for Meaning,* one of the earliest and most hopeful accounts to come out of the

Holocaust. What he learned and taught the world through his experiences spread not only to mental health professionals but also to millions of adults and young people. *Man's Search for Meaning* is the second most read book about the Holocaust after *The Diary of Anne Frank*. Viktor had thought he had to choose between caring for his parents and pursuing his life's work. In the end, choosing to care for his mother and father furthered his work in ways he couldn't have imagined.

★ ★ ★

Although God is not named in the Book of Esther, I think that the deep meaning of Esther's story hangs on what Mordecai said—that Esther had come to the throne "for just such a time as this." The implication is that there can be divine purpose in the things that often seem to just happen to us. Things that appear to be coincidences—joyful things, our passions, difficult and painful things, suffering and even evil, may be used to guide us into fulfilling God's purpose for us.

I'm not suggesting that God engineers the painful, evil things in order to guide us. Those things most often come from human error. I'm reminded of the words Joseph spoke to his brothers when they came to buy grain from him in Egypt, long after selling him into slavery: "Even though you intended to do harm to me, God intended it for good, in order to preserve a numerous people, as he is doing today." It is God who takes the horrific situations and through us, his people, transforms them into good.

★ ★ ★

The stories of Esther and Viktor are about big meaning. Esther's big purpose turned out to be huge and resulted in the festival of Purim, which Jews still celebrate today. Frankl's big purpose lay in helping the world make some sense of the horrors of the Holocaust and in enabling us to see that we can create meaning even in the most horrific situations.

Finding our life work, our life purpose, sometimes does happen through suffering, or through closed doors that God transforms into openings. Other times we find our big purpose through recognizing our God-given passions, our interests, our talents and skills. The thirteenth century Muslim mystic and poet Rumi wrote:

"There is one thing in this world that you must never forget to do. If you forget everything else and not this, there is nothing to worry about, but if you remember everything else and forget this, then you will have done nothing in your life. It is as if a king has sent you to some country to do a task, and you perform a hundred other services, but not the one he sent you to do."

So human beings come to this world to do *particular work.* That work is the purpose, and each is specific to the person. Remember the deep root of your being, the presence of your Lord. Give your life to the one who already owns your breath and your moments.

★ ★ ★

In addition to the big purpose, there is simple, everyday purpose, how we live our ordinary lives. This lies in giving our lives to the one who already owns our lives and holds our moments. Frankl believed that his everyday purpose lay in helping others find their purpose. Throughout our lives, we come to many crossroads, transition times. We're given opportunities to ask ourselves, "What does this time in my life, this time in the world around me, ask of me?"

★ ★ ★

At St. Andrew, we find ourselves at a crossroads as a faith community. In New Beginnings, we are continuing to ask God for guidance as to our communal purpose. We hope to find the mission that is specific to us, a mission that no other faith community can fulfill in exactly the same way as we can—*at just such a time as this.* And this comes back around to each of us, to asking ourselves what is our individual purpose within St Andrew's mission, asking ourselves where our individual gifts and passions, and also our commitment, enter into the communal mission. We are seeking to know how God will move through us.

* * *

Thanks be to God for the transformative, empowering work of the Spirit, offering us guidance, granting us the discernment to recognize guidance when we receive it. May the Holy Spirit grant us the openness and the courage of those who have gone before us—Joseph in Egypt, Esther in the kingdom of Persia, Rumi in thirteenth-century Turkey, and Viktor Frankl in the time of the Holocaust.

About Anna Redsand

RAISED BY FUNDAMENTALIST MISSIONARIES on the Navajo reservation, Anna Redsand was forced to leave the faith and family that had always supported her and embark on a decades-long quest for a new spiritual home that would accept her as both a lesbian and someone committed to social justice.

She is the award-winning author of *Viktor Frankl: A Life Worth Living,* as well as a published writer of essays, stories, and newspaper columns. Her essay "Naturalization" was listed in *Best American Essays 2014.* She also has taught writing at the public school and university levels, and created and presented workshops on the writing of a spiritual journey. Much of her work explores the fluidity of identity, the effects of colonization, race relations, the morality of missions, and the dynamics of cultural contact. Redsand lives in Albuquerque, New Mexico.